Essentials of Treatment Planning

Essentials of Mental Health Practice Series

Founding Editors, Alan S. Kaufman and Nadeen L. Kaufman

Essentials of Interviewing
by Donald E. Wiger and Debra K. Huntley

Essentials of Outcome Assessment
by Benjamin M. Ogles, Michael J. Lambert, and Scott A. Fields

Essentials of Treatment Planning
by Mark E. Maruish

Essentials

of Treatment Planning

Mark E. Maruish

John Wiley & Sons, Inc.

Author's Note:
Portions of this book are adapted from the following sources: "Introduction," in M. E. Maruish (Ed.), *The Use of Psychological Testing for Treatment Planning and Outcomes Assessment* (2nd ed.) (1999), with permission of Lawrence Erlbaum Associates, Mahwah, NJ; "Introduction," in M. E. Maruish (Ed.), *Handbook of Psychological Assessment in Primary Care Settings* (2000), with permission of Lawrence Erlbaum Associates, Mahwah, NJ; M. E. Maruish, *Psychological Testing in the Age of Managed Behavioral Health Care* (2002), with permission of Lawrence Erlbaum Associates, Mahwah, NJ.

MMPI-2™ is a trademark of The Regents of the University of Minnesota, Minneapolis, MN.
PAI™ is a trademark of Psychological Assessment Resources, Inc.
SF-36® and *SF-12*® are registered trademarks of The Medical Outcomes Trust.
BDI®*-II* is a registered trademark of The Psychological Corporation.
Rorschach® is a registered trademark of Verlag Hans Huber, AG, Bern, Switzerland.
SCL-90-R® and *BSI*® are registered trademarks of Leonard R. Derogatis, Ph.D.
OQ-45® is a registered trademark of American Professional Credentialling Services, LLC.
Basis-32® is a registered trademark of McClean Hospital, Belmont, Massachusetts.

This publication is designed to provide accurate and authoritative information in regard to the subject matter covered. It is sold with the understanding that the publisher is not engaged in rendering professional services. If legal, accounting, medical, psychological or any other expert assistance is required, the services of a competent professional person should be sought.

Wiley also publishes its books in a variety of electronic formats. Some content that appears in print may not be available in electronic books.

Library of Congress Cataloging-in-Publication Data

Maruish, Mark E. (Mark Edward)
    Essentials of treatment planning / Mark E. Maruish
        p. cm. — (Essentials of mental health practice series)
    Includes bibliographical references and index.
    ISBN 0-471-41997-4 (pbk. : alk. paper)
        1. Psychiatry—Differential therapeutics. I. Title. II. Series.

RC480.52 .M37 2002
616.89'14—dc21

                                              2002066368

To Rick and Dodie Shifley,
for all the care they showed me over the years

We would like to sincerely thank Irving B. Weiner, Ph.D., ABPP, for his assistance as a consulting editor on this project.

Dr. Weiner completed his doctoral studies at the University of Michigan in 1959 and went on to write and edit over 20 books, as well as countless chapters and journal articles. A Diplomate of the American Board of Professional Psychology in both Clinical and Forensic Psychology, he currently serves as Clinical Professor of Psychiatry and Behavioral Medicine at the University of South Florida. Dr. Weiner serves as Chairman of the Wiley Behavioral Sciences Advisory Board and is Editor-in-Chief of the 12-volume Handbook of Psychology, which published in December 2002.

CONTENTS

Series Preface ix

One Introduction 1

Two Patient Assessment 14

Three Contributions of Psychological Testing to Clinical
Assessment and Treatment Planning 54

Four Case Formulation 107

Five Developing a Treatment Plan 122

Six Monitoring Treatment Progress: Implications for
Treatment Planning 185

References 217

Annotated Bibliography 229

Index 233

About the Author 243

SERIES PREFACE
Essentials of Mental Health Practice

I n the *Essentials of Mental Health Practice* series, our goal is to provide readers
with books that will deliver key practical information in an efficient and accessible style. The series features books on a variety of critical practice topics, such as interviewing, treatment planning, and outcomes assessment, to
name a few. For the experienced professional, books in the series offer a concise yet thorough overview of a specific area of expertise, including numerous
tips for best practices. Students will find here a prioritized assembly of all the
information and techniques that must be at one's fingertips to practice knowl-
edgeably, efficiently, and ethically in today's behavioral health environment.

Wherever feasible, visual cues highlighting key points are utilized alongside
systematic, step-by-step guidelines. Chapters are focused and succinct. Topics
are organized for an easy understanding of the essential material related to a
particular practice area. Theory and research are continually woven into the
fabric of each book, but always to enhance the practical application of the material, rather than sidetrack or overwhelm readers. With this series, we aim to
challenge and assist readers engaged in providing mental health services to as-
pire to the highest level of proficiency in their particular discipline by arming
them with the tools they need for effective practice.

In *Essentials of Treatment Planning,* the author presents an atheoretical approach to the development and implementation of treatment plans in behavioral health care settings. First, a discussion of treatment planning—its role
and benefits in clinical settings—is presented. This is followed by a detailed
guide to conducting a comprehensive assessment of the patient, with special
attention given to the use of psychological testing for gathering information
important to the completion of that assessment. Next is a discussion regarding the use of assessment information to develop a case formulation—the ba-

sis of the treatment plan. With the completion of the case formulation, the clinician is prepared to develop the treatment plan, and a general structure and process for developing treatment plans are presented in detail. Finally, acknowledging the importance for clinicians to continually evaluate and (as necessary) revise the treatment plan, a process for monitoring and evaluating the patient during the course of treatment is discussed.

Alan S. Kaufman, PhD, and Nadeen L. Kaufman, EdD, Founding Editors
Yale University School of Medicine

Essentials of Treatment Planning

One

Psychologists, psychiatrists, clinical social workers, and other behavioral health care professionals practicing in this new millennium are all aware of the importance of having a specific, individualized plan to guide the treatment of their patients. Many of these same people might be surprised to know that formalized treatment planning is a relatively new component of mental health and substance abuse treatment. Harkness and Lilienfeld (1997) note that in the 1950s and 1960s, this part of the therapeutic endeavor was often allowed to develop from the treatment sessions themselves. Moreover, in some schools of thought, the development of a formalized plan would have been considered contradictory to the basic tenets of the theoretical approach (e.g., the importance of free association in psychodynamic approaches, the genuineness of client-centered approach). According to Jongsma and Peterson (1999), the treatment plans developed for mental health and substance abuse patients were of a bare-bones type and generalizable across most patients. Naglieri and Pfeiffer (1999) have made similar observations. Treatment goals and objectives were not clear, interventions were not patient specific, and outcomes were not measurable.

It was not until the 1970s and 1980s that formal treatment planning in behavioral health care began to grow in importance as a standard part of good clinical care. Jongsma and Peterson (1999) attribute the increased recognition of the importance of treatment-plan development during this period to the beginning of two significant movements in the behavioral health care industry. The first was the pursuit of accreditation from organizations such as the Joint Commission for the Accreditation of Healthcare Organizations (JCAHO) by mental health and substance abuse treatment facilities and agencies. Such accreditation was necessary to qualify for third-party reimbursements. The accreditation standards of JCAHO and other accrediting bodies required providers to be more thorough in their development and documentation of individual treatment plans. JCAHO and organizations such as the National Committee for Quality Assurance (NCQA) continue to maintain treatment-planning standards for initial and reaccreditation of behavioral health care organizations.

The other significant movement identified by Jongsma and Peterson (1999) as influencing the growing importance of treatment planning was the advent of managed care in the 1980s. As they most succinctly summarize the matter,

> Managed care systems *insist* that clinicians move rapidly from assessment of the problem to the formulation and implementation of the treatment plan. The goal . . . is to expedite the treatment process by prompting the [patient] and the treatment provider to focus on identifying and changing behavioral problems as quickly as possible. Treatment plans must be specific as to the problems and interventions, individualized to meet the client's needs and goals, and measurable in terms of setting milestones that can be used to chart the patient's progress. (p. 1)

It is unfortunate that external pressures have served as a major impetus for behavioral health care professionals to be more attentive to what is now considered a basic part of clinical service delivery. However, as will be discussed later in this chapter, there are many other reasons that the development of an individualized treatment plan is an important part of the standard care that should be delivered to mental health and substance abuse patients.

TREATMENT PLANNING: A BRIEF OVERVIEW

What is treatment planning? Why do we do it? The answers to these questions provide a context for understanding, completing, and successfully implementing this important component of any behavioral health intervention.

What is Treatment Planning?

Treatment planning is a term that may mean different things to different people. At one level, treatment planning can be defined as "an organized conceptual effort to design a program *outlining in advance* the specific steps by which the therapist will help the patient recover from his or her presenting dysfunctional state" (Makover, 1992, p. 338). At another level, however, treatment planning might be described as "a complex process involving sequential decisions, with weighting of information concerning patient characteristics (including, but not limited to, patient diagnoses and problem areas), treatment context, relation variables, and treatment strategies and techniques" (Clarkin & Kendall, 1992, p. 906). This latter definition highlights the fact that treatment planning is not the application of a cookie-cutter, one-size-fits-all approach to intervention. Rather, it is an activity that, if performed properly, requires serious deliberation and clinical skill on the part of the clinician. This fact is borne out by the content of this book.

Growing Importance of Treatment Planning in Contemporary Behavioral Health Care

As discussed earlier, the emergence of managed care and, in particular, of managed behavioral health care, served as major impetus for placing more emphasis on treatment planning as an important part of clinical service delivery. Managed care's focus on providing quality care in the most efficient and effective way possible necessitates the careful planning of interventions in order to accomplish what it sees as its general goals for treatment. These goals include educating patients and their families or other support systems about the nature of the problem, options for intervention, and the role of the patient in treatment process; reducing core symptoms and dysfunctional behaviors; returning the patient to the baseline level of functioning; and preventing a relapse (United Behavioral Health [UBH], 2000).

From a managed care perspective, treatment planning serves multiple purposes. As summarized in Rapid Reference 1.1, the following

Rapid Reference 1.1

Purposes of Treatment Planning for MBHOs

- To clarify treatment focus
- To set realistic expectations
- To establish a standard for measuring treatment progress
- To facilitate communication among professionals
- To support treatment authorization
- To document quality assurance efforts
- To facilitate communication with external reviewers

Note. From UBS (1994).

are those identified by one large managed behavioral health care organization (United Behavioral Systems [UBS], 1994).

To Clarify the Focus of Treatment

The nature of any *treatment plan* is such that it must specify what the treatment will be working to accomplish and the means by which it will do so. Initially, it can be viewed as a tool to ensure that both the therapist and the patient agree on the goals that they will be working toward and how they will go about doing so. During the course of treatment, the treatment plan can serve as a reference that both parties can consult in order to verify that treatment is indeed on track relative to these goals. Certainly, the focus of treatment can change as new information becomes available or the patient's life circumstances change. In these cases, such changes would be reflected in a revised treatment plan.

To Set Realistic Expectations for Treatment

People seeking mental health or substance abuse treatment may have any of a multitude of expectations about behavioral health interventions. These expectations may center around various treatment-related issues, including the degree to which they will be cured, so to speak, of the symptoms or problems that led them to seek treatment; the clinician's approach to and degree of involvement in the treatment; the degree to which they must be involved in treatment in order for it to be effective; and the need to involve collaterals (spouse, friends, teachers, etc.) at some point during the episode of care. A formal treatment plan can help the patient understand prior to treatment what he or she can realistically expect to occur during the course of treatment and what should be accomplished at the end of treatment. Thus, clarifying patient and clinician roles, setting the ground rules for therapy, and establishing achievable goals before therapy begins can help minimize the chance that the patient will be disappointed either during or at the end of the therapeutic experience.

To Establish a Standard Against Which to Judge Therapeutic Progress

It is difficult to determine whether and how much progress is being made during treatment unless one first knows what the patient's status was at the beginning of treatment and what one hopes it will be at the end of treatment. The treatment plan permits such an assessment. Through the documentation of criteria of successfully completed treatment—that is, mutually agreed upon treatment goals—the treatment plan also provides the criteria for terminating an episode of care.

To Inform Other Professionals Involved in the Patient's Treatment

In many instances a patient undergoing mental health or substance abuse treatment will be receiving care from multiple providers. This situation is likely to be the case when the treatment is being provided in an inpatient or other nonambulatory setting. In inpatient settings, for example, a patient should expect care from the admitting psychiatrist, the nursing staff, and other mental health or substance abuse professionals responsible for individual or group treatment. Other ancillary services (e.g., speech pathology, occupational therapy, recreational therapy, vocational rehabilitation, physical therapy) might also be required. The coordination of treatment being given by multiple providers is critical if the patient is to achieve maximum therapeutic benefit from the episode of care. Here, the treatment plan provides a common guide to direct the efforts of all members of the behavioral health treatment team. However, it can also give direction to other providers responsible for different aspects of the patient's health and well-being.

It is unfortunate that many behavioral health professionals have not been trained in the importance of communicating with other professionals who also are providing some form of medical (physical) health care to their patients. At the same time, it is encouraging that communication between clinicians and their patients' medical health care providers is on the increase. There are at least two reasons for this. One has to do with the recognition that much of behavioral health care is provided by nonpsychiatric medical specialties. As Maruish (2000) has noted,

> the situation that exists in the United States today is one in which (a) behavioral health problems of various degrees of severity exist in significant number; (b) about half of the people with these problems seek treatment from their family physician or other primary care provider; and (c) a significant proportion of these same people are among the highest utilizers of medical resources. (p. 12)

The other reason has to do with the standards of NCQA, JCAHO, and other accrediting bodies, which require providers of mental health and substance abuse services to convey (with informed, written consent) information to their patients' primary care or referring physicians about the services that are being rendered. Communication between the behavioral health clinician and the physician responsible for the patient's overall health care allows for better coordination and facilitation of each professional's efforts to provide the best care to his or her patient in the safest and most efficient manner. Again, the treatment plan can serve as an excellent tool for facilitating collaboration between behavioral and medical health care providers.

To Support Requests to MBHOs for Treatment Authorization

It is not uncommon for managed behavioral health care organizations (MBHOs) to require that requests for authorization for initial or continued treatment be accompanied by a written treatment plan. Frequently, the treatment plan must be written in such a way or must use such a format that information important for decision making (of both the MBHO and the clinician) is provided and specific aspects of the proposed care are addressed. Not only does this allow the MBHO to determine whether the health plan member is or will be receiving the appropriate treatment for his or her problem, it also is a means of holding the clinician accountable for delivering the necessary services. Moreover, the MBHO may use the information reported in a treatment plan as a means of determining the reasonableness of a later request for additional services.

In one sense, the treatment plan also serves as means of prompting consultation from the MBHO regarding the treatment that the clinician is proposing. A review of treatment plan information by an MBHO care manager can be used as an opportunity for the clinician to obtain feedback regarding such important clinical issues as the appropriateness of the patient's diagnosis, treatment goals, planned level of care (LOC), and projected length of treatment (as reflected in the requested number of treatment sessions or days). As a consequence, the care manager and clinician may arrive at a more effective approach to the patient's problems.

To Provide a Record for Quality Assurance Purposes

Treatment plans provide documentation against which MBHOs can help ensure that health plan members are receiving quality care. The review that takes place during the treatment authorization process helps determine whether patients are getting the *individualized* treatment that they need for their particular problems, both at the initiation of treatment and periodically thereafter. At the same time, the treatment plan can serve as a vehicle for planning and documenting general interventions. For example, one large MBHO has two system-wide quality initiatives: screening all patients aged 12 years and older for substance abuse, and informing every patient's primary care physician (PCP) that the patient is receiving services from the MBHO. Every treatment plan submitted to the MBHO for review must document whether the provider has completed these quality-improvement activities.

To Provide a Means of Communication with External Reviewers

Periodically, MBHOs are audited by state and federal regulatory bodies, as well as by accrediting organizations such as JCAHO and NCQA. As part of their requirements for continued licensure or accreditation, these oversight bodies require evidence that the MBHO is providing quality care to the health plan members it serves. Sometimes, the MBHO is required to have copies of written treatment plans on file and accessible for review by auditing teams. Such treatment plans can be used in other instances to demonstrate that certain quality improvement activities (such as substance abuse screening or PCP communication) are currently taking place.

There are two other ways in which treatment planning is important to MBHOs (Jongsma & Peterson, 1999). First, it provides one means of achieving uniformity in the documentation of treatment records. This is especially the case when the MBHO has adopted a standardized format for the development and submission of these plans. Standardization can help streamline the processing of requests for authorization of care and thus can facilitate patients' receiving the care they need. In addition, treatment plans ensure that providers are meeting the MBHO's demands for accountability by requiring the documentation of measurable objectives, which can also be used for outcome assessment purposes. Indeed, as Naglieri and Pfeiffer (1999) have observed, the ability to demonstrate the value of mental health (and substance abuse) care is dependent upon having reliable treatment outcomes data that "necessitate a more carefully crafted treatment plan that meets the [patient's] needs, is individualized and specific, and measurable in terms of setting goals and objectives that can be used to chart the [patient's] ongoing progress and ultimate outcome" (p. 553).

Benefits of Treatment Planning

It should be clear from the foregoing discussion how treatment planning serves the purposes of the MBHO—but how do the direct participants in the therapeutic process profit from the time and effort that are required to develop a plan for improving the patient's life?

To the Clinician

Both Naglieri and Pfeiffer (1999) and Seligman (1993) view treatment planning as providing a road map that can guide the treatment process—something that helps keep the clinician on course to the agreed upon goals. Jongsma and Peterson (1999) point out how it forces the clinician to analytically and critically consider which interventions are best for the patient and the desired treatment outcomes. It can be used to guide treatment, rather than allowing treatment to follow the patient as many traditionally trained clinicians have been taught. This is certainly an important development in an era in which clinicians no longer have the luxury of planning treatment on a session-to-session basis. Also, as alluded to earlier, it helps meet the demands for accountability made by MBHOs and other third parties with a stake in the patient's treatment, and assists in the coordination of the patient's care with multiple care providers.

Moreover, the development of a written, formal treatment plan can serve as one form of protection against certain types of legal action that might be brought against the clinician (Jongsma & Peterson, 1999; Seligman, 1993). This is not an unimportant consideration in a behavioral health care environment serving a clientele that appears to be growing more litigious. Having documentation of mutually agreed upon treatment goals and interventions can, in some cases, save the clinician from professional and financial disaster.

Rapid Reference 1.2 summarizes the benefits of treatment planning to the clinician.

To the Patient

For patients, the benefits of having a treatment plan are straightforward: It specifies what the focus of the treatment will be and what outcomes the patient and the clinician will be collaboratively working to-

===Rapid Reference 1.2

Benefits of Treatment Planning for Clinicians

• Provides a road map to guide treatment

• Forces critical thinking in formulating interventions

• Helps meet MBHO requirements for accountability

• Assists in coordinating care with other health care professionals (e.g., primary care physicians)

• Provides protection from certain types of litigation

Note: From Jongsma and Peterson (1999); Naglieri and Pfeiffer (1999); Seligman (1993).

ward (Naglieri & Pfeiffer, 1999). Consequently, instead of treatment's being no more than a vague contract between the patient and the clinician, it becomes a cooperative effort in which both parties work toward specific goals using specific interventions (Jongsma & Peterson, 1999).

TREATMENT PLANNING ASSUMPTIONS

The introduction to this chapter presented a broad overview of the importance and benefits of the development and successful implementation of treatment plans for behavioral health care patients. The following are some general assumptions underlying the treatment planning process.

1. As Tillett (1996) has observed, "Not all patients (and not all mental health professionals) are suited to the psychotherapeutic endeavor" (p. 11).
2. The patient is experiencing behavioral health problems that have been either self-identified or identified by another party. Common external sources of problem identification include the patient's spouse, parent, teacher, or employer, and the legal system.
3. The patient experiences some degree of internal or external motivation, or both, to eliminate or reduce the identified problems. An example of external motivation to change is the potential loss of a job or dissolution of a marriage if problems are not resolved to the satisfaction of the other party.
4. The goals of treatment are tied either directly or indirectly to the identified problems.
5. The goals of treatment have definable criteria for achievement, are indeed achievable by the patient, and are developed by the patient in collaboration with the clinician.
6. The prioritizing of goals is reflected in the treatment plan.
7. The patient's progress toward the achievement of the treatment goals can be tracked and compared against an expected path of improvement in either a formal or informal manner. This expected path of improvement may be based on either the clinician's experience or (ideally) on objective data gathered on similar patients.
8. Deviations from the expected path of improvement may require a

DON'T FORGET

Assumptions About Treatment Planning

• The patient is experiencing behavioral health problems.
• Not all patients are suited for psychotherapy (Tillett, 1996).
• The patient is motivated to work on the identified problems.
• Treatment goals are tied to the identified problems.
• Treatment goals have criteria for achievement, are achievable, and are collaboratively developed and prioritized.
• Progress toward the treatment goals can be tracked.
• Deviations from expected improvement may require modifications in the treatment plan.

modification in the treatment plan, followed by subsequent monitoring to determine the effectiveness of the alteration.

The preceding assumptions should not be considered exhaustive, nor are they likely to reflect what actually occurs in all situations. For example, some patients seen for therapeutic services have no motivation to change. As may be seen in juvenile detention settings or in cases in which children are brought to treatment by the parents, their participation in treatment is forced; consequently, they may exert no effort to change. In the more extreme cases, they might in fact engage in intentional efforts to sabotage the therapeutic intervention. In other cases, some clinicians continue to identify and prioritize treatment goals without the direct input of the patient. Regardless, the preceding assumptions should have a direct bearing on treatment-planning efforts.

PURPOSE OF THIS BOOK

In addition to the recognition of its place in the provision of quality behavioral health care, the realization of the benefits of and the importance that is currently being placed on treatment planning by the behavioral health care industry and the behavioral health care professions have served as the impetus for this book. The purpose of this book is to provide both graduate students and seasoned clinicians from the behavioral health professions a practical, easy-to-use guide to the development and use of treatment plans for behavioral health care patients. Realizing the variability of treatment plan development that accompanies many of the theoretical approaches to therapeutic intervention, the approach taken here is one that is general and atheoretical. The focus of this book will be directed to the planning of treatment for adults voluntarily seeking outpatient psychotherapeutic or other intervention services for a mental health or substance abuse problem. However, issues related to treatment planning for other populations—children, inpatients, and those involuntarily engaged in treatment—will also be addressed. When appropriate, treatment planning issues as they specifically relate to the provision of services in an MBHO system of care will be given additional consideration, given the dominant presence of managed care in the delivery of behavioral health care services.

It is important to acknowledge that the treatment planning process and resulting product that are described herein should be considered ideals. It is recognized that, particularly in the age of managed behavioral health care, clinicians may not have the luxury of time and resources needed to complete the type of treatment planning to the full extent recommended in the chapters that follow. However, this information still can assist in the development of the type of treatment planning that is required and enabled by the particular setting and circumstances in which the clinician practices.

As with other volumes in the *Essentials* series, various aids to learning or for quick reference to important information are included in each chapter. These include boxes presenting concise key information *(Rapid References)*, exceptions or caveats to particular ideas *(Caution)*, information central to theory or critical to implementation of ideas *(Don't Forget)*, and a hypothetical case study developed to demonstrate the application of chapter-specific information *(Putting It Into Practice)*. Several questions to test one's knowledge about and ability to apply information presented *(Test Yourself)* are also included at the end of each chapter.

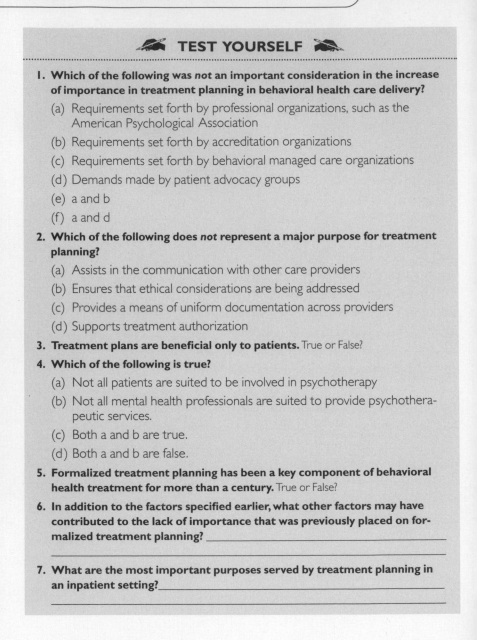

TEST YOURSELF

1. **Which of the following was *not* an important consideration in the increase of importance in treatment planning in behavioral health care delivery?**
   (a) Requirements set forth by professional organizations, such as the American Psychological Association
   (b) Requirements set forth by accreditation organizations
   (c) Requirements set forth by behavioral managed care organizations
   (d) Demands made by patient advocacy groups
   (e) a and b
   (f) a and d

2. **Which of the following does *not* represent a major purpose for treatment planning?**
   (a) Assists in the communication with other care providers
   (b) Ensures that ethical considerations are being addressed
   (c) Provides a means of uniform documentation across providers
   (d) Supports treatment authorization

3. **Treatment plans are beneficial only to patients.** True or False?

4. **Which of the following is true?**
   (a) Not all patients are suited to be involved in psychotherapy
   (b) Not all mental health professionals are suited to provide psychotherapeutic services.
   (c) Both a and b are true.
   (d) Both a and b are false.

5. **Formalized treatment planning has been a key component of behavioral health treatment for more than a century.** True or False?

6. **In addition to the factors specified earlier, what other factors may have contributed to the lack of importance that was previously placed on formalized treatment planning?** _____
   _____

7. **What are the most important purposes served by treatment planning in an inpatient setting?**_____
   _____

8. What rationale could one provide to an MBHO that would help justify reimbursement for time spent in treatment planning? _____

_____

Answers: 1. f; 2. b; 3. False; 4. c; 5. False; 6. insurance companies did not require clinicians to submit treatment plans for reimbursement, patients were not as involved in the planning of their own treatment; graduate students were not taught the importance of treatment planning, clinicians were not generally held accountable for their services, ongoing unlimited treatment was commonplace; 7. to facilitate clear communication among all professionals involved in the patient's treatment, to set realistic expectations for treatment, to set goals for discharge to a lower level of care, to support requests for treatment authorization from MBHOs; 8. helps ensure that the patient is receiving appropriate and effective treatment, can establish criteria for treatment termination, provides patients with opportunities to become immediately involved in their own treatment.

Two

PATIENT ASSESSMENT

The importance of assessment in the development of a treatment plan cannot be overestimated. Beutler (1991) described it as the first step in systematic treatment selection, whereas Jongsma and Peterson (1999) referred to it as the "foundation of an effective treatment plan" (p. 3). Butcher (1997) identified assessment of the patient's problems, symptoms, and personality makeup as "the primary factor that the therapist can use to prevent some of the [potentially negative factors impinging on treatment] . . . or at least try to counterbalance them" (p. 332). He also pointed to the need for assessment at the beginning of treatment in order to have data with which to gauge patient progress during treatment or upon its completion.

What is assessment? *Assessment* involves the gathering of relevant information about patients and their environments, their problems, and what they hope to accomplish through therapeutic intervention. The information gained through assessment answers some of the more basic questions, such as the following:

- For what problems is the patient seeking help?
- How have these problems affected the patient's life?
- What is maintaining these problems?
- What does the patient hope to gain from treatment?

Moreover, what are the goals of assessment? According to Tillett (1996, p. 12),

Assessment should enable both patient and assessor collaboratively to answer certain key questions:
   a) Is treatment of any kind required?
   b) If treatment is indicated, what are the relative merits of medical, psychological and social interventions?

  c) If psychological intervention is indicated
      i) Which types of approach might be appropriate?
      ii) What depth of therapy is needed?
      iii) Who should therapy involve?

It is only through having this type of information that the clinician is able to arrive at a formulation of the patient and the patient's problems, which in turn will enable the development of an appropriate treatment plan.

MEANS OF ASSESSMENT

The way an assessment of a patient seeking mental health or substance abuse treatment is conducted can vary considerably from one clinician to another. Several factors can contribute to this variation. One has to do with the *professional training* of the clinician. Each behavioral health profession tends to view assessment from a difference perspective. This, in part, is a reflection of the differences among the professions. For example, psychiatrists are more likely to be medically oriented in their approach to assessment, focusing on a more thorough medical history and being more interested in the results of medical tests (e.g., lab results, electroencephalograms [EEG], magnetic resonance imaging). Clinical social workers are more likely to assess patients from a perspective of the patients' relationships to others and their surroundings. For this reason, they may place more emphasis on information obtained from collaterals (e.g., family members, school officials). With expertise in psychological testing considered their unique and distinguishing characteristic among the behavioral health care professions, psychologists have greater interest in findings from psychological testing.

Another possible factor playing into the means by which clinicians assess patients is their *theoretical orientation,* or how they conceptualize behavioral health disturbances. A behaviorist will be interested in the antecedents and reinforcers of the problematic behavior, whereas a cognitive therapist will be more interested in what patients tell themselves about their experiences that tend to trigger the problematic behaviors.

Yet another factor is a more practical one. This has to do with *the situation itself.* The ability of clinicians to conduct an interview may be limited by external limitations and circumstances that are beyond their control. A example can be seen in the differences in the assessment procedures that may be exhibited by the same clinician seeing self-pay patients versus patients that are being seen under a managed care contract. Clinicians know that they can bill their usual hourly or per-procedure rate with self-pay patients and not be concerned with health care benefit limitations. With MBHO patients, however, the amount or type of care authorized for the patient, as well as the MBHO's treatment philosophy or expectations (e.g., an emphasis on brief problem-oriented therapy) may lead the clinician to forgo his or her usual approach to assessing patients requesting treatment.

Regardless of any of the factors just mentioned, the core of any assessment should be the *clinical interview.* Findings from psychological testing, a review of medical and other pertinent records of historical value (e.g., school records, court records), collateral contacts (e.g., family, teachers, work supervisors), and other sources of information about the patient all are important and can help one understand patients and their problems. However, nothing can substitute for the type of information that can be obtained only through face-to-face, one-to-one contact with the patient.

THE CLINICAL INTERVIEW: GENERAL CONSIDERATIONS

As suggested earlier, any number of approaches can be taken in conducting the clinical interview. Nonetheless, there are several factors that should be taken into consideration with regard to the clinical interview. Doing so will help ensure that the limited time typically allotted for direct assessment of the patient will yield the most valid, useful, and comprehensive information.

The Clinical Interview Within the Context of the Assessment

Although the clinical interview is at the core of the assessment, in most cases it is only one component of the process. Other sources of information about the patient (e.g., collateral interviews, psychological testing, record reviews) may be available and the clinician certainly should capitalize on these as appropriate. Referral to another behavioral health professional for needed information should also be considered when called for. For instance, the presence of concomitant seizures, blackouts, severe memory lapses, or other signs or symptoms pathognomonic of disorders of the central nervous system should lead to a referral for a neurological or neuropsychological evaluation to help rule out a neurological basis for the presenting problem.

The primacy of the clinical interview over the other means used to gather assessment information cannot be emphasized heavily enough. Information from other sources is important, but it often is indirect, second-hand information that either has been colored by others' perceptions of the patient, is inferred from other information, or lacks the degree of detail or specificity that the clinician would have pursued if the clinician were the one who gathered the information. None of these sources of information can provide the same sense of the patient and his or her circumstances that the clinical interview can provide. Moreover, as Beutler (1995) points out, "The interview is usually the first assessment procedure administered, because it is the easiest method of facilitating the patient's cooperation and is readily adapted to providing a context in which the other instruments can be selected and interpreted" (p. 101). The clinical interview therefore helps establish a relationship with the patient and sets the tone and expectations for the remainder of the assessment process.

Goal of the Clinical Interview

What one hopes to accomplish during the clinical interview will vary from clinician to clinician. Some may view it as only a formality required by the patient's MBHO and that will make little difference in the patient's treatment. Others may view it as a means of gathering necessary (but not, in itself, sufficient) information for the assessment of the patient. Still others may view it as being the only legitimate source of information. Makover (1992) indicates that by the end of the initial interview, the clinician should be able to answer three important questions:

1. *Why did the patient come here?* Knowing why patients seek services from a behavioral health professional as opposed to other treatment sources (e.g., Alcoholics Anonymous, clergy, primary care physician) can provide insight into both how patients conceptualize their problems and what their expectations are of both themselves and the clinician in the therapeutic relationship.
2. *Why did the patient come now?* Most patients probably experience prob-

lems for some time prior to seeking help. They could have sought help earlier, or at some later time. Information about their motivation for seeking help *now* can help identify those problems and issues most pressing to them and for which they are most amenable to treatment.

3. *What does the patient want?* As Makover (1992) notes, "This goes to the heart of treatment planning, for in order to arrive at the 'therapeutic contract,' the patient's perceived or stated requests must be clarified and then either agreed to or modified. In a sense, addressing this issue is the first piece of therapeutic work to be done" (p. 341). He also notes that answering this question may require more than one interview and may be subject to change over time. However, at least a tentative answer should be obtained prior to the development of an initial treatment plan.

Unstructured, Structured, and Semistructured Clinical Interviews

There are a few ways in which clinicians can conduct the clinical interview. The first is what is referred to as the *unstructured interview*. The approach taken here is just as the term implies: It is one that follows no rigid sequence or direction of inquiry; rather, it is tailored more to the individual patient's problems and relies heavily on the clinician's competence, judgment, creativity, and skills (Beutler, 1995). The reliance on individual clinician skills makes the unstructured interview the least reliable and possibly the least valid of the assessment procedures.

At the other end of the continuum is the *structured interview*. As defined by Beutler (1995), the structure interview is one in which the patient is asked a standard set of questions in a specific order. Beutler identified two types of structured interview: The first is the *omnibus diagnostic interview*, in which decision trees are used to determine which among a pool of potential questions the patient should be asked. In essence, the responses to previous questions guide the clinician in selecting which questions to ask next. Two examples are the Diagnostic Interview Schedule (DIS; Robins, Helzer, Croughan, & Ratcliff, 1981) and the Structured Clinical Interview for *DSM-III-R* (SCID; Spitzer, Williams, & Gibbon, 1986). The second type of structured interview is focused more on assessing a broad or narrow array of symptomatology and its severity rather than being tied closely to a diagnostic system. Examples include the structured versions of the broad-based Mental Status Examination (Amchin, 1991) and the narrowly focused Hamilton Rating Scale for Depression (HRSD; Hamilton, 1967).

Although the structured interview provides the best means of obtaining valid and reliable information about the patient, there are drawbacks to its use. As Beutler (1995) points out, structured interviews generally tend to be rather lengthy and require extensive training to ensure proper use. For this reason, they tend to be used less in clinical applications than in research applications in which standardization in data gathering and empirical demonstration of data validity and reliability are critical.

Viewed from another perspective, Meyer et al. (2001) see the problem of structured versus unstructured interviews as follows:

> When interviews are unstructured, clinicians may overlook certain areas of functioning and focus more exclusively on presenting complaints. When interviews are highly structured, clinicians can lose the forest for the trees and make precise but errant judgments. . . . Such mistakes may occur when the clinician focuses on responses to specific interview questions (e.g., diagnostic criteria) without fully considering the salience of these responses in the patient's broader life context or without adequately recognizing how the individual responses fit together into a symptomatically coherent pattern. (p. 144)

What is the best way to deal with the dilemma posed by structured and unstructured interviews? The solution is a compromise between the two, that is, the *semistructured interview.* Employing a semistructured interview provides clinicians with a means of ensuring that all important areas of investigation are addressed while allowing them the flexibility to focus more or less attention on specific areas, depending on their relevance to the patient's problems. In essence, the clinician conducts each interview according to a general structure addressing common areas of biopsychosocial functioning. At the same time, the clinician is free to explore in greater detail the more salient aspects of the patient's presentation and history as they are revealed. This exploration may be *horizontal* (dealing with establishing temporal relationships) or *vertical* (dealing with establishing the meaning or interpretation of affect or behavior) in nature (Mumma, 1998). Moreover, this semistructured approach allows for the insertion of therapeutic interventions if such opportunities arise during the course of the interview.

In addition, Makover (1992) has observed that one reason for the failure of clinicians to understand the key issues or crises that lead the patients to seek treatment

> may be the kind of aimless or disconnected history-taking fostered by training programs that require an exhaustive history for the initial evaluation. The attempt to gather all relevant (and irrelevant) information diffuses the interviewer's focus and makes it more difficult to decide what issues are most important to the patient's life situation. [Makover] encourages trainees to concentrate on the most important issues first and to have confidence that important historical information will emerge at a later time when its significance can be more easily assessed. (p. 341)

For these reasons, the semistructured approach is the one that is advocated by this author and therefore serves as the recommended method for gathering the interview information discussed later in this chapter.

Some Keys to Good Clinical Interviewing

Conducting a good, useful clinical interview requires more that just knowing what areas to query the patient about. It requires skills that are usually taught in graduate-level practicum and internship experiences and later honed through down-in-the-trenches experience. It is beyond the scope of this book to go into depth on the art of interviewing, even at the most basic level. However, there are some general tips that should help the clinician extract the greatest amount of useful information possible during the clinical interview.

Beutler (1995) provides several recommendations pertaining to conducting the clinical interview, regardless of the setting or circumstances in which it is conducted. First, there are recommendations pertaining to setting the stage for the interview. Included here is a discussion of such things as the purpose of the clinical interview and (assuming the interview is the first procedure in the process) the assessment in general; the questions that will be addressed during the course of the assessment; the patient's impressions of the purpose of the assessment and how the results will be used; matters pertaining to the patient's right to confidentiality and right to refuse to participate in the evaluation or treatment; and any questions the patient may have as a result of this preliminary discussion. Questions regarding the administrative aspects of the service (e.g., completion of standard intake forms, insurance information) can also be addressed. In all, this preliminary discussion serves to instill in the patient a sense of reassurance and freedom regarding the assessment process.

As for the interview itself, Beutler (1995) recommends the following:

- Avoid a mechanical approach to covering the desired interview content areas. Maintain a conversational approach to asking questions and eliciting information, modifying the inquiry (as necessary) to ensure a smooth flow or transition from one topic to another.
- Begin exploration of content areas with open-ended inquiries, and proceed to closed-ended questions as more specificity and detail are required.
- Consistent with the previous recommendations, move from general topic areas to the more specific ones.
- At the end of the interview, invite the patient to add other information that he or she feels is important for the clinician to know. Also invite questions and comments about anything related to the interview or the assessment process.
- Provide at least preliminary feedback to the patient based on the information presented during the interview. Arrange for another feedback session after all assessment procedures have been completed in order to review the final results, conclusions, and recommendations of the assessment.

ASSESSMENT CONTENT AREAS IMPORTANT FOR TREATMENT PLANNING

This section presents a discussion of the content areas that *ideally* would

---

DON'T FORGET

Keys to Good Clinical Interviewing

- Avoid a mechanical approach to questioning.
- Move from open-ended inquiries to closed-ended inquiries.
- Move from general topics to specific topics.
- Invite the patient to add information and ask questions.
- Provide feedback to the patient.

Note. From Beutler (1995).

be addressed during the course of every assessment (these areas are outlined in Rapid Reference 2.1). However, the content areas or patient issues addressed in a given assessment will vary, depending on a number of factors. Among these are the patient's willingness to be involved in the assessment, the nature and severity of the patient's problems, the clinician's training and experience, the setting in (or for which) the assessment is being conducted, and

═Rapid Reference 2.1

Recommended Outline for a Semistructured Clinical Interview

1. Presenting problem or chief complaint
2. History of the problem
3. Family and social history
4. Educational history
5. Employment history
6. Mental health and substance abuse history
7. Medical history
8. Important patient characteristics
   a. Functional impairment
   b. Subjective distress
   c. Problem complexity
   d. Readiness to change
   e. Potential to resist therapeutic influence
   f. Social support
   g. Coping styles
9. Patient strengths
10. Mental status
11. Risk of harm to self and others
12. Diagnosis and related considerations
13. Treatment goals
   a. Patient-identified goals
   b. Third-party goals
14. Motivation to change

time and reimbursement considerations. Consistent with the semistructured approach to clinical interviewing, flexibility and clinical judgment are called for. In some cases, one will want to ensure that particular content areas are thoroughly explored, while in other cases efforts should be directed at obtaining information about other content areas.

The methods for gathering the assessment information also will vary according to a number of patient, clinician, and other factors. Some clinicians feel confident in their ability to elicit all necessary assessment information through the clinical interview. (Indeed, some types of assessment information, such as that pertaining to the patient's affect and continuity of thought, are accessible only through the clinical interview.) Others may find it useful or critical to employ adjuncts to the interview process. For example, some psychologists may administer an MMPI-2 to every patient they assess, regardless of the patient or the patient's presenting problems. Similarly, some psychiatrists may order an EEG for anyone suspected of being neurologically impaired. Thus, in the discussion that follows, no one means of gathering specific information for a given content area is required. However, certain methods or sources of information are recommended because they have been found to be useful or otherwise important for obtaining information about specific content areas.

It is recognized that much of this book's intended audience is likely to have a strong inclination for using psychological testing as a means of obtaining assessment information. Thus, chapter 3 is devoted to the use of testing in general as well as individual tests in the assessment process.

Presenting Problem or Chief Complaint

One of the first bits of information that the clinician will want to obtain is the chief problem or complaint that led the patient to seek treatment. This is usually elicited by fairly standard questions, such as "What brings you here today?" or "Why do you think you need to see a psychologist [or other behavioral health professional]?" Responses to questions such as these can be quite telling and thus should be recorded verbatim. Besides providing immediate insight into what the patient considers the most pressing problems, the responses to questions such as these can provide clues as to how distressing these problems are, whether the patient is entering treatment voluntarily, how motivated the patient may be to work in therapy, and what the patient's expectations for treatment are. Moreover, the contrast among the patient's report, that of the referring professional, and the clinician's observations can provide additional verification of the degree to which the patient is likely to engage in the therapeutic endeavor (Beutler, 1995). In addition, the verbatim statement can serve as a kind of baseline against which to measure the gains made from treatment.

History of the Problem

Thorough knowledge and understanding of the problem's history can greatly facilitate its treatment. This knowledge should include when the patient began experiencing the problem, the patient's perception of the cause of the problem, significant events that occurred at or around that time, antecedents or precipitants of the problem, what has maintained its presence, and its course over time. Also important is the effect that the problem has had on the patient's ability to function, what the patient has done to try to deal with the problem, and what has and has not been helpful in ameliorating it.

Beutler (1995) recommends that historical information obtained from the patient be cross-validated through other sources of information. This might necessitate interviewing family members or other significant collaterals, reviewing records of past treatment attempts, or reviewing school or employment records. Again, knowing the perceptions of the problem from multiple perspectives permits a more comprehensive understanding of its nature and course.

Family and Social History

Many would argue that understanding the patient's problems requires an understanding of the patient within a social context. How did the person who is currently seeking behavioral health care intervention get to this point? What experiences have shaped the patient's ability to interact with others and cope with the demands of daily living? Knowing where the patient came from and where the patient is now vis-à-vis the patient's relationship with the world is critical when developing a plan to improve or at least come to terms with that relationship.

Important aspects of the family history include the occupation and education of parents; number of siblings and birth order; quality of the patient's relationship to parents, siblings, and significant extended family members; parental approach to child rearing (e.g., punitive, demeaning, or abusive vs. loving, supportive, and rewarding); and parental expectations for the patient's educational, occupational, and social accomplishments. Also important is the physical environment (type of housing and neighborhood) in which the child was reared, and whether the family was settled or subjected to uprooting or frequent moves (e.g., military families).

The patient's interaction with and experiences in the social environment outside the protection of the home provide clues to the patient's perception of the world, ability to derive comfort and support from others, and ability to cope with the daily, inescapable demands that accompany living and working with others. Information about the general number (a lot vs. a few) and types (close vs. casual) of friendships; participation in team sports; involvement in clubs or other social activities; being a leader versus a follower; involvement in religious or political activities; and other opportunities requiring interpersonal interaction can all be insightful. Pointing to the work of Luborsky and Crits-Christoph (1990), Beutler (1995) recommends that key relationships—parents or parental figures, siblings, significant relatives, and major love interests—should be explored, in that

to the degree that similar needs and expectations are found to be working across the different relationships described, the clinician can infer that the pattern observed is pervasive and ritualistic. That is, the patient's relationships are more dominated by his/her fixed needs than by the nature of the person to whom the patient is relating. Alternatively, if different needs and expectations are found to be expressed in different relationships, it may be inferred that the patient has the ability to be discriminating, flexible, and realistic in social interactions. (p. 113)

Beutler adds that

the patient's subjective responses to early friendships, love relationships, and sexual attachments are specifically sought. In eliciting such information, the clinician is not only seeking to determine past and present patterns in the way the patient deals with others, but also to form an impression about his/her capacity for forming a therapeutic or treatment alliance. (p. 112)

In addition, as relevant, the patient's legal history and experiences stemming from being a member of a racial or ethnic minority should be explored because both can have a significant bearing on the current problems and coping styles. They also may provide information related to the patient's ability to relate well with and take direction from perceived authority figures (such as clinicians).

Educational History

The patient's educational history generally provides limited yet potentially important information. When not readily obvious, the attained level of education can yield a rough estimate of the patient's level of intelligence, an important factor in considering certain types of therapeutic intervention. It also speaks to the patient's aspirations and goals, ability to gain from learning experiences, willingness to make a commitment and persevere, and ability to delay gratification. Participation in both academic and school-related extracurricular activities (e.g., debate or theater clubs, school paper or yearbook staff, varsity sports) are also worth noting in this regard.

Employment History

A patient's employment history can provide a wealth of information that can be useful in understanding the patient and developing an effective treatment plan. Interactions with supervisors and peers provide additional insights into the patient's ability to get along with others and take direction. Also, the type of position the patient holds relative to past educational or training experiences or level of intelligence can be enlightening in terms of the patient's being a success versus a failure, being an overachiever versus an underachiever, being motivated to succeed versus doing only the minimum, being an initiator versus needing to be told what to do and when to do it, or being internally versus externally motivated. In addition, the patient's ability to assume the role and meet the expectations of a hired employee (e.g., being at work on time, giving a full day's work, adhering to company policies, respecting company property) may have implications for assuming the role of a patient and complying with treatment recommendations.

Mental Health and Substance Abuse History

It should go without saying that a previous history of behavioral health problems and treatment thereof (if any) is important to know. This would include any episodes of care for mental health or substance abuse problems, regardless of the level of care (e.g., inpatient, outpatient, residential) at which treatment for these problems was provided. Records pertaining to previous treatment, including psychological test results, are important in this regard and therefore should always be requested. Obtaining a thorough mental health and substance abuse history can shed light on whether the current problem is part of a single or recurrent episode, or a progression of behavioral health problems over a period of time; what treatment approaches or modalities have worked or not worked in the past; and the patient's willingness to engage in therapeutic interventions.

The cooccurrence of both mental health and substance abuse disorders is not uncommon, with estimates of past-year comorbidity prevalence running as high as 4.7% (Kessler, et al., 1994). However, patients seeking services for mental health problems might not always know that they have an accompanying substance abuse problem, or they simply may not feel that it is worth mentioning since that is not what they are seeking help for. For these reasons, history taking should always include an inquiry about the patient's use of alcohol and other substances. A detailed exploration is called for when either current or past use suggests it is or has been problematic for the patient. Dual-diagnosis patients often present unique challenges and warrant special considerations. It is therefore important to identify these individuals early on and ensure that they receive the specialized treatment that is warranted.

Medical History

Obtaining a medical history is always in order, regardless of the problems that the patient presents. At the minimum, one should inquire about any significant illnesses or hospitalizations, past and current physical illnesses or conditions (e.g., breast cancer), chronic conditions (e.g., diabetes, asthma, migraine headaches), and injuries or disorders affecting the central nervous system (e.g., head injury, stroke), as well as any functional limitations they may impose on the patient. Not only may this provide clues to the presenting symptomatology and functioning (see Maruish, 2000, for a discussion of comorbid psychiatric and medical disorders), but it may also suggest the need for referral to a psychiatrist or other medical professional (e.g., a neurologist) for evaluation, treatment, or management. It is also important to identify any current prescribed and over-the-counter medications that the patient is taking, as well as any medications to which the patient is allergic.

In addition, at least a cursory family history for significant medical problems is recommended. Information about blood relatives can reveal a history of genetically transmitted disorders of which the patient may be unaware. This could have a bearing on the patient's current problems, or it may suggest a predisposition to develop medical problems in the future that could have negative consequences for the patient's mental health. A family history of illness might also provide insight into the environment in which the patient was reared and the impact of the demands of that environment.

Important Patient Characteristics

From the foregoing discussion, it should be obvious that assessment for the purpose of treatment planning should go beyond the identification and description of the patient's symptoms or problems. The patient's family, social, psychiatric, medical, educational, and employment histories provide a wealth of information for understanding the origin, development, and maintenance of behavioral health problems. At the same time, other types of information can be quite useful in developing a treatment plan.

During the past decade, Beutler and his colleagues (Beutler & Clarkin, 1990; Beutler, Goodrich, Fisher, & Williams, 1999; Fisher, Beutler, & Williams, 1999; Gaw & Beutler, 1995) have worked to develop and promote the use of a system of patient characteristics considered important for treatment planning. According to Beutler et al. (1999),

> In an effort to bring some order to the many variables and diverse hypotheses associated with the several models of differential treatment assignment and to place them in the perspective of empirical research, Beutler and Clarkin (1990) grouped patient characteristics presented by the different theories into a series of superordinate and subordinate categories. This classification included seven relatively specific classes of

patient variables that are distinguished both by their susceptibility to measurement using established psychological tests and by their ability to predict differential responses to psychosocial treatment. (p. 85)

For this reason, the seven patient characteristics that power Beutler's *systematic treatment selection model* merit investigation by the clinician.

Functional Impairment

The degree to which behavioral health patients are impaired in their social, environmental, and interpersonal functioning has been identified as one of the most important factors to consider during an assessment, particularly for the purposes of treatment outcomes programs (Maruish, 1999, 2002). Much of the information needed for this portion of the assessment can be obtained during the investigation of the patient's family, social, employment, and educational history. However, more in-depth questioning may be required. Not only is social functioning information important for treatment planning and outcomes assessment purposes, it also is critical for arriving at the Global Assessment of Functioning (GAF) rating for Axis V of the *Diagnostic and Statistical Manual of Mental Disorders* (4th ed., text revision) (*DSM-IV-TR* [American Psychiatric Association, 2000]; discussed later). Indicators of functional impairment are listed in Rapid Reference 2.2.

≡Rapid Reference 2.2

Clinical Indicators of Functional Impairment Exhibited or Reported During Assessment

- Problem interferes with patient's functioning during interview.
- Patient cannot concentrate on interview tasks.
- Patient is distracted even by minor events.
- Patient appears incapacitated by problem and has difficulty in functioning.
- Patient has difficulty in interacting with the interviewer as a result of problem severity.
- Multiple areas of performance are impaired in daily life.

Note. From "Integrating Treatment Recommendations: The Clinical Interview," by K. F. Gaw and L. E. Beutler, 1995, in *Integrative Assessment of Adult Personality* (p. 295), ed. L. E. Beutler and M. R. Berren, New York: Guilford Press. Copyright 1995 by Guilford Press. Adapted with permission.

Subjective Distress

Subject distress "is a cross-cutting, cross-diagnostic index of well-being ... [that] is poorly correlated with external measures of impairment. ... [It] is a transitory or changeable symptom state" (Beutler et al., 1999, p. 88). It might be considered a measure of internal functioning separate from the external or objective measure just described, with its importance lying in its relationship with the patient's level of motivation to engage in the therapeutic process (Gaw & Beutler, 1995). Subjective distress essentially refers to a *state* phenomenon; however, an assessment of the patient's *trait* level of distress may also yield information important to treatment planning (Fisher et al., 1999). Rapid Reference 2.3 provides a list of indicators of both high and low subjective distress.

Problem Complexity

Gaw and Beutler (1995) have indicated that problem severity is related to another important patient characteristic: *problem complexity*. The difference be-

---

≡Rapid Reference 2.3

Clinical Indicators of Subjective Distress Exhibited or Reported During Assessment

High Distress	Low Distress
• High emotional arousal	• Low emotional arousal
• High symptomatic distress	• Low symptomatic distress
• Motor agitation	• Reduced motor activity
• Difficulty in maintaining concentration	• Low investment in treatment
• Unsteady faltering voice	• Low energy level
• Autonomic symptoms	• Blunted or constricted affect
• Hyperventilation	• Unmodulated verbalizations
• Hypervigilance	• Slow verbalizations
• Excited affect	
• Intense feelings	

Note. From "Integrating Treatment Recommendations: The Clinical Interview," by K. F. Gaw and L. E. Beutler, 1995, in *Integrative Assessment of Adult Personality* (p. 299), ed. L. E. Beutler and M. R. Berren, New York: Guilford Press. Copyright 1995 by Guilford Press. Adapted with permission.

tween complex and noncomplex problems (or problems with a high or low level of complexity) is explained as follows:

> The symptoms associated with complex problems are indirect or symbolic expressions of the initiating or provoking stimuli, and these stimuli are unseen internal events rather than circumstances of the environment; the problems recur in somewhat different but related forms whenever the conflict is activated; and they spread across a variety of symptoms and situations. On the other hand, noncomplex problems are situationally evoked, infrequently recurrent unless the same situation is encountered again, and reflected in complexes of common symptoms. (p. 300)

Whether the patient's presenting problems are high or low with respect to complexity can have a important bearing on treatment planning. Ascertaining the level of problem complexity can be facilitated by historical information about other aspects of the patient's life (e.g., mental health and substance abuse history, family and interpersonal history, employment history). This information can allow for the revelation of "recurrent patterns or themes arising within objectively different but symbolically related relationships" (Gaw & Beutler, 1995, p. 301) that characterize high problem complexity. Indicators of complex and noncomplex problems are presented in Rapid Reference 2.4.

Readiness to Change

The importance of the patient's readiness to change in the therapeutic process comes from the work of Prochaska, DiClemente, and their colleagues (Brogan, Prochaska, & Prochaska, 1999; DiClemente & Hughes, 1990; DiClemente & Prochaska, 1998; McConnaughy, DiClemente, Prochaska, & Velicer, 1989; McConnaughy, Prochaska, & Velicer, 1983; Prochaska, 1995; Prochaska & DiClemente, 1982, 1992; Prochaska, DiClemente, & Norcross, 1992; Prochaska, Velicer, DiClemente, & Fava, 1988; Velicer, Hughes, Fava, Prochaska, & DiClemente, 1995; Velicer, Norman, Fava, & Prochaska, 1999; Velicer et al., 2000). They identified five stages through which individuals go when changing various aspects of their lives. These stages apply not only to change that is sought through mental health or substance abuse treatment, but also in nontherapeutic contexts. These stages, in their order of progression, are labeled *precontemplation, contemplation, preparation, action,* and *maintenance.* The distinguishing features of each stage are described in Rapid Reference 2.5. The

Rapid Reference 2.4

Clinical Indicators of Problem Complexity Exhibited or Reported During Assessment

Noncomplex Problem Indicators	Complex Problem Indicators
• Chronic habits and transient responses. • Behavior repetition is maintained by inadequate knowledge or by ongoing situational rewards. • Behaviors have a direct relationship to initiating events. • Behaviors are situation specific.	• Behaviors are repeated as themes across unrelated and dissimilar situations. • Behaviors are ritualized (yet self-defeating) attempts to resolve dynamic or interpersonal conflicts. • Current conflicts are expressions of the patient's past rather than present relationships. • Repetitive behavior results in suffering (rather than gratification). • Symptoms have a symbolic relationship to initiating events. • Problems are enduring, repetitive, and symbolic manifestations of characterological conflicts.

Note. From "Integrating Treatment Recommendations: The Clinical Interview," by K. F. Gaw and L. E. Beutler, 1995, in *Integrative Assessment of Adult Personality* (p. 302), ed. L. E. Beutler and M. R. Berren, New York: Guilford Press. Copyright 1995 by Guilford Press. Adapted with permission.

further along in the progression of these stages the individual is, the greater the effort that individual is likely to exert to effect the desired change. The stage at which the patient is at any point in treatment can have an important bearing on the selection of the most appropriate psychotherapeutic approach.

Potential to Resist Therapeutic Influence

Two different types of resistance are subsumed under this characteristic. One is *resistance*, which might be considered a state-like quality in which patients fail to comply with external recommendations or directions (Fisher et al., 1999). In some cases, this may be an indicator of their motivation to engage in treatment. The other is *reactance*, which reflects a more extreme, trait-like form of resistance that stems from patients' feeling that their freedom or sense of con-

≡Rapid Reference 2.5

Prochaska's Stages of Change

Stage	Distinguishing Features
Precontemplation	Little or no awareness of problems; little or no serious consideration or intent to change; often presents for treatment at the request of or pressure from another party; change may be exhibited when pressure is applied, but patient reverts to previous behavior when pressure is removed. *Resistance to recognizing or changing the problem* is the hallmark of the precontemplation stage.
Contemplation	Awareness of problem and serious thoughts about working on it, but no commitment to begin to work on it; weighing pros and cons of the problem and its solution. *Serious consideration of problem resolution* is the hallmark of the contemplation stage.
Preparation	Intention to take serious, effective action in the near future (e.g., within a month) but has already made small behavioral changes have already been made. *Decision making* is the hallmark of this stage.
Action	Overt modification of behavior, experiences, or environment in an effort to overcome the problem. *Modification of problem behavior to an acceptable criterion* and *serious efforts to change* are the hallmarks of this stage.
Maintenance	Continuation of change to prevent relapse and consolidate the gains made during the action stage. *Stabilizing behavior change* and *avoiding relapse* are the hallmarks of this stage.

Note. From Prochaska, DiClemente, and Norcross (1992).

trol is being challenged by external forces. It is manifested in their active opposition (i.e., in their doing the opposite of what they are requested or directed to do), rather than through a passive, do-nothing response during times of perceived threats to personal control. Rapid Reference 2.6 lists indicators of the low and high reactance.

Social Support

Beutler et al. (1999) discussed the importance of assessing the patient's social support system from both objective and subjective perspectives. *Objective social*

≡ Rapid Reference 2.6

Clinical Indicators of Reactance Exhibited or Reported During Assessment

Low-Reactance Indicators	High-Reactance Indicators
• Readily agrees to complete home-work assignments.	• Does not comply with homework assignments.
• Completes homework assign-ments.	• Has intense need to maintain au-tonomy.
• Is compliant with therapist direc-tions.	• Resists external influences.
• Accepts therapist's interpretations.	• Therapeutic interventions have paradoxical results.
• Is tolerant of events outside of own control.	• Refuses therapist's interpretations.
• Seeks direction.	• Is dominant.
• Is submissive to authority.	• Displays anxious resistance.
• Is nondefensive.	• Previous response to treatment was poor.
	• Has a history of social or interper-sonal conflict.

Note. From "Integrating Treatment Recommendations: The Clinical Interview," by K. F. Gaw and L. E. Beutler, 1995, in *Integrative Assessment of Adult Personality* (p. 306), ed. L. E. Beutler and M. R. Berren, New York: Guilford Press. Copyright 1995 by Guilford Press. Adapted with permission.

support can be assessed from external evidence of resources that are available to the patient. This would include such things as marriage, physical proximity to relatives, a network of identified friends, membership in social organizations, and involvement in religious activities. *Subjective social support* refers to the self-report of things such as the *quality* of the patient's social relationships. In essence, it has to do with the patient's perception of potential sources of psychological and physical support that the patient can draw upon during the episode of care and thereafter.

Coping Styles

Few would disagree with Beutler and his colleagues' identification of the patient's coping style as an important consideration for treatment planning. Here, *coping style* is defined as "an enduring trait that relates to the way one copes with personal or interpersonal threats" (Beutler et al., 1999, p. 828). It is conceived as a mechanism falling along a continuum of internalizing and externalizing behaviors that are employed during times of psychological distress. According to Gaw and Beutler (1995), *internalization* is suggested in patients who tend to (a) avoid, deny, repress, or compartmentalize sources of anxiety; (b) be overly introverted, introspective, self-critical, and self-controlled; and (c) be emotionally constricted. *Externalization* is suggested by a tendency to (a) directly avoid, rationalize, project, or act-out onto their environments; (b) exhibit a degree of insensitivity to their own and others' feelings; and (c) be spontaneous, impulsive, extraverted, and sometimes manipulative. Indicators of both types of coping styles are presented in Rapid Reference 2.7.

Patient Strengths

Typically, assessments are focused on uncovering the negative aspects of the patient, often to the neglect of the patient's more positive aspects. For treatment planning purposes, it is just as important to focus on revealing the patient's strengths as it is to focus on his or her deficits. Many may find this a difficult thing to do, because, as Lehnhoff (1991) indicated in speaking about *strength-focused assessment,* clinicians typically are not trained in uncovering patient successes. As he noted,

> Clinicians traditionally ask themselves, What causes the worst moments and how can we reduce them? They might then go on to scrutinize the pathology and the past. But one could also ask, What causes the patient's best moments and how can we increase them? Or similarly, Why is the patient not having more bad moments, how does the patient regain control after losing it, and why doesn't he lose control more often? Clearly, the strength-focused view of a patient seeks, for one thing, to uncover the reasons the pathology is not worse. The view assumes that almost any clinical condition varies in its intensity over time. (p. 12)

At the same time, Lehnhoff (1991) noted how the inclusion of the highest-level-of-functioning rating provided on Axis V into the multiaxial schema of the *DSM-IV-TR* is evidence of the behavioral health care field's recognition of the importance of patient coping strengths. He provides a number of examples of questions that can be used to help both the clinician and the patient

Rapid Reference 2.7

Clinical Indicators of Coping Style Exhibited or Reported During Assessment

Internalization Indicators	Externalization Indicators
• Undoing	• Ambivalence
• Self-punishment	• Acting out
• Intellectualization	• Blaming others and self
• Isolation of affect	• Low tolerance for frustration
• Emotional overcontrol or constriction	• Difficulty in differentiating emotions
• Low tolerance for feelings or sensations	• Avoidance or escape (or both)
• High resistance for feelings or sensations	• Projection
• Denial	• Conversion symptoms
• Reversal	• Paranoid reactions
• Reaction formation	• Unsocialized aggression
• Repression	• Manipulation of others
• Minimization	• Ego-syntonic behaviors
• Unrecognized wishes or desires	• Stimulation seeking
• Introversion	• Extraversion
• Social withdrawal	• Somatization (seeking of secondary gain via physical symptoms)
• Somatization (autonomic nervous system symptoms)	

Note. From "Integrating Treatment Recommendations: The Clinical Interview," by K. F. Gaw and L. E. Beutler, 1995, in *Integrative Assessment of Adult Personality* (p. 308), ed. L. E. Beutler and M. R. Berren, New York: Guilford Press. Copyright 1995 by Guilford Press. Adapted with permission.

identify strengths that might not otherwise come to light. Some of these questions are presented in Rapid Reference 2.8.

It is important to recognize that the benefits of assessing patient strengths go beyond their value to the development of the treatment plan. Lehnhoff (1991) noted that the act of forcing patients to consider their psychological assets can have therapeutic value in itself. In essence, strength-focused assessment can serve as an intervention before formal treatment actually begins.

≡ Rapid Reference 2.8

Questions That Help Assess Patient Strengths

- I've been hearing mostly about how bad things are for you, but I'd like to balance the view I have of you. What kinds of things do you do well?
- Now that we've discussed some things about your symptoms and stresses, I'd like to learn more about some of your satisfactions and successes. What are some good things you have enjoyed doing well?
- To get a more complete picture of your situation, I now need to know more about when the problem does *not* happen.
- What have you noticed you do that has helped in the past?
- Which of your jobs lasted the longest? What did you do to help this happen?
- Right now, some things are keeping you from doing worse than you are. What are they?
- Which of your good points do you most often forget?

Note. From Lehnhoff (1991, pp. 13–14).

Consequently, it can help build self-esteem and self-confidence, reinforce patients' efforts to seek help, and increase their motivation to return to engage in the work of treatment.

Mental Status Examination

Any clinical assessment should include a mental status examination (MSE). Completion of the MSE usually takes place at the end of the clinical interview. For the most part, the information needed for an MSE comes from the clinician's observations of and impressions formed about the patient during the course of the clinical interview and as a result of other assessment procedures (e.g., psychological testing). However, some aspects of the MSE usually require specific questioning that typically would not be included during the other parts of the assessment.

The MSE generally addresses a number of general categories or aspects of the patient's functioning, including descriptions of the patient's appearance and behavior, mood and affect, perception, thought processes, orientation, memory, judgment, and insight (see Rapid Reference 2.9). Trzepacz and Baker

Rapid Reference 2.9

Outline for the Mental Status Examination

1. Appearance (level of arousal, attentiveness, age, position, posture, attire, grooming, eye contact, physical characteristics, facial expression)

2. Activity (movement, tremor, choreoathetoid movements, dystonias, automatic movements, tics, mannerisms, compulsions, other motor abnormalities or expressions)

3. Attitude toward the clinician

4. Mood (euthymic, angry, euphoric, apathetic, dysphoric, apprehensive)

5. Affect (appropriateness, intensity, mobility, range, reactivity)

6. Speech and language (fluency, repetition, comprehension, naming, writing, reading, prosody, quality of speech)

7. Thought process (circumstantiality, flight of ideas, loose associations, tangentiality, word salad, clang associations, echolalia, neologisms, perseveration, thought blocking)

8. Thought content (delusion, homicidal or suicidal ideation, magical thinking, obsession, rumination, preoccupation, overvalued idea, paranoia, phobia, poverty of speech, suspiciousness)

9. Perception (autoscopy, déjà vu, depersonalization, hallucination, illusion, *jamais vu*)

10. Cognition (orientation, attention, concentration, immediate recall, short-term memory, long-term memory, constructional ability, abstraction, conceptualization)

11. Insight

12. Judgment

13. Defense mechanisms (altruism, humor, sublimation, suppression, repression, displacement, dissociation, reaction formation, intellectualization, splitting, externalization, projection, acting out, denial, distortion)

Note. From Trzepacz and Baker (1993).

(1993) provide an excellent description of the detailed aspects of each of these general categories. As Ginsberg (1985) has indicated, the manner in which the MSE is conducted will depend on the individual clinician, who may decide to forgo certain portions of the examination because of the circumstances of the particular patient. At the same time, he recommended that the MSE be conducted in detail, and that the patient's own words be recorded whenever possible.

Risk of Harm to Self and Others

Assessment of suicidal or homicidal ideation and potential should always be assessed, even if it consists of no more than asking the question, "Have you been having thoughts of harming yourself or others?" If the answer is yes, one should inquire further about how long the patient has been having these thoughts, how frequently they occur, previous and current plans or attempts, and opportunities to act on the thoughts (e.g., whether the patient owns a gun). Even when the patient denies any such thoughts, one may wish to carefully pursue this line of questioning with patients who have a greater likelihood of suicidal or homicidal acting out. For example, patients with major depression, especially when there is a clear element of hopelessness to the clinical picture, and paranoid patients who perceive potential harm to themselves or have a history of violent acts both would justify further exploration for signs of potential suicidal or homicidal tendencies.

Suicide risk factors have been identified in numerous publications. Some of those identified in recent publications by Rains, Kukor, Myers, Bobbitt, and Davis (1996), Sanchez (2001), and Sommers-Flanagan and Sommers-Flanagan (1995) are presented in Rapid Reference 2.10. Note that the presence

≣Rapid Reference 2.10

....

Examples of Commonly Identified Suicide Risk Factors

- Male
- Caucasian
- Over 45 years old
- Unmarried
- History of previous suicide attempt
- Presence of a mental disorder, especially an affective disorder
- Current state of distress
- Poor impulse control
- Comorbid physical problems
- Recent job, financial, or other loss
- Clues given or admission to suicidal ideation, intent, or plan

Note. From Rains et al. (1996); Sanchez (2001); Sommers-Flanagan and Sommers-Flanagan (1995).

CAUTION

- Cross-validate historical information reported by patients for accuracy.
- Remember that mental health patients might not always know when a comorbid substance abuse problem exists.
- Don't overlook the patient's strengths.
- Always assess for suicidal and homicidal ideation.

of any given risk factor should always be considered in light of all available information about the patient.

Diagnosis and Related Considerations

With the assessment information in hand, the clinician is prepared to determine the appropriate diagnoses. Assignment of diagnoses to mental health and substance abuse patients has long been an objectionable activity for many behavioral health care professionals. Some feel that it demeans patients to label them as belonging to a specific group to which general, often negative characterizations and expectations have been assigned. This problem is exacerbated by the fact that labels (and the implications thereof) may accompany patients throughout their lives. Others feel that labeling patients causes their individuality to be ignored.

Still other clinicians feel that diagnoses have no bearing on the treatment that patients receive. As Jongsma and Peterson (1999, p. 6) note, "The issue of differential diagnosis is admittedly a difficult one that research has shown to have rather low interrater reliability. Psychologists have also been trained to think more in terms of maladaptive behavior than disease labels." Beutler and his colleagues (Beutler, 1989; Beutler et al., 1999) would support this latter contention. As they have noted, "even if a diagnosis is reliable (and there is still debate about this . . .), it provides little information on which to develop a differentially sensitive psychotherapeutic program" (Beutler et al., p. 83). At the same time, there have been efforts by the American Psychological Association (APA) to identify efficacious treatments that are tied to specific diagnostic groups (see Chambless et al., 1997; Chambless et al., 1996; Task Force on Promotion and Dissemination of Psychological Procedures, 1995). Although such efforts are not without criticism or concern (e.g., see Garfield, 1996), they do suggest that at least in some instances, an accurate diagnosis can have important implications in the development of an effective course of treatment. A discussion of *empirically supported treatments* is presented in chapter 5.

Regardless, the fact is that third-party payers and many other stakeholders who are influential in the treatment of patients (e.g., accreditation bodies, regulatory agencies) require that patients be assigned a diagnosis. Currently, the use of the diagnostic classification system presented in the *DSM-IV-TR* is commonly required in the United States and several other countries. The World Health Organization's (WHO's) *International Classification of Diseases and Related Health Problems, Tenth Revision (ICD-10;* WHO, 1992) is yet another common classification system. Although it is similar to *DSM-IV-TR,* and at times it is required or permissible to employ the *ICD* system, the *DSM-IV-TR* is considered the standard means of communicating diagnostic information in behavioral health care systems. Its multiaxial system permits a more descriptive, individualized presentation of the patients than may be found in other diagnostic systems. Consequently, the use of the *DSM-IV-TR*'s five axes to report diagnosis-related information about the patient can provide a means addressing some of the limitations and objections raised by critics of diagnostic systems.

DON'T FORGET

DSM-IV Multiaxial Diagnostic System

Axis	Domain	Examples
Axis I	Clinical disorders, other conditions that may be a focus of attention	Anxiety disorders, mood disorders, schizophrenia, adjustment disorders, mental disorders due to general medical condition
Axis II	Personality disorders, mental retardation	Antisocial personality disorder, avoidant personality disorder, mental retardation
Axis III	General medical conditions	Neoplasms, diseases of the digestive system, congenital anomalies, injury
Axis IV	Psychosocial and environmental problems	Problems with primary support group, occupational problems, problems related to the social environment
Axis V	Global assessment of functioning	GAF scale rating

Note. From American Psychiatric Association, 2000.

In spite of their likely limitations with regard to the selection of a specific psychotherapeutic intervention, diagnoses can have implications for other aspects of treatment. For instance, a diagnosis of schizophrenia or major depressive disorder by itself would suggest that adjunctive psychopharmacological intervention should at least be considered. A GAF rating on *DSM-IV-TR* Axis V that falls in the lower quartile would probably indicate the need for inpatient or a partial hospitalization level of care. Furthermore, the identification of a personality disorder on Axis II with or without an accompanying Axis I disorder would have a bearing on the projected length of treatment. Thus, though often maligned, the assignment of a diagnosis is commonly required and can frequently provide useful information for the planning of treatment.

Jongsma and Peterson (1999) have observed that MBHOs' interest in behavioral indexes over diagnoses is growing, but it is this author's opinion that managed care's requirement for a diagnosis will not disappear any time in the foreseeable future—nor should it. Diagnoses based on a common system of classification criteria continue to be important, efficient tools for communicating among professionals and organizations, a fact that has tremendous implications for those involved in the clinical, research, or administrative aspects of behavioral health care provision.

Treatment Goals

No assessment would be complete without the identification of treatment goals. In some cases, one or two goals might be identified; in others, several goals might come to light. In cases of multiple goals, they can be prioritized by the importance and immediacy with which they need to be attended in treatment (an issue that is addressed in chapter 5). Goals can be classified as being either patient-identified goals or goals identified by third parties that have a stake in the patient's treatment.

Patient-Identified Goals
In most cases, the goals for treatment are obvious. For example, for a patient who complains of anxiety or depression, cannot touch a door knob without subsequently washing his or her hands, hears voices, or feels that the spouse is trying to kill him or her, it goes without saying that the amelioration of the unwanted behaviors or other symptomatology that led the patient to seek treat-

ment becomes a goal. This may not be the only goal, however, nor may it be even the primary goal from the patient's standpoint.

There is a quick, efficient way to obtain at least a preliminary indication of the patient's goals for treatment: Ask the patient directly. One MBHO (UBS, 1994, p. 8) recommends using three simple questions:

- What do you see as your biggest problem?
- What do you want to be different about your life at the end of your treatment?
- Does this goal involve changing things about yourself?

The inclusion of the last question can serve a couple of purposes. First, it forces patients to think through their problems and realize the extent to which these problems have control over their thoughts, feelings, and behavior. In short, it can provide a means for patients to gain insight into their problems— a therapeutic goal in and of itself. In addition, it elicits information about their motivation to engage in and become active participants in the therapeutic endeavor. Other helpful questions are presented in Rapid Reference 2.11.

To assist in clarifying and setting goals, it is important to have patients identify what the anticipated or hoped-for results of achieving their goals will be.

═Rapid Reference 2.11

Questions to Help Patients Set Realistic Treatment Goals

- What is your biggest problem?
- Is there a problem that needs to be addressed immediately?
- What do you consider your primary goal for therapy?
- How will you know when you have achieved this goal?
- What, if anything, will you have to change about yourself to achieve this goal?
- What problems might keep you from achieving this goal?
- If you achieve this goal, how will things be different? What positive things will you start doing? What negative things will no longer be present?
- What skills or other aspects about yourself will help you achieve this goal?

Note. Adapted from UBS (1994).

UBS (1994, p. 9) recommends that clinicians ask their patients the following questions related to establishing objective outcome criteria for goal achievement:

- How will you know when things are different?
- What kinds of things will you be doing differently?
- What negative things will no longer be present?
- What positive things will you be doing?

As before, questions such as these offer patients an opportunity to gain insight into their problems. Moreover, feedback from the clinician helps patients see how realistic their expectations for treatment are and determine whether those expectations should be modified.

Third-Party Goals

Treatment goals set by nonpatient stakeholders in the treatment process must always be considered. These third-party goals can come from many sources. In the case of child patients, these goals most frequently come from parents or teachers, although other parties (e.g., the legal system) may also have a vested interest in what should be addressed during treatment. The legal system's input also might be involved in adult cases, as might that of other third parties. A good example is the patient's employer in cases where the patient's problems interfere with his or her ability to get along with supervisors and or peers, result in lower productivity, or have other financial implications for the company.

One faction that always has a say in the goals established for all but self-pay patients is the party that provides the behavioral health care benefits. Whether it be an MBHO, indemnity company, Medicare, or other insurer, there is always the expectation, and thus the goal, that the patient will return to a level of functioning that will no longer necessitate the need for mental health or substance abuse treatment services.

As with patient-identified goals, third parties' expectations for the

CAUTION

- Be sure to assess goals from the perspectives of both the patient *and* relevant third-party stakeholders.
- Clarify the expectations of relevant third-party stakeholders.
- Patients' goals are not always obvious, so be sure to conduct a thorough inquiry regarding what the patient wishes to accomplish in treatment.

outcomes of goal achievement should be elicited. Similarly, these too may be modified based on the clinicians' evaluation of how realistic they are.

Motivation to Change

An important factor to assess for treatment-planning purposes is the patient's motivation to change. A good estimate of the level of motivation can be derived from several pieces of information. One, of course, is whether seeking treatment stems from the patient's desire for help or from the request (or demand) of another party. Another obvious clue is the patient's stated willingness to be actively involved in treatment, regardless of whether the treatment is voluntarily sought. Answers to questions such as "What are you willing to do to solve your problems?" can be quite revealing.

There are also other types of information that can assist in the assessment of patient motivation to change. Among them are the patient's subjective distress and reactance, as well as the patient's readiness for (or stage of) change, both of which were discussed earlier. In discussing the issue, Morey (1999) pointed to seven factors identified by Sifneos (1987) that should be considered in the evaluation of motivation to engage in treatment. Morey summarized them as follows:

1. A willingness to participate in the diagnostic evaluation.
2. Honesty in reporting about oneself and one's difficulties.
3. Ability to recognize that the symptoms experienced are psychological in nature.
4. Introspectiveness and curiosity about one's own behavior and motives.
5. Openness to new ideas, with a willingness to consider different attitudes.
6. Realistic expectations for the results of treatment.
7. Willingness to make a reasonable sacrifice in order to achieve a successful outcome. (p. 1098)

The clinician may not be able to assess some of these factors until treatment has actually begun. However, the clinician should be able to form at least a tentative opinion about the patient on each of these factors from the interactions that take place during the assessment.

Putting It Into Practice

Case Study of Mary Smith

Following is the clinical assessment report of a hypothetical mental health patient, Mary Smith. This is the first part of a case study that was developed to illustrate the application of the recommendations presented in this book. Relevant portions of the remainder of this case study are presented in each of the chapters that follow.

CLINICAL ASSESSMENT

Mary Smith

Identifying Information

Mary Smith is a 28-year-old, white, married female who is a student at the Acme University School of Law. She was referred to this clinic by the university's student counseling center after it was determined that Ms. Smith is experiencing problems that the counseling center would not be able to treat effectively.

Presenting Problem

When asked what prompted her to seek psychological treatment, Ms. Smith indicated, "I can't get these thoughts out of my head. I can't concentrate. It's getting worse and it's affecting my ability to study. I don't know what I'll do if I flunk out of school."

History of the Problem

Ms. Smith described a history of obsessive thinking and accompanying compulsive behavior dating back to the beginning of puberty in early adolescence. Messages about sex that were conveyed by her religious parents and her parochial school teachers made her feel guilty and anxious about the normal thoughts, feelings, and desires related to the burgeoning sexuality that typically accompanies adolescence. Thoughts about boys and sex took on a taboo quality, and she attempted to control them by turning her attention to other things or by distracting herself (e.g., by counting to 25). Ms. Smith also began having thoughts about unintentionally harming others in various ways. For example, she felt that people might get sick if she touched eating and cooking utensils with her "dirty" hands; or as she got older, she became fearful that she would accidentally run over a pedestrian while driving. She soon learned that she could better control these thoughts through ritualistic behaviors, such as excessive hand washing, touching certain objects (e.g., her watch), moving parts of her body (e.g., tapping her foot to a specific rhythm), or saying silent prayers to God for forgiveness for these "sins."

Ms. Smith found that these problematic behaviors could also be used to control the anxiety and nervousness she felt when she did not live up to the other expectations that come with being a "good Catholic girl," or when her academic work fell short of her parents' goals. In addition, these behaviors began to be employed when her parents began to delegate increasing responsibility for the care of her younger siblings. Taking on these child-care and other household responsibilities began when she about 15 years old, when her mother was diagnosed with ovarian cancer. Initially, she expressed protest and resentment for having to do these chores "instead of being with my friends and having fun." However, this rebellious behavior soon dissipated as her parents made her feel guilty about her anger and resentment by continually reminding her of her obligations as the oldest child and of how they had sacrificed for her. Ms. Smith assumed full "woman-of-the-house" responsibilities when her mother died 3 years later. Since then, obsessive-compulsive behavior in one form or another began to appear in other aspects of life in which she felt she had not done her best, or had not done "the right thing."

The relief provided by these approaches to coping has not been without a cost. Over the past few years, trying to meet the expectations that she perceives from her husband as well as those she sets for herself has been quite wearing for Ms. Smith. She reports feeling tired much of the time, has lost interest in formerly pleasurable activities (e.g., sex, playing the piano), and has experienced difficulties in sleeping and concentrating. During the past 6 months, concentration has become even more difficult. It was at about this time that her husband started expressing a desire to have a child as soon as possible. At the same time, more demands to care for her ailing father began to be placed on her. This has included taking time out of her busy class and study schedule to make daily visits to her father's home. Because of these increased difficulties, there has been an increase in the frequency and intensity of her obsessive-compulsive symptoms. Ms. Smith has also had problems concentrating on class lectures and completing reading assignments. Moreover, she has become forgetful in other aspects of her life, which has led to conflicts with her husband, father, and her younger siblings.

Mr. Smith accompanied his wife to this assessment and was able to provide additional information. He reported that for the past several months his wife has been spending more time studying because "she can't keep her mind focused on her books." Also, she has also seemed to be more irritable, tense and withdrawn, and less interested in having sexual relations. This latter problem appears to be of greater concern to Mr. Smith than it is to Ms. Smith, especially since he is eager to have a child. He attributes the more frequent occurrence of arguments to the disruption in their sexual relationship as well as to the amount of time she devotes to the demands of law school and her family. Mr. Smith also noted that his wife is not sleeping well and that she seems to be skipping meals more frequently than usual.

Family and Social History

Ms. Smith was born, reared, and currently resides here in Plainville. Her father is a 59-year-old retired sheet-metal worker who is receiving disability benefits for emphysema and cardiac problems. Her mother, a former administrative as-

(continued)

sistant at Acme University, died of ovarian cancer 10 years ago. Neither parent attended college. She grew up in a household with deeply religious, Catholic parents who expected strict adherence to church teachings and instilled a strong sense of commitment to family and achievement in the world. She describes her parents as having been strict but loving as she was growing up. She now sees her father as being very dependent on her.

She is the oldest of her parents' three children. Her brother, age 20, is a sophomore at Acme University and her sister is a senior at the local high school. Both live with their father at the family home located a few miles from her and her husband's house. As alluded to earlier, Ms. Smith assumed increasing responsibility for the care and raising of her siblings after her mother's death and continues to do so. She provides her sister and brother with emotional support and help with academic assignments when they request it. In addition, she makes sure that all of her father's bills are paid, his house is clean, and that he receives the required medical care.

Ms. Smith met and began dating John, now her 29-year-old husband, in college while she was a junior and he was a senior at Acme. After receiving his bachelor's degree in business administration, he continued for two more years at the Acme business school until he received his MBA. Upon graduation, he began working for a local bank, and he and Ms. Smith were married. He is now a senior loan officer and is said to be "on the fast track" to move up in the ranks of bank management. Ms. Smith describes her husband as a loving husband who is intent on making sure that his and his wife's financial needs are provided for both now and in the future. Mr. Smith is also described as a gregarious, ambitious person who is very focused on achieving his professional goals. They have been married for almost 5 years and have no children.

Ms. Smith says that she has a few friends, most of whom she works with or are married to people who work with or otherwise know her husband. For the most part, her time is occupied by attending and studying for law classes and keeping up two households (hers and her father's). When she does have free time and can concentrate, she prefers to spend it alone reading; otherwise, she watches TV or goes for a long walk in order to relax.

Educational History

Ms. Smith was a member of the National Honor Society and graduated in the top 2% of her high school class. Because of her responsibilities at home, she was not able to participate in any extracurricular activities during high school. Her grades and test scores were good enough to earn her a full scholarship at Acme University, where she majored in art history. She graduated with a bachelor's degree 6 years ago. Her grade point average (GPA) for the four years at Acme was 3.92. Three years ago, she was admitted to Acme's school of law. She is currently a second-year law student with a GPA of 3.75.

Employment History

Ms. Smith is attending law school full-time and currently is unemployed. She has had only one job outside of the home. Upon graduating with a bachelor's degree, she went to work for the Gotham County Art Museum as an assistant to the curator. Her primary responsibilities were to assist the curator in his daily duties and to lead one or two tour groups each day. Ms. Smith enjoyed this work, reporting that "When I was at work, I was surrounded by all of those beautiful works of art. I could forget about meeting everyone else's needs and focus on what pleases me. I hardly ever had any of those crazy thoughts or did those crazy things when I was there." She said that she hated to leave that job 2 years ago to go to law school. When asked why she did so, she indicated that she did it at her husband's encouragement. She reported, "He kept telling me that I was too smart for that type of work, that I could make a lot more money if only I lived up to my potential, that lawyers can make a whole lot of money doing a lot of important and different things. He said that he would be so proud of me if I would just make something of myself."

Behavioral Health History

Ms. Smith sought help for her problems twice during her undergraduate years: once during her sophomore year and then again during her junior year. These were described as the most academically demanding of her undergraduate years. In both instances, she experienced an exacerbation of her "usual" concentration difficulties and obsessive-compulsive behaviors. Both times, treatment consisted of time-limited, goal-focused psychotherapy provided by the school's student counseling center. According to Ms. Smith, each of the episodes of care was apparently effective enough to "get me back on the right track."

Medical History

Ms. Smith's medical history is unremarkable. Generally, she attained developmental milestones at the appropriate ages, had the usual childhood illnesses, and reports no hospitalizations or treatment for any chronic illnesses. There is a family history of cardiac disease on her father's side of the family, as well as a family history of cancer on her mother's side. Because of this, she reports that during each of the past 4 years she has had a routine physical examination. Ms. Smith also tries to exercise regularly but says that it is now hard to do because of the demands or needs of school, her husband, and her family.

Important Characteristics

The information presented by Ms. Smith and her husband is indicative of an individual who has been experiencing distress to varying degrees for many years. Her problems are complex from the standpoint of their being a means of controlling anger and resentment that arise as she tries to meets the needs and expectations of others. Her coping style has been to internalize her anxieties. With few exceptions, this approach allowed her to adapt to their presence successfully in that the accompanying distress generally has not significantly interfered with her functioning as wife, student, and caregiver. However, the re-

(continued)

cent addition of even more stress appears to have pushed her to the point that she is now beginning to experience difficulties. In her favor is the fact that she appears to be ready to make changes in her life and likely to show little resistance to therapeutic efforts. On the other hand, the amount of support for her efforts that she will receive from her husband or others is likely to be minimal, given that those closest to her are, in one way or another, at the source her problems.

Strengths

Ms. Smith is a very bright woman who displays an awareness of her problems and how they interfere with multiple aspects of her functioning. Her ability to successfully meet the rigors and demands of law school and her family while coping with intrusive thoughts and behaviors attests to her perseverance and determination not to allow her psychological problems to interfere with goals that she has set for herself. This level of ego strength bodes well for positive treatment outcomes.

Mental Status

Ms. Smith is an attractive young woman of medium build who looks her stated age of 28. She came to this assessment session after attending a law class, neatly dressed in jeans, a sweater, and sandals. Initially, she sat rigidly in her chair, appeared nervous and made only occasional eye contact, but she began to relax and became more engaged with this therapist as the assessment session progressed. Rapport with Ms. Smith was established in a relatively short amount of time. Although she was dysphoric in mood, her affect was appropriate to the topics of discussion. She exhibited no unusual speech patterns or language deficits, nor were there any observations or reports of perceptual distortions or impairments in her thought processes. Ms. Smith did report long-standing problems with obsessive thinking and compulsive behavior that appear to worsen during conflictual or other stressful events. These are often accompanied by magical thinking. Cognitively, she was attentive and oriented to time, place, and person. There were no apparent deficits in her abstraction, conceptualization, or constructional abilities, and her immediate, short-term, and long-term memory all seemed to be intact. Although she was able to successfully perform serial-seven subtraction from 100 within average time limits, difficulties in concentrating were occasionally noted throughout the interview. Ms. Smith displayed adequate judgment and insight into her problems. Intellectualization, repression, suppression, and undoing are frequently employed defense mechanisms.

Risk of Harm to Self and Others

There are no indications that Ms. Smith is currently at risk of harming herself or anyone else.

Diagnostic Impression

Based on information obtained during this assessment, Ms. Smith meets the *DSM-IV-TR* criteria for Axis I diagnoses of obsessive-compulsive disorder

(300.3) and dysthymic disorder (300.4). There are also traits of Axis II obsessive-compulsive personality disorder (301.4) but it is not clear whether she meets all criteria for this diagnosis.

Treatment Goals

Ms. Smith's stated goals for treatment include the following:

1. Amelioration or alleviation of obsessions, compulsions, depressed mood, and concentration problems
2. Increased ability to say no to others and meet her own needs
3. Improvement in her marital relationship

Important to the achievement of each of these goals is Mary's ability to learn to recognize and express anger and resentment in appropriate, effective ways.

Motivation to Change

Mary has actively sought help for her problems and appears willing to work to make changes in her life. She is likely to become an active participant in her treatment and thus appears to be an excellent candidate for psychotherapy.

SUMMARY

The goal of developing a useful and effective treatment plan can be achieved only through a good assessment of the patient. The manner in which the assessment is conducted will vary from one clinician to another, depending on any number of factors related to the patient, the clinician, and the situation. In all cases, however, the clinical interview should serve as the core of the information-gathering process.

A semistructured format is recommended as the best means of gathering the information from the patient. This approach ensures that all interview information that is generally helpful or needed in formulating a clinical picture of the patient is obtained; at the same time, it allows the clinician flexibility in the manner in which information is gathered. The focal areas or content of the interview include the nature and history of the patient's presenting problem, as well as other historical information important to understanding the problem's development, maintenance, and effects on the patient's current functioning. Included here is the patient's medical and behavioral health history.

Information regarding other patient characteristics is also important to know for treatment-planning purposes. Some of those characteristics were identified by Beutler as part of his systematic treatment selection model for treatment planning. Others include the patient's strengths or assets that can be mobilized in the service of effecting change, and the motivation to engage in a therapeutic relationship and work to effect change in one's life. Information obtained from a mental status examination and assessment of the patient's risk of harm to self or others can assist in determining various aspects of care, including the level of care that is most appropriate for the patient at the time. The mental status examination can also facilitate the assignment of a diagnosis. Although of limited value for treatment planning, diagnoses are a necessary evil that enable communication among professionals and the fulfillment of third-party requirements for reimbursement.

Finally, no assessment would be complete without the therapist's and patient's knowing the desired goals of treatment. Except in some cases of involuntary treatment, patients will be able to state one or more goals for themselves. At the same time, other parties (e.g., relatives, insurers, employers) may have additional goals in mind and these are also important to know.

TEST YOURSELF

1. **Which of the following is *not* one of Prochaska's stages of change?**
    (a) Contemplation
    (b) Decision making
    (c) Action
    (d) Maintenance

2. **What can be described as being at the core of assessment?**
    (a) Psychological testing
    (b) Mental status examination
    (c) Clinical interview
    (d) Feedback provided to the patient

3. **Which of the following is *not* an important area for assessment?**
    (a) Psychiatric history
    (b) Motivation
    (c) Current abuse of alcohol or other substances
    (d) Ability to pay for extended treatment
    (e) Insight into the problem

4. **Problem complexity reflects or refers to**

   (a) having multiple problems.

   (b) having multiple problems that have an exacerbating effect on one another (i.e., they create a vicious cycle).

   (c) the degree to which the problems are symbolic of internal stimuli.

   (d) the degree to which the problems are symbolic of external stimuli.

   (e) the number of complications that the problem presents to the patient in his or her daily living.

5. **The patient's diagnosis is critical to the development of an effective treatment plan.** True or False?

6. **An MBHO's goals for the treatment of patients are important considerations in developing treatment plans for those patients.** True or False?

7. **How do *structured, unstructured,* and *semistructured* interviews differ from one another?** _____

8. **Under what circumstances would each type of interview in question 7 have an advantage over the other two?** _____
   _____

9. **What types of assessment information might be more easily or reliably obtained using psychological testing?** _____
   _____

10. **A patient is unable to identify any strengths that might be helpful in his treatment. Which content areas of the assessment, if explored in greater detail, might be helpful in this regard?** _____
    _____

11. **Are there times when it might be more appropriate for the clinical interview to take place at the end of an assessment rather than at the beginning? If so, when?** _____
    _____

Answers: 1. b; 2. c; 3. d; 4. c; 5. False; 6. True; 7. structured interviews require a standard set of questions be asked in a specific order, unstructured interviews follow no rigid set of questions or order of presentation, semistructured interviews employ a general structure but permit flexibility to focus more or less attention on specific areas; 8. structured interviews would be important to employ in cases where the assessment might undergo close scrutiny by a third party (e.g., forensic cases), unstructured interviews have an advantage in cases where the assessment is used as a therapeutic intervention itself or when time for assessment or treatment of a patient is limited, and semistructured interviews are most advantageous in routine daily practice where session limitations are not a major concern; 9. intellectual functioning, academic abilities, symptom severity level, neuropsychological functioning; 10. educational history, employment history, social history, coping styles; 11. yes, in cases where direct interaction with another may be problematic but the patient is willing to engage in other, less threatening assessment activities (e.g., psychological testing).

Three

CONTRIBUTIONS OF PSYCHOLOGICAL TESTING TO CLINICAL ASSESSMENT AND TREATMENT PLANNING

Psychological testing can play a significant role in planning a course of treatment for behavioral health care problems. When employed by a trained clinician, it can yield information that can greatly facilitate and enhance the planning of a specific therapeutic intervention by providing some of the assessment information recommended in chapter 2. For example, Butcher (1990) indicated that information available from instruments such as the MMPI-2 not only can assist in identifying problems and in establishing communication with the patient, it also can help ensure that the plan for treatment is consistent with the patient's personality and external resources. In addition, psychological assessment may reveal potential obstacles to therapy, areas of potential growth, and problems of which the patient may not be consciously aware. Other benefits of psychological assessment identified by Appelbaum (1990) include assistance in identifying patient strengths and weaknesses, identification of the complexity of the patient's personality, and establishment of a reference point during the therapeutic episode. Moreover, both Butcher and Appelbaum view testing as a means of quickly obtaining a second opinion.

The type of treatment-relevant information that can be derived from psychological testing and the manner in which it is applied are quite varied—a fact that will become evident later. Regardless, Strupp (see Butcher, 1990) probably provided the best summary of the potential contribution of psychological assessment to treatment planning, stating that "careful assessment of a patient's personality resources and liabilities is of inestimable importance. It will predictably save money and avoid misplaced therapeutic effort; it can also enhance the likelihood of favorable treatment outcomes for suitable patients" (pp. v–vi).

Before proceeding further, a particularly important point of clarification

54

needs to be made. This has to do with the use of the terms *psychological testing* and *psychological assessment.* Using the distinction made by Meyer et al. (2001), psychological testing can be defined as the administration of one or more psychological tests for the purpose of obtaining a score or set of scores. Psychological assessment, on the other hand, involves the integration of these test-derived data with data from other sources of information (e.g., clinical and collateral interviews, review of medical and other historical documentation, behavioral observations) into a "cohesive and comprehensive understanding of the person being evaluated" (p. 8). In other words, psychological testing is a component of psychological assessment. For this reason, the term *testing* is used throughout this book to emphasize the fact that it is only one specific component of the assessment activity (as described in chapter 2).

CURRENT STATUS OF PSYCHOLOGICAL TESTING IN HEALTH CARE: THE IMPACT OF MANAGED BEHAVIORAL HEALTH CARE

The 1990s saw tremendous growth in managed behavioral health care. Kiesler (2000) reported that of the 170 million people enrolled in some form of managed mental health care, 150 million (88%) are served by a behavioral health care specialty *(carve-out)* plan. The growth of managed care as the predominant form of general health care delivery has had an enormous impact not only on patients, but also on practitioners, insurers, employers, and other parties that have a stake in the care and well-being of patients.

Adapting to this system of health care has not been an easy one for mental health and substance abuse professionals, particularly psychologists. In addition to limitations placed on the other clinical services they provide, psychologists have seen dramatic restrictions imposed by MBHOs on their use of psychological testing. Ben-Porath (1997), reporting on Griffith's survey of nine large managed care companies, noted that the findings indicated that "the prevailing view among these companies was that [psychological testing] in general and comprehensive psychological test batteries in particular are not cost-effective tools for psychodiagnosis and treatment planning. ... [M]anaged care companies view interviews as a cost-effective and preferred alternative to psychological [testing]" (p. 361). At the same time, psychological testing con-

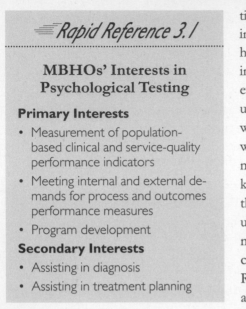

Rapid Reference 3.1

MBHOs' Interests in Psychological Testing

Primary Interests
- Measurement of population-based clinical and service-quality performance indicators
- Meeting internal and external demands for process and outcomes performance measures
- Program development

Secondary Interests
- Assisting in diagnosis
- Assisting in treatment planning

tinues to play an important role in psychological practice and behavioral health care service delivery in MBHO settings. Consequently, even though MBHOs may view the use of psychological testing in the way it typically was used in the past with some degree of skepticism and may restrict its use, they also acknowledge that it can bring value to the organization in serving individual patients, in meeting external demands, and in surviving in a highly competitive marketplace (see Rapid Reference 3.1). For these reasons, an understanding of managed care's views and attitudes toward psychological testing is important in any discussion on the use of testing for treatment-planning purposes.

MBHOs' Primary Interests

Given the day-to-day processes for authorizing and managing the care of MBHO customers, where does psychological testing—for any purpose—fit into the priorities of MBHOs? The results of the numerous surveys (Miller, 1996; Murphy, DeBernardo, & Shoemaker, 1998; Phelps, Eisman, & Kohout, 1998; Rothbaum, Bernstein, Haller, Phelps, & Kohout, 1998) bear out the deemphasis that MBHOs have placed on psychological testing as part of the routine care offered to those seeking services. Usually, reimbursable psychological testing requires special or separate authorization, something that is not granted unless specific criteria are met. However, the deemphasis on individual, clinically related testing does not mean that all measurement is relegated to the back burner of MBHO priorities.

Even though it is not always apparent, MBHOs do indeed rely on and value psychological testing and measurement for many purposes. As it happens, however, the purposes for which MBHOs are most interested in testing and for which they find it most useful are not the same as those generally valued by their network of care providers. MBHOs generally view psychological test data from *groups* of patients rather than individual patients as more useful in helping to assure that the people they serve are receiving quality services. This is consistent with a move toward a population-based focus in the delivery of behavioral health care (Schreter, 1997) as well as with the growing interest in measuring the outcomes of behavioral health care.

Measurement of Population-Based Quality Performance Indicators

Today, MBHOs are dedicating considerable resources to measurement activities. The focus is more on population-based measurement of structure and process indicators of both clinical and service quality, rather than on the measurement of the symptomatology, functioning, and so on of the individual patient. These indicators provide the organization with a gauge of its ability to meet both the clinical and nonclinical needs of its covered lives. Thus, this type of measurement is typically tied to formal and informal quality-improvement activities.

Meeting Internal and External Demands for Process and Outcomes Performance Measures

Psychological testing and other measurement-required activities can help the organization fulfill external requirements. For example, JCAHO and NCQA both require accredited MBHOs to conduct studies and activities aimed at improving the quality of their clinical and nonclinical services. Here again, measurement has a population focus, but individual testing may play an important role in studies or programs in which the identification of patients with specific characteristics or symptoms is a key component. Measurement activities are also needed for external requirements to demonstrate treatment outcomes. The source of these requirements may be the purchasers of the services, regulatory or accrediting bodies, market demands, or other forces.

Program Development

Another area in which this author has observed a growth in testing in MBHO settings is that of program development. Testing is more frequently becoming a part of specialized programs that MBHOs are developing. In particular, there is an increasing interest in developing behavioral medicine programs or supporting medical disease management programs being developed by the health plans with which MBHOs contract. In disease management programs, screeners might be administered to individuals upon entry into the program to assist in identifying program participants who may have a comorbid behavioral health disorder—such as depression—that could interfere with the patient's treatment and, more importantly, may have a direct impact on the morbidity and mortality of the patient.

MBHOs' Secondary Interests

It is both interesting and unfortunate that the unique knowledge, skill, and experience in psychological testing held by psychologists and other trained behavioral health professionals are related to applications that most MBHOs would probably consider secondary in utility to those just discussed. *Routine* testing of patients is essentially a thing of the past. Only under specific circumstances are MBHOs likely to consider authorizing reimbursable testing, the most common of these being for diagnostic and treatment-planning purposes.

Testing to Assist in Diagnosis

It is probably safe to say that most people seeking mental health or substance abuse services present with problems that are fairly clear-cut. The clinician is most likely to encounter affective and anxiety disorders that are relatively easy to diagnose and generally responsive to psychotherapeutic (e.g., individual psychotherapy) or psychopharmacologic interventions, or to both. There are those times, however, when the picture the patient presents is unclear, containing signs and symptoms that might be indicative of more than one type of disorder. Even with extensive data gathered from patient and collateral interviews, a review of medical charts, and contacts with other potential sources of information, a determination of exactly what is going on with the patient can remain elusive. In a behavioral health care system that is oriented toward problem-focused treatment, an accurate diagnosis may not always be as important as the resolution of the presenting problem. However, as previously mentioned, the accuracy of the diagnosis at the onset of treatment can have a tremendous impact on the treatment that is provided to the patient and, consequently, on the outcomes of that treatment. Rapid Reference 3.2 presents some of the more common differential diagnostic questions that Schaefer, Murphy, Westerveld,

Examples of Implications of Common Differential Diagnostic Questions

Referral Question	Implications
ADHD vs. anxiety	• Stimulant vs. anxiolytic or SSRI • Structured vs. insight-oriented therapy
ADHD vs. PTSD	• Emphasis on external or environmental controls vs. capacity for internal control
Psychosis vs. anxiety	• Neuroleptic vs. anxiolytic or SSRI
Psychosis vs. PTSD	• Supportive and structured treatment vs. insight-oriented and/or cognitive-behavioral (e.g. desensitization) treatment
Psychosis vs. MDD, psychotic features	• Supportive or structured treatment vs. IPT (adolescent) vs. insight-oriented treatment
Psychosis vs. PDD	• Neuroleptic vs. skills training • Prognosis; long-term management
Psychosis vs. bipolar disorder; psychosis vs. language or cognitive disorder	• Neuroleptic vs. mood stabilizer • Choice and level of intervention (educational, social skills, psychotherapy) • Treatment modality
Bipolar or unipolar disorder vs. borderline traits	• Medication indications • Therapeutic (e.g., DBT vs. CBT, insight-oriented therapy) • Selection of treatment program (individual or group therapy, level of intensity)
PDD vs. anxiety disorder	• Anxiolytic vs. SSRI • Treatment modality and setting • Selection of treatment program
Antisocial traits vs. intermittent explosive disorder	• Impulsivity vs. character disorder, therapeutic and disorder prognosticators • Indication for medication • Level of containment
Mood or anxiety disorders vs. ODD	• Medication indications • Therapeutic modality (structured vs. supportive vs. insight-oriented therapy)

Note. ADHD = attention-deficit/hyperactivity disorder, SSRI = selective serotonin reuptake inhibitor, PTSD = posttraumatic stress disorder, MDD = major depressive disorder, PDD = pervasive developmental disorder, IPT = interpersonal therapy, DBT = dialectic behavioral therapy, CBT = cognitive-behavioral therapy, ODD = oppositional defiant disorder. From slides presented in *Psychological Assessment and Managed Care: Guidelines for Practice with Children and Adolescents*, workshop conducted by M. Schaefer, R. Murphy, M. Westerveld, and A. Gewirtz at the annual meeting of the American Psychological Association, August, 2000, Washington, D.C. Copyright 2000 by the authors. Adapted with permission.

and Gewirtz (2000) have identified in their dealings with MBHO systems, along with some of the possible treatment implications for each.

Testing to Assist in Treatment Planning

Another way in which MBHOs have found testing useful is in uncovering non-diagnostic information that can assist in (a) developing an initial treatment plan and (b) modifying treatment plans for patients who are not making the expected progress toward their treatment goals. In the latter cases, testing may be able to elicit insight into barriers to progress that might not otherwise be available to the clinician or MBHO care manager. For example, a patient being treated for anxiety may be found to be experiencing a hitherto unknown co-morbid depressive disorder that has prevented him from returning to his previous level of functioning. In other instances, neuropsychological, cognitive, and attention-deficit/hyperactivity disorder (ADHD) evaluations may be authorized to determine the extent to which associated deficits may interfere with both the patient's functioning and his or her ability to benefit from therapeutic interventions. As in the case of differential diagnosis, the value-added aspect of psychological testing for treatment planning lies in the empirical research that enables access to information that may not be easily accessible to even the most experienced clinicians.

Reasons for Decline in Psychological Assessment in MBHOs

It is quite apparent that the introduction of managed care has affected what Meyer et al. (2001) have described as "a vital element of psychology's professional heritage and a central part of professional practice today" (p. 155). The profession needs to do much work in order to reclaim the level of acceptance and value that psychological testing had held at in previous years. To step back for a moment, however, it is important to ask why MBHOs are hesitant to authorize testing for their health plan members (see Rapid Reference 3.3). Understanding this will be the key to regaining psychological testing's former status as an invaluable component of behavioral health care services, including its use for treatment planning purposes.

General Emphasis on Streamlining Interventions and Containing Costs

First and foremost among the reasons for the decline of psychological testing in MBHOs is the general emphasis on streamlining interventions and containing costs. In pursuit of this emphasis, MBHOs have adopted what Schreter (1997) refers to as the *principle of parsimony*, which holds that "each patient should receive the least intensive, least expensive treatment at the lowest level of care that will permit a return to health and function" (p. 653).

It is important to keep in mind that the managed care movement arose from the need to control health care costs. Managed care was and will continue to be (at least in the foreseeable future) a viable solution to runaway costs. It is therefore

> ≡ *Rapid Reference 3.3*
>
> **Reasons for the Decline in Psychological Testing in MBHOs**
>
> - Emphasis on streamlining interventions and containing costs
> - General attitude toward psychological testing
> - Lack of empirical demonstration of cost effectiveness of testing and assessment
> - Use of medication trials to arrive at diagnosis

incumbent upon MBHOs to trim as much unnecessary cost from its expenses as is possible without compromising quality of care. One way of reducing costs is to eliminate services unnecessary for patient improvement. Given MBHOs' questions surrounding the validity and cost-effectiveness of testing (discussed in the next section), as well as psychologists' sometimes indiscriminant or inappropriate use of testing in the past, it is not surprising that psychological testing has come under close scrutiny and is authorized by MBHOs only when certain criteria are met. Moreover, with limited health plan benefits and the fact that the typical patient terminates treatment after only five to six sessions, it seldom makes sense to devote an authorized visit or hour of time to an activity, such as psychological testing, that may yield no long-term benefit for the patient. This is particularly the case when, for the reasons just cited, treatment tends to be problem focused.

MBHOs' Attitude Toward Psychological Testing

During the latter part of the last decade, the APA's Board of Professional Affairs appointed the Psychological Assessment Work Group (PAWG; Kubiszyn et al., 2000) to examine evidence of the utility of psychological testing. Earlier, Ambrose (1997) summarized what the PAWG concluded to be a common attitude of MBHOs toward psychological assessment:

Typically, when a clinician is asked why third-party payers should pay for personality assessment measures, their response generally falls into one of the following categories:

- It improves diagnosis.
- It improves treatment outcomes.
- It shortens treatment.
- I have children in college, and I need the money. (p. 66)

He adds that

while these responses appear to be logical, there is no conclusive, un-equivocal research that demonstrates that objective personality assessment in and of itself does any of the above. Intuitively, we anticipate that the more information we gather about a patient, the better likelihood we will be able to improve diagnosis. With a better diagnosis, we can increase treatment outcomes and shorten treatment duration. Yet, most research has never been aimed at a cost benefit analysis of objective personality assessment. Instead, most research is based on a goal of diagnostic or triage verification. (p. 66)

Although Ambrose specifically addresses objective personality assessment, his comments and conclusions also apply to other types of psychological testing.

Ambrose's (1997) view is consistent with Schaefer et al.'s (2000) observation that MBHOs find limited evidence for the claims that are made about the utility of psychological assessment. However, the PAWG (Kubiszyn et al., 2000) contests the claims made by Ambrose, stating that

considerable empirical support exists for many important clinical health care applications of psychological assessment instruments. For such applications psychological assessment can enhance diagnosis and treatment. Health care cost savings would be expected to follow from enhanced diagnosis and treatment, an outcome that third-party payers would be expected to be seriously interested in. (p. 120)

They cite several studies and meta-analyses supporting their claims for the validity and utility of psychological testing for several applications. The applications that are noted include symptom description and differential diagnosis; description and prediction of role functioning; prediction of health, medical, mental health, psychotherapeutic, and forensic outcomes; identification of characteristics that can affect the outcomes of treatment; and psychological assessment as a treatment technique.

Certainly, this author is in agreement with the PAWG. Why, then, do the findings reported in the professional literature seem to fall on deaf ears? The PAWG members contend that the psychological profession has not done a good job of educating MBHOs and other third-party payers about the empirical support that exists for psychological testing and assessment. Consequently, MBHOs are asking psychologists to *show me the data!*

Cost-Effectiveness and Value of Assessment Not Empirically Demonstrated
One major point made by the PAWG that this author disagrees with is its contention that psychological testing is cost-effective (Kubiszyn et al., 2000). There really has been no *empirical* demonstration of the direct value and (most importantly) the cost-effectiveness of psychological testing and assessment in MBHOs. This claim is not new and, to the best of this author's knowledge, cannot be disputed at this time. Even the PAWG stops short of disputing the claim, making statements that indicate only the possibility or likelihood of cost-effectiveness. For example, the PAWG indicates that "health care costs *would be expected* to follow from enhanced diagnosis and treatment" (p. 120) stemming from psychological assessment; that "neuropsychological tests . . . are useful . . . for *facilitating accurate diagnosis toward cost-effective treatment*" (p. 120); that "psychological assessment instruments can identify patients who are likely to utilize health care services more often than average" (p. 124); and that "health care utilization *clearly influences* third-party payer 'bottom line' decision making" (p. 124; emphasis added to each quotation). Yet MBHOs are crying, *show me the money!* The industry will not accept a "trust me, it works" attitude by psychologists or other test users, particularly when other behavioral health care professionals render effective treatment without it. Use of psychological tests must show actual cost or treatment effectiveness, or both, *beyond* what treatment yields without using the same assessment process.

Use of Medication Trials to Arrive at Diagnoses
Another PAWG report (Eisman et al., 1998, 2000) identified an increase in the use of medication trials as one more reason for the decline in psychological testing—at least for diagnostic purposes. Here, the fact that positive responses to certain medications are expected in certain disorders, but not in others,

might be used to differentiate between those disorders. A good example might be the use of methylphenidate (Ritalin) to differentiate ADHD from other possible disorders, such as anxiety, depression, or a psychotic disorder. However useful this might seem, there is a downside of such a practice—for example, the possibility of developing serious medication side effects, or of delaying or restricting a patient's access to other, more appropriate types of treatment, such as psychotherapy.

BENEFITS OF PSYCHOLOGICAL TESTING FOR TREATMENT PLANNING

As has already been touched on, there are several ways in which psychological testing can assist in the planning of treatment for behavioral health care patients. The more common and evident contributions can be organized into four general categories: *problem identification, problem clarification, identification of important patient characteristics,* and *monitoring treatment progress.*

Problem Identification

Probably the most common use of psychological testing in the service of treatment planning is for problem identification. Often, the use of psychological testing per se is not needed to identify what problems the patient is experiencing. Patients either will tell the clinician directly without questioning, or they will readily admit their problem(s) when questioned during a clinical interview. However, this is not always the case. The value of psychological testing becomes more apparent when patients are hesitant or unable to identify the specific nature of their problems. Moreover, even with motivated and engaged patients who respond openly and honestly to items on a well-validated and reliable test, the process of identifying what led them to seek treatment may be greatly facilitated by psychological testing. Cooperation shown during testing may be attributable to the nonthreatening nature of questions presented on printed testing materials or a computer monitor (as opposed to those posed by another human being); the subtle, indirect qualities of the questions themselves (compared to direct questions posed by the clinician); or a combination of these factors.

In addition, the nature of some of the more commonly used psychological test instruments allows for the identification of secondary, but significant, problems that might otherwise be overlooked. Multidimensional inventories such as the MMPI-2 and the Personality Assessment Inventory (PAI; Morey, 1991, 1999) are good examples of these types of instruments. Moreover, these instruments may be sensitive to other patient symptoms, traits, or characteristics that may exacerbate or otherwise contribute to the patient's problems.

Problem Clarification

Psychological testing can often assist in the clarification of a known problem. Through tests designed for use with populations presenting problems similar to those of the patient, aspects of the identified problems can be elucidated. Information gained from these tests can improve the patient's and clinician's understanding of the problem, and lead to the development of a better treatment plan. The three most important types of information that can be gleaned for this purpose are the *severity* of the problem, the *complexity* (i.e., multidimensionality) of the problem, and the degree of *impairment* that the problem poses for the patient's ability to function in one or more life roles.

The manner is which a patient is treated depends a great deal on the severity of the problem. In addition to any other consideration identified by Beutler and his colleagues (see chapter 2), problem severity plays a particularly important role in determining the setting in which the behavioral health care intervention is provided. Those patients whose problems are so severe that they are considered a danger to themselves or others are often best suited for inpatient treatment, at least until dangerousness is no longer an issue. Similarly, problem severity may be a primary criterion that signals the necessity of evaluation for a psychopharmacological adjunct to treatment. Severity also may have a bearing on the type of psychotherapeutic approach that is taken by the clinician. For example, it may be more productive for the clinician to take a supportive role, at least initially, with severe cases; all other things being equal, a more confrontive approach may be more appropriate with patients whose problems are mild to moderate in severity.

As alluded to previously, the problems of patients seeking behavioral health care services are frequently multidimensional. Patient and environmental factors that play into the formation and maintenance of a psychological problem, along with the problem's relationship with other conditions, all contribute to its complexity. (Note that the problem complexity as discussed here is different from the complexity to which Beutler et al., 1999, refer.) Knowing the complexity of the target problem is invaluable in developing an effective treatment plan. Again, multidimensional instruments or batteries of tests, each measuring specific aspects of psychological dysfunction, serve this purpose well.

As with knowledge of problem severity, knowledge of the complexity of a patient's problems can help the clinician and patient arrive at many important treatment-planning decisions, including the determination of the appropriate setting, therapeutic approach, and the need for medication. However, possibly of equal importance to the patient and other concerned parties (wife, employer, school, etc.) is the extent to which these problems affect the patient's ability to carry out the roles of parent, employee, student, friend, and so on. Information gathered from the administration of measures such as the SF-36 Health Survey (SF-36; Ware, Snow, Kosinski, & Gandek, 1993), which was designed to assess the impact of health status on role functioning, can help clarify the impact of the patient's problems and establish role-specific goals. In general, the most important role-functioning domains to assess are those related to work or school performance, interpersonal relationships, and self-care, as reflected in activities of daily living (ADLs).

Identification of Important Patient Characteristics

The identification and clarification of the patient's problems are of key importance in planning a course of treatment. However, numerous other types of patient information that are not specific to the identified problem can be useful in planning treatment and are easily identified through the use of psychological testing instruments. Some of these were discussed in chapter 2. The vast majority of treatment plans are developed or modified with consideration to at least some of these nonpathological characteristics. The exceptions are generally found with clinicians or programs that take a one-size-fits-all approach to treatment—an approach not advocated by this author.

In addition to the information about those characteristics identified by Beutler et al. (1999), probably the most useful type of information not specific to the identified problem that can be gleaned from psychological testing is the identification of characteristics that can serve as assets or areas of strength for patients in working to achieve their therapeutic goals. For example, Morey and Henry (1994) point to the utility of the PAI's Nonsupport scale in identifying whether the patient perceives an adequate social support network, this being a predictor of positive therapeutic progress. Other examples include "normal" personality characteristics, such as that which can be obtained from Gough, McClosky, and Meehl's Dominance (1951) and Social Responsibility (1952) scales developed for use with the MMPI or MMPI-2. Greene (1991) indicated that those with high scores on the Dominance scale are described as "being able to take charge of responsibility for their lives. They are poised, self-assured, and confident of their own abilities" (p. 209). Gough and his colleagues interpreted high scores on the Social Responsibility scale as being indicative of individuals who, among other things, trust the world, are self-assured and poised, and believe that each individual must carry his or her share of duties. Thus, scores on these and similar types of scales may reveal important aspects of patient functioning that can be used to effect therapeutic change.

Similarly, knowledge of the patient's weaknesses or deficits may impact the type of treatment plan that is devised. Greene and Clopton (1999) provided examples of numerous types of deficit-relevant information from the MMPI-2 content scales that have implications for treatment planning. For example, a clinically significant score ($T > 64$) on the Anger scale should lead one to consider the inclusion of training in assertiveness or anger control as part of the patient's treatment. On the other hand, one's uneasiness in social situations, as suggested by a significantly elevated score on either the Low Self-Esteem or Social Discomfort scale, suggests that a supportive approach to the intervention would be beneficial, at least initially.

Moreover, use of specially designed scales and procedures can provide information related to the patient's ability to become engaged in the therapeutic process. For example, the Therapeutic Reactance Scale (Dowd, Milne, & Wise, 1991) and the MMPI-2 Negative Treatment Indicators content scale (Butcher, Graham, Williams, & Ben-Porath, 1989) may be useful in determining whether the patient is likely to resist therapeutic intervention. Morey and Henry (1994) presented algorithms utilizing PAI T scores that may be useful in determining the presence of characteristics that bode well for the therapeutic endeavor (e.g., sufficient distress to motivate engagement in treatment, the ability to form a therapeutic alliance).

Other types of patient characteristics that can be identified through psychological testing have implications for selecting the best therapeutic approach for a given patient. Moreland (1996) pointed out how psychological testing can assist in determining whether the patient deals with problems through internalizing or externalizing behaviors. He noted that all other things being equal, internalizers would probably profit most from an insight-oriented approach rather than a behaviorally oriented approach. The reverse would be true for externalizers. Furthermore, as discussed in chapter 2, Beutler and his colleagues (Beutler & Clarkin, 1990; Beutler, Wakefield, & Williams, 1994; Beutler & Williams, 1995) have identified several patient characteristics that are important to matching patients and treatment approaches for maximized therapeutic effectiveness.

Monitoring of Treatment Progress

Information from repeated testing during the treatment process can help the clinician determine whether the treatment plan continues to be appropriate for the patient at a given time. Thus, many clinicians use psychological testing any number of times during the course of treatment to determine whether their patients are showing the expected improvement. If not, adjustments can be made. Any modifications to the treatment plan require later reassessment of the patient to determine whether the revised treatment plan has impacted patient progress in the expected direction. This process also can provide information relevant to the decision of when to terminate treatment. Chapter 6 addresses the matter of treatment monitoring in detail.

DON'T FORGET

The benefits of psychological testing derive from its ability to help
- identify problems,
- clarify problems,
- identify important patient characteristics, and
- monitor treatment.

Advantages of Psychological Test Data Over Other Assessment Data

Many would argue that psychological test data have several advantages over other types of assessment data. Ben-Porath (1997) noted that in comparison to interview data, psychological test data are more reliable and valid. Also, the interpretation of test data is more easily automated. In addition, the availability of test data facilitates the systematic assessment of patients for treatment-monitoring purposes as well as for determining when they have reached their treatment goals. It is probably safe to say that these same points continue to hold true with respect to other types of assessment data (e.g., medical and school records). The key, in part, lies in the standardization of the testing procedures. One can feel more confident with data that is gathered in a standardized fashion and can be compared to a body of other (normative and research) data that was gathered in the same manner.

Meyer et al. (2001) also identify validity and reliability, standardization, and availability of normative data as being advantages of psychological testing, or as ways in which testing can overcome problems associated with clinical interview data. In addition, they point to the ability of psychological testing to measure a number of characteristics simultaneously and the ability to cross-check hypotheses when batteries of tests are administered.

Combining Test Data With Other Assessment Data

Can one rely solely on psychological testing for the type of assessment that is recommended in chapter 2? The answer is clearly *no*. Derogatis and Savitz (1999) have noted that

> before an effective treatment plan can be developed, a clinician must know as much as possible about the nature and magnitude of the patient's presenting condition. Diagnostic interviews, medical records, psychological testing, and interviews with relatives all represent sources of information that facilitate the development of an effective treatment plan. Rarely is information from a single modality (e.g., psychological testing) definitive. Ideally, each source provides an increment of unique information that, taken collectively with data from other sources, contributes to an ultimate understanding of the case at hand. (pp. 690–691)

Essentially, data from psychological testing and other sources of information complement each other. In addition to the unique contribution alluded to previously, test data may serve as a source of hypotheses about the patient while data from other sources can be used to support or reject those hypotheses. Similarly, test data can be used to validate information obtained from other sources. Moreover, as Meyer et al. (2001) have observed, "using just test scores, a growing body of findings supports the value of combining data from more than one type of assessment method, even when these methods disagree within or across individuals" (p. 153).

Just as it its important to remember that psychological test data should not be used in isolation from other data, it is also important to remember that there are times when psychological testing may not be called for in the assessment of a mental health or substance abuse patient. Meyer et al. (2001) have noted that "the key that determines when [psychological testing] is appropriate is the rationale for using specific instruments with a particular patient under a unique set of circumstances to address a distinctive set of referral questions" (p. 129). They also address the different types of information that various methods can provide to the clinician, "under optimal conditions." These are summarized in Rapid Reference 3.4.

CRITERIA FOR SELECTING PSYCHOLOGICAL TESTS FOR TREATMENT-PLANNING PURPOSES

Test publishers and other developers of psychological measures (e.g., universities, government agencies) regularly release new instrumentation that can facilitate treatment planning. Thus, availability of instrumentation for this purpose is not an issue. However, selection of the best or most appropriate instrument(s) to aid in planning a course of treatment is a matter requiring careful consideration. Inattention to the instrument's intended use, its demonstrated psychometric characteristics, its limitations, and other aspects related to its practical application can result in misguided treatment and potentially harmful consequences for a patient.

CAUTION

- Psychological test results should never be the sole source of assessment data.
- There are times when psychological testing may not be appropriate.

General Considerations for Instrument Selection

Regardless of the type of instrument one might consider using, clinicians frequently must choose among many product offerings. What are the general criteria for the selection

≡ Rapid Reference 3.4

Key Strengths of Assessment Methods

Assessment Method	Types of Information Provided	Limitations/ Constraints
Unstructured interviews	Information relevant to thematic life narratives	The range of topics considered and ambiguities inherent when interpreting this information
Structured interviews	Details concerning patients' conscious understanding of themselves and overtly experienced symptomatology	Patients' motivation to communicate frankly and their ability to make accurate judgments
Self-report instruments	Details concerning patients' conscious understanding of themselves and overtly experienced symptomatology	Patients' motivation to communicate frankly and their ability to make accurate judgments
Performance-based personality tests (e.g., Rorschach, TAT)	Data about behavior in unstructured settings or implicit dynamics and underlying templates of perception and motivation	Task engagement and the nature of the stimulus materials
Performance-based cognitive tasks	Findings about problem solving and functional capacities	Motivation, task engagement, and setting
Observer rating scales	Informant's perception of the patient	Parameters of the particular types of relationship (e.g., spouse, coworker, therapist) and the setting in which the observations transpire

Note. TAT = Thematic Apperception Test. From Meyer et al. (2001, p. 145).

of any instrument for psychological testing? What should guide the clinician's selection of an instrument for treatment planning or other purpose? As part of their training, psychologists and other appropriately trained professionals from related behavioral health fields have been educated about the psychometric properties that are important to consider when determining the appropriateness of an instrument for its intended use. However, this is only one of several considerations that should be taken into account in evaluating a specific instrument for any clinical application. Following are criteria that are recommended for the selection of tests and other assessment instruments for treatment-planning purposes. These criteria are also summarized in Rapid Reference 3.5. Some of these criteria may seem obvious, but one may be surprised how easily some of these considerations can be overlooked.

Brevity

One of the most important characteristics of any instrument under consideration should be brevity. This is particularly the case in MBHO settings. Lengthy instruments do not fit well in a behavioral health care delivery system in which time-limited, problem-oriented intervention is the primary approach to patient treatment. In addition, to maximize the patient's cooperation with the testing process, the length of the instrument should be acceptable to most

≡Rapid Reference 3.5

General Considerations for the Selection of Psychological Instruments for Treatment Planning

- Brevity
- Psychometric integrity, especially test-retest reliability
- Relevancy to intended purpose of testing
- Availability of relevant normative data
- Cost
- Required reading level
- Content
- Ease of use
- Comprehensibility of results
- Patient-completed vs. observer-completed format

patients. Keep in mind that what clinicians consider short for a test may seem unreasonable long to the patient. Overall, one must consider the wisdom of employing lengthy, expensive instruments or batteries of instruments that either provide little useful information or represent overkill with a patient who may be seen for only five or six sessions.

Psychometric Integrity

Brevity is meaningless unless the instrument is valid and reliable. In fact, the briefer the instrument, the more one should be concerned with its psychometric properties, given that brief instruments tend to be less valid and reliable than longer instruments. Thus, although the psychometric characteristics of all psychological instruments should be carefully evaluated, particular scrutiny is called for with brief measures of any construct.

In selecting a test, one must ask, "Is the instrument a valid and reliable measure of what it purports to measure?" In addition, should specific aspects of validity and reliability be attended to more than other aspects when evaluating psychological measures? There is no one, clear answer to this question. All relevant aspects of validity and reliability are important to consider in selecting a test, but depending on the intended use, particular types of validity or reliability might be given more weight in the decision. For example, as will be discussed later, if the intended use is for treatment monitoring, one would like to see empirical data that demonstrate good test-retest reliability. The reader is referred to the *Standards for Educational and Psychological Testing* (American Educational Research Association, APA, & National Council on Measurement in Education, 1999) for further guidance on this matter. Also, Cicchetti (1994) provides guidelines for evaluating the validity and reliability of psychological measures being considered for clinical use.

Relevancy to Intended Purpose of Assessment

Validity and reliability are important considerations with regard to the next desired test characteristic—relevancy to the intended purpose of administering the instrument. Administering a Beck Depression Inventory-II (BDI-II; Beck, Steer, & Brown, 1996) to assess levels of general distress is not the most appropriate way to accomplish the task—unless, of course, it has been empirically shown to be effective when used this way. Regardless of its psychometric integrity, a measure lacking empirical support for the clinician's intended use should not warrant further consideration.

CAUTION

- A psychological test should never be so brief as to compromise its psychometric integrity.
- A psychological test should never be used with a population or for purposes other than those for which it was developed and validated.
- The face validity of a psychological test is not as important as other types of validity.

Availability of Relevant Normative Data

Tied to the relevancy and psychometric soundness of the instrument is the issue of whether normative data are available for the particular population with whom the measure will be used. Using the Geriatric Depression Scale (GDS; Yesavage et al., 1983) to determine the presence and severity of depression in geriatric patients is quite appropriate. However, use of this same instrument with patient populations consisting primarily of young adults and adolescents should be avoided unless its use with those other populations has been demonstrated to be valid.

Cost

Cost is always a factor. One does not want to use a great deal of the reimbursement for testing to cover the cost of expensive test forms or scoring services. Fortunately, valid, reliable, and useful instruments are becoming more available for little or no cost. Some of these instruments have been in the public domain for a number of years; other cost-free instruments have become available only during the past few years. Still other instruments, such as the SF-36, are provided by their developers for a nominal licensing fee. Finally, some instrumentation is available from the party that is paying for the service (e.g., an MBHO) at no charge. This is likely to be the case when the MBHO wishes to implement a program that will, in the end, provide improved services for the patient or cost savings, or both, to the organization.

Reading Level

For instruments that are completed via paper-and-pencil or online computer-administration format, reading level is a major consideration. In general, test developers have become more sensitive to the issue of the reading level of the intended patient population. Part of this may be due to the fact that software is available to determine the reading level of material, thus providing a means of easily identifying problematic text. However, one is still amazed at the reading level of some instrumentation that is intended for a general patient audience. For clinicians who cater to the care of patients with various levels of education, the recommendation is to try to select an instrument with a reading level no higher than eighth grade. Tests requiring no more that a sixth-grade reading level are preferable, but these may be difficult to find. Alternatives, of course, are those instruments that have available an oral administration mode, such as audiotape or an interactive voice response (IVR) system.

Instrument Content

Aside from its importance as another aspect of validity, the content of the test—what the test is asking the patient to report on—is also important in achieving acceptability to the patient. Questions that are not considered relevant by the patient (i.e., questions having face invalidity) or that are informative but unnecessary or potentially offensive should be avoided. Patients' perceptions of what is appropriate or useful to inquire about can have a direct bearing on the probability that they will give valid (if any) responses to any or all of the questions being asked.

Ease of Use

One selection criterion that many professionals may overlook, or at least minimize in its importance, is the ease with which the test is administered and scored either by the clinician or (in cases in which he or she is not going to be directly engaged in these activities) by other staff members. Considerations here can include how easily the person who will be administering, scoring, or interpreting the instrument can become skilled in its use. It also extends to how acceptable it is to the payer, that is, to the degree to which the payer sees the value in and is willing to reimburse for the instrument's use.

Comprehensibility of Results

Another often overlooked criterion in instrument selection is how easily the test results can be understood by the payer or other relevant individuals, such as patients and their families. The clinician should be able to easily explain the results to the payer, the patient, and the patient's family in order that they more clearly understand the problems and the implications they have for the patient's day-to-day functioning. In some cases, the results may reveal areas of strength, which, if understood by the patient, may facilitate efforts toward positive change. Comprehensibility of results is particularly important when the clinician utilizes test results–driven interventions, such as Finn's (1996) therapeutic assessment technique, during the course of treatment.

Patient-Completed Versus Observer-Completed Instrument

Sometimes, the only available instrumentation for assessing a particular aspect of the patient's history or functioning is patient self-report measures. At other times, instrumentation completed by a clinician or other observer (e.g., parent, teacher) is the only available tool. At these times, the source of the information is not an issue: If one wants to use a standardized instrument, one uses what is available. However, there are occasions when the clinician will have the option of choosing between patient- and other-completed instrumentation to obtain the information being sought. Which type of instrument is better? The answer to that question will vary according to the patient being assessed, the type of information that is being sought, and the psychometric characteristics of the instruments being considered.

In many cases, the most important data will be obtained directly from the patient using self-report instruments. Underlying this assertion is the assumption that valid and reliable instrumentation, appropriate to the needs of the patient, is available; the patient can read (or understand questions presented orally) at the level required by the instrument; and the patient is motivated to respond honestly to the questions asked. If one or more of these conditions is not fulfilled, other options should be considered.

Patient self-report data may be viewed with suspicion by some (see Beutler, 2001; Strupp, 1996). These suspicions may be based on the potential problems just mentioned (see Bieber, Wroblewski, & Barber, 1999) or others. This author has personally witnessed the rejection of outcomes information that contradicted staff impressions, merely because it was based on patient self-report data. The implication was that such data are not valid. Generally, such concerns are not justified. As Strupp has noted,

> Patients may exaggerate benefits [of treatment] or distort their recollections in other ways, but unless they are considered delusional, there seems to be no reason for questioning their reports. To be sure, one would like to obtain collateral information from therapists, clinical evaluators, significant others, as well as standardized tests, but the information from collateral sources is intrinsically no more valid than the patients' self-reports. None the less, society is biased in favor of "objective" data and skeptical of "subjective data." (p. 1022)

Rating scales completed by the clinician or other members of the treatment staff may provide information that is as useful as that elicited directly from the patient. In those cases in which the patient is severely disturbed, is unable to give valid and reliable answers (e.g., as with younger children), is unable to read, or is an otherwise inappropriate candidate for a self-report measure, clinical rating scales can serve as a valuable substitute for gathering information about the patient. Related to these clinical rating instruments are parent-completed inventories for child and adolescent patients. These are particularly useful in obtaining information about the behavior of children or adolescents that might not otherwise be known. Information might also be obtained from other patient collaterals, such as siblings, spouses, teachers, coworkers, employers, and (in some cases) the justice system, which can be valuable by itself or in combination with other information.

Regardless of these variables, there are some generalities that one should keep in mind in deciding whether to opt for a self-report or other-report instrument. In addition to providing information from the patient's perspective, self-report instruments can allow access to a large amount of patient information using a minimum amount of expensive clinician time, which is frequently at a premium. Moreover, depending on the instrument being used, self-report measures may lead to the identification of problems or strengths that might not otherwise be known. At the same time, there is a downside to the use of self-report instruments. For instance, Fisher et al. (1999) point out that self-report instruments must be restricted to use with motivated and educated individuals, can consume a large amount of patient time, and frequently yield a great deal of unrelated or superfluous information. Furthermore, as Beutler (2001, *Source of Assessment* section, para. 3) has observed,

Although self-reports make sense from a clinical perspective, given that clinicians dislike adding time to their own schedules and because most assessments are based on patient self-report, methods

CAUTION

Considerations for self-report psychological tests:

- Make sure that the patient can read and understand the item content.
- Verify that alternate forms of self-report psychological tests (e.g., translations, audio or oral administrations) have been validated.
- Ensure that the item responses are those of the patient, *not* those of others who may be present at the time the patient is completing the test.
- Validate that the patient has responded to the test items openly and honestly.

that are less likely to be directly affected by patient motivation and benefit are likely to provide a sounder basis for research that transfers to clinical decision making. Although they are likely to have their own biases, especially if reimbursement is tied to effectiveness, clinicians' ratings would be likely to provide for less confounding of patient factors and outcomes than self-reports, even if they do not produce higher rates of compliance.

Although this author's experience has not borne out these concerns, they may be relevant with some types of patients in some situations and thus warrant consideration when one is selecting psychological test instruments.

SELECTED PSYCHOLOGICAL ASSESSMENT INSTRUMENTS FOR TREATMENT PLANNING

There are numerous instruments that can be helpful in assessing individuals seeking psychological treatment. The selection of the right psychological instrumentation for planning and monitoring treatment will depend on a number of variables. All other things being equal, however, there are a number of low-cost and public domain instruments that were developed to measure variables that are quite useful for assessing and monitoring change in the types of problems that are commonly seen in many types of clinical settings.

It is beyond the scope of this book to identify, much less describe in detail, how each potentially useful instrument can provide information that will assist the clinician in understanding patients and their problems and strengths, and in monitoring their progress in treatment. However, the following is an overview of several of those instruments that this author would recommend for consideration. They meet most or all of the previously indicated criteria for acceptable treatment-planning instruments. Many of them also offer the advantage of assessing multiple domains of functioning and being quite useful for monitoring progress during the course of treatment (see chapter 6). As appropriate, general guidelines developed by experts for interpreting individual scales and indices of these measures for treatment planning are also presented. In all cases, a more detailed discussion of these instruments, including information pertaining to their validity and reliability, can be found in the works of Maruish (1999, 2002). The reader also is encouraged to refer to the cited sources for more detailed information about the use and interpretation of these instruments

Minnesota Multiphasic Personality Inventory–2 (MMPI-2)

The Minnesota Multiphasic Personality Inventory (MMPI; Hathaway & McKinley, 1943) and, more recently, its revision, the MMPI-2 (Butcher, Dahlstrom et al., 1989), has proven itself to be one of the most useful psychological tests for more than 50 years. It is generally considered the gold standard by which other clinical instruments are compared and validated. Its large item pool (567 items) and resulting sets of validity, clinical, content, and supplemental scales, along with the volumes of published articles, books, and book chapters supporting its psychometric integrity and clinical use, make it an excellent source of information for patient assessment, particularly as it relates to treatment planning.

The research supporting the use of the MMPI-2 and its predecessor, the original MMPI, is voluminous. In addition, there are several available works that are helpful in interpreting the results derived from the administration of the MMPI-2. Butcher (1990) and Greene and Clopton (1999) have published works that specifically address the use of the MMPI-2 for treatment planning. Rapid Reference 3.6 presents a summary of the prototypical meaning of clinically significant scores for the MMPI-2 validity, clinical, content, and selected supplemental scales, as well as for over- and underreporting and response consistency, as presented by Greene and Clopton. These are accompanied by associated treatment implications. This summary table should be considered as a very general guide to the interpretation and use of MMPI-2 results for assessment and treatment planning. Butcher and Williams (1992), Friedman, Lewak, Nichols, and Webb (2001), Graham (2000), Greene (2000), and Nichols (2001) provide a more extensive discussion of this topic.

Rorschach Inkblot Method

Aside from the MMPI-2, probably no other measure of abnormal personality or psychopathology can compare to the level of international use and acceptance as that enjoyed by the Rorschach inkblot method. Although relatively labor intensive for the clinician (a major consideration in the age of managed

≡ Rapid Reference 3.6

MMPI-2 Response Styles, Scales, and Indices Useful for Treatment Planning

Response Style	Potential Treatment Implications
Item endorsement	
Consistent	Compliant with the assessment process, boding well for all interventions; should be able to read any treatment materials that are provided.
Inconsistent	May lack the necessary reading skills/intellectual ability to endorse items consistently; suggests any reading within the treatment process should be de-emphasized. Alternately, may indicate unwillingness to engage in the treatment process; noncompliance should be the first focus of treatment.
Accuracy of reporting pathology	
Overreporting	More severe or extensive psychopathology than would be expected; likely to terminate treatment prematurely despite the patient's report of severe problems. Determine whether there is any apparent motivation for overreporting.
Accurate reporting	Good insight into his or her behavior; willing to provide accurate evaluation of self; engaged in the assessment process and would be expected to be engaged in treatment.
Underreporting	Not reporting any form of psychopathology despite presence in treatment setting; problems likely to be chronic and not distressing; experiencing little motivation for any type of intervention.

Scale	Potential Treatment Implications
	Basic Validity Scales
Lie (L)	
L > 64T	Likely to be naive, defensive, and psychologically unsophisticated; when found with a within-normal-limits profile in an inpatient setting, likely to be psychotic or seriously disturbed.
Infrequency (F)	
F > 80T	Experiencing severe psychopathology unless overreporting. May be necessary to lower level of distress before making specific treatment interventions.

Scale	Potential Treatment Implications
F < 50T	Either not reporting or not experiencing any form of discomfort or distress; probably underreporting the full extent and severity of problems.

Correction (K)

K > 60T	Defensive and guarded; reluctant to acknowledge psychological problems; will be resistant to any type of intervention.
K < 40T	Sees self as having few coping resources and is fearful of being overwhelmed by problems. Initially, supportive interventions will be needed.

Basic Clinical Scales

Hypochondriasis (Hs)

Hs > 64T	Focused on vague physical complaints and resistant to the possibility of psychological problems; argumentative and pessimistic about being helped. Conservative intervention and reassurance that ailments will not be ignored are indicated.

Depression (D)

D > 64T	Experiencing distress and likely to be depressed. Determine whether mood state is due to internal or external factors and plan treatment accordingly.
D < 45T	Not reporting any types of emotional distress either as a result of treatment or as symptoms that led to treatment; little motivation for any type of intervention. Evaluate the possibility of acting out in an impulsive manner.

Hysteria (Hy)

Hy > 64T	Naive, suggestible, lacking in insight, and denying psychological problems; specific physical ailments develop under stress; limited motivation; looks for simplistic, concrete solutions. Focus on short-term goals.
Hy < 45T	Caustic, sarcastic, and socially isolated; has few defenses for coping with problems. Well-structured, behavioral interventions indicated when possible.

Psychopathic Deviate (Pd)

Pd > 64T	In conflict with family members or persons in authority; egocentric with little concern for others. Focus on short-term goals with emphasis on behavioral change rather than verbalized intent to change.

(continued)

Scale	Potential Treatment Implications
$Pd < 45T$	Rigid, conventional, and lacking in psychological insight. Use explicit, behavioral directives if patient is motivated to follow them.
Masculinity-Femininity (Mf)	
$(Mf) > 64T$	Does not identify with traditional gender role and is concerned about sexual issues; men frequently worry and feelings are easily hurt; women are confident and self-satisfied.
$Mf < 40T$	Identifies with traditional gender role.
Paranoia (Pa)	
$Pa > 64T$	Suspicious, hostile, and overly sensitive. Institute intervention slowly because of difficulty in developing trust-based relationship.
$Pa < 45T$	Narrow interests and insensitive to the motives of others. Use explicit, behavioral directives if patient is motivated to follow them.
Psychasthenia (Pt)	
$Pt > 64T$	Tense, worried, indecisive; obsessive or ruminative behaviors may be seen. May be necessary to lower the level of anxiety before treating other symptoms.
$Pt < 45T$	Level of security and comfort with self may augur poorly for any type of clinical intervention.
Schizophrenia (Sc)	
$Sc > 64T$	Feelings of alienation and remoteness from others and the environment, with possible difficulties with logic and judgment at the higher scale elevations. Directive and supportive interventions are required, and psychotropic medications may be needed.
$Sc < 45T$	Conventional, concrete, and unimaginative. Intervention should be behavioral, directive, and focused on short-term goals.
Hypomania (Ma)	
$Ma > 64T$	Overactivity, impulsivity, lability, and euphoria with occasional anger outbursts are seen. Evaluate for manic mood disorder and focus on short-term goals.
$Ma < 45T$	Low energy and activity level. Evaluate for serious depressive disorder and for suicidal potential, particularly as the patient starts to feel better.

Scale	Potential Treatment Implications
Social Introversion (Si)	
Si > 64T	Introverted, shy, and socially insecure; avoids significant others that exacerbate distress. Interventions should address tendency to withdraw and avoid others.
Si < 45T	Extroverted, gregarious, socially poised; at very low levels (T < 35), difficulty forming intimate relationships; unlikely to have a thought disorder; increased probability of acting out. Group therapies are useful.

Content Scales

Scale	Potential Treatment Implications
Anxiety (ANX) > 64T	Reports general symptoms of anxiety, worry, and difficulty with sleep and concentration. Psychotropic medication or other anxiety-reducing techniques may be required before implementing other interventions.
Fears (FRS) > 64T	Reports a large number of specific fears and generalized fears. Specific fears may respond well to systematic desensitization if they are not part of a larger set of fear and anxiety symptoms.
Obsessiveness (OBS) > 64T	Experiences excessive worry and rumination, difficulty making decisions, and intrusive thoughts; good candidate for insight-oriented therapies.
Depression (DEP) > 64T	Has a negative self-concept; has depressive mood and thoughts with an angry component that involves blaming others; experiences difficulty in getting going or getting things done. Evaluate for suicide potential.
Health Concerns (HEA) > 64T	Reports physical concerns and symptoms (e.g., gastrointestinal, neurological) that may be a manifestation of emotional distress. Assure patient that the symptoms are being taken seriously.
Bizarre Mentation (BIZ) > 64T	Reports overtly psychotic symptoms (e.g., paranoid ideation, hallucinations) and peculiar experiences. Psychotropic medication, hospitalization, or both may be indicated.
Anger (ANG) > 64T	Reports irritability, impatience, and explosive tendencies. Implement assertiveness training, anger control techniques, or both as part of treatment.
Cynicism (CYN) > 64T	Is suspicious of or doubts others' motives and feels others are interested only in their own welfare. Imperative to establish a trusting relationship if progress is to be made in therapy.

(continued)

Scale	Potential Treatment Implications
Antisocial Practices (ASP) > 64T	Has attitudes similar to those of persons who break the law, even if the patient does not engage in antisocial behavior. Determine whether problem behaviors and antisocial practices displayed during school years are being currently displayed. Group interventions with similar patients will be most productive.
Type A (TPA) > 64T	Hard-driving, competitive individual who frequently becomes impatient, grouchy, and annoyed. Rule out the possibility of a manic mood disorder.
Low Self-Esteem (LSE) > 64T	Has low opinions about self, is uncomfortable if people say nice things about him or her, and gives in easily to others. Interventions should be supportive. Allow ample time for change.
Social Discomfort (SOD) > 64T	Sees self as shy and uncomfortable in social situations; happier being alone. Needs support and encouragement to participate in treatment until comfortable in interacting with others.
Family Problems (FAM) > 64T	Reports considerable family discord and alienation from family; family seen as lacking love and support. Family involvement in treatment important unless patient needs emancipation from them.
Work Interference (WRK) > 64T	Reports being unable to work as before; tired, works under a great deal of tension, and is sick of what has to be done. Determine whether symptoms and behaviors actually interfere with work because this scale is primarily a measure of general distress.
Negative Treatment Indicators (TRT) > 64T	Unmotivated, dislikes going to doctors, prefers not to discuss personal problems; would rather take medication because talking does not help. Use caution in interpreting this as a characterological trait because depressed mood may elevate this scale, which is primarily a measure of general distress.
Factor Scales	
Anxiety (A) > 69T and Repression (R) > 59T	Aware of general distress and maladjustment and is trying to control overt expression of these; motivated for most types of psychological intervention.
A > 69T and R < 40T	Aware of general distress and maladjustment but is unconcerned about these problems; little motivation for treatment once distress has passed. Treatment should be focused on short-term goals.

Scale	Potential Treatment Implications
$A < 50T$ and $R > 59T$	Not reporting distress and is confident in his or her own abilities; denial and repression of any problems that may exist, and reluctant to examine own behavior. Short-term, behaviorally oriented interventions are indicated.
$A < 50T$ and $R < 40T$	Not reporting distress and is confident in own abilities; little awareness of possibility of problems that need to be repressed or denied; chronic ego-syntonic behaviors make any type of intervention difficult.

Note: From "Minnesota Multiphasic Personality Inventory–2 (MMPI-2)," by R. L. Greene and J. R. Clopton, 1999, in *The Use of Psychological Testing for Treatment Planning and Outcomes Assessment* (pp. 1023–1049), ed. M. E. Maruish, Mahwah, NJ: Lawrence Erlbaum Associates. Copyright 1999 by LEA. Adapted with permission.

care), the Rorschach can provide information important to the conceptualization and understanding of the patient's personality makeup and problems that generally is unavailable through other sources. As for the discussion at hand, Weiner (1999) notes that

> Rorschach assessment contributes to treatment planning in three ways. First, data provided by the Rorschach Inkblot Method help identify a prospective patient's levels of personality integration and subjectively felt distress, both of which have known implications for the intensity of psychotherapy people can tolerate and their likelihood of becoming active participants in the treatment relationship. Second, the Rorschach distinguishes among various styles of personality that make patients differentially responsive to particular kinds of treatment and approaches with psychotherapy. Third, Rorschach protocols assist in delineating the kinds of personality change that are likely to be most beneficial for an individual patient (treatment targets) and anticipating personality-based interference with such changes that might arise in the course of therapy (treatment obstacles). (p. 1131)

Weiner (1999) presents a list of Rorschach indicators of adjustment difficulty that represent maladaptive personality characteristics. Changes in these variables, studied by Weiner and Exner (1991) in their investigation of the Rorschach's sensitivity to change in short- and long-term psychotherapy patients and presented in Rapid Reference 3.7, can serve as targets for the outcomes of treatment. Note how the type of information provided here differs from that yielded by instruments such as the MMPI-2, or even a clinical interview, and thus can provide a unique perspective of patients and their current levels of functioning.

Weiner (1999) also notes that some treatment targets can actually become obstacles to therapeutic progress. For example, an active : passive (a:p) ratio that exceeds 2:1 in either direction suggests rigidity in personality functioning and thus a person who is unlikely to consider changing his or her perspective. For individuals in treatment, $D > 0$ is indicative of self-satisfaction and of feeling little need to change, and thus suggests chronic disorders, characterological difficulties, or an ego-syntonic symptom formation. The lack of Dimensionality ($FD = 0$) in Rorschach protocols is suggestive of patients who are not inclined to examine themselves (nonintrospectiveness), thus limiting the amount and significance of the information that is revealed during treatment. In addition, lack of a texture response ($T = 0$) is indicative of interpersonal distancing, which can interfere with the development of a trusting therapeutic relationship with the clinician. Weiner notes that each of these obstacles must be addressed within the therapeutic context if one expects behavioral or personality change to occur.

Symptom Checklist–90–R (SCL-90-R) and Brief Symptom Inventory (BSI)

Probably the most widely used of the brief, multidimensional measures of psychiatric symptomatology are the Derogatis family of symptom checklist instruments. These include the original Symptom Checklist–90 (SCL-90; Derogatis, Lipman, & Covi, 1973) and its revision, the SCL–90–R (Derogatis, 1983). Each of these instruments contains a checklist of 90 psychological symptoms. The Brief Symptom Inventory (BSI; Derogatis, 1992) is a 53-item, abbreviated version of the SCL-90-R. In a health care environment that is cost conscious and unwilling to make too many demands on a patient's time, the BSI is gaining popularity over its longer, 90-item parent instrument.

Both the SCL-90-R and the BSI yield T scores on nine scales and three summary indices. The nine scales measure the following symptom domains: Somatization (SOM), Obsessive-Compulsive (OBS), Interpersonal Sensitivity

Rorschach Adjustment Difficulty Indices Useful for Treatment Planning

Variable	Implication
$D < 0$[a, b]	Subjectively felt distress resulting from inadequate resources to meet experienced demands.
$AdjD < 0$[a, b]	Persistently felt distress extending beyond transient or situational difficulties in meeting experienced demands.
$EA < 7$[a, b]	Limited resources for implementing deliberate strategies of resolving problematic situations.
$CDI > 3$[a, b]	General deficit in capacities for coping with demands of daily living.
Ambitence[a, b]	Lack of commitment to a cohesive coping style leading to a personal sense of uncertainty.
$Zd < -3.0$[a, b]	Insufficient attention to the nuances of one's experience, with superficial scanning of environmental events and hastily drawn conclusions about their significance.
Lambda $> .99$[a, b]	Narrow and limited frames of reference and an inclination to respond to situations in the simplest possible terms.
$X+\% < 70$[a, b]	Inability or disinclination to perceive objects and events as most people would.
$X-\% > 20$[a, b]	Inaccurate perception of one's circumstances and faulty anticipation of the consequences of one's actions.
$SumSh > FM + m$[a, b]	Negative emotional experiences of dysphoria, loneliness, helplessness, and/or self-denigration.
$DEPI = 5$[a, b]	Depressive concerns.
$DEPI > 5$	Likelihood of diagnosable depressive disorder.
$Afr < .50$[a, b]	Avoidance of emotional interchange with the environment and reluctance to become involved in affect-laden situations.
$CF + C > FC + 1$[a, b]	Overly intense feelings and unreserved expression of affect.
Sum 6 Sp Sc > 6[a]	Tendency toward loose and arbitrary thinking.
$M- > 0$[a, b]	Strange conceptions of the nature of human experience.

(continued)

Variable	Implication
$Mp > Ma$[a,b]	Excessive use of escapist fantasy as a replacement for constructive planning.
Intellect > 5[a]	Excessive reliance on intellectualization as a defensive measure.
$Fr + rF > 0$	Narcissistic glorification of oneself and tendencies to externalize blame.
$3r + (2) / R > .43$[a]	Excessive self-focusing and preoccupation with oneself.
$3r + (2) / R < .33$[a,b]	Low regard for oneself in comparison with others.
$FD > 2$	Unusual extent of introspection.
$p > a + 1$[a,b]	Passivity in relation to other people and an inclination to avoid taking initiative and responsibility.
$T = 0$[a]	Lack of expectation or reaching out for close, psychologically intimate, nurturant, and mutually supportive relationships with others.
$T > 1$[a,b]	Unmet needs for close and comforting relationships with other people, leading to feelings of loneliness and deprivation.
Pure H < 2[a,b]	Disinterest in and/or difficulty identifying with other people.
$H < (H) + Hd + (Hd)$[a,b]	Uneasiness in contemplating relationships with real, live, and fully functional people.

Note. From Weiner and Exner (1991).

[a]Became significantly less frequent among patients receiving long-term psychotherapy.

[b]Became significantly less frequent among patients receiving short-term psychotherapy. From "Rorschach Inkblot Technique," by I. B. Weiner, 1999, in *The Use of Psychological Testing for Treatment Planning and Outcomes Assessment* (pp. 1137–1138), ed. M. E. Maruish, Mahwah, NJ: Lawrence Erlbaum Associates. Copyright 1999 by LEA. Reprinted with permission.

(I-S), Depression (DEP), Anxiety (ANX), Hostility (HOS), Phobic Anxiety (PHOB), Paranoid Ideation (PAR), and Psychoticism (PSY). The three summary indices of symptom count, symptom intensity, or both include the Positive Symptom Total (PST), the Positive Symptom Distress Index (PSDI), and the Global Severity Index (GSI), respectively.

Derogatis advocates SCL-90-R and BSI interpretation that incorporates summary index-, scale-, and item-level information (Derogatis, 1994; Derogatis & Savitz, 1999). In terms of specific algorithms or interpretive rules, however, little is offered. There is an algorithm for determining psychiatric "caseness" (that being a GSI T score greater than or equal to $63T$, or two or more of the nine symptom domain scales greater than or equal to $63T$). Otherwise, the GSI reflects both the number and intensity of the reported symptoms and may be viewed as the best indicator of current level of psychological distress. As an indication of the number of symptoms endorsed, the PST reflects the breadth of symptomatology. PSDI reflects the mean intensity level of the symptoms reported. In addition to their unique contributions, both PSDI and PST can help identify patients who may be over- or underreporting symptomatology. Elevations of $60T$ or greater (i.e., ± 1 standard deviation above the mean) on the individual symptom domain scales can probably be interpreted as being indicative of a high probability of the presence of significant symptomatology in the domain suggested by the scale title. As well, it is probably safe to use the same T-score cutoff in interpreting the scores of each of the three summary indices.

Outcome Questionnaire – 45 (OQ-45)

Over the past decade, the Outcome Questionnaire, or OQ-45 (Lambert et al., 1996) has gained widespread acceptance and popularity in MBHOs and other behavioral health care settings as a useful tool for identifying, tracking, and measuring the outcomes of behavioral health treatment. Contributing to this acceptance is its brevity, low cost, and focus on multiple areas of functioning that are generally deemed important in evaluating those seeking behavioral health care services. These same characteristics make it a good candidate for treatment monitoring.

The 45 items selected for inclusion in the OQ-45 were chosen because they "addressed commonly occurring problems across a wide variety of disorders . . . , tap the symptoms that are most likely to occur across patients, regardless of their unique problems . . . , [and] measure personally and socially relevant characteristics that effect the quality of life of the individual" (Lambert & Finch, 1999, p. 832). These items comprise three scales. The Symptom Distress (SD) scale consists of 25 items that measure the presence and severity of anxious and depressive symptomatology (Lambert & Finch). The anxiety and depression symptom domains were selected because of their prevalence in one large epidemiological study as well as in diagnostic data from one large MBHO. Because research has shown these two types of symptomatology are not easily separated, there was no attempt by the test authors to distinguish them in the OQ-45. In addition to anxiety and depression items, there are also two of items that screen for substance abuse.

The Interpersonal Relations (IR) scale comprises 11 items dealing with satisfaction with and problems in interpersonal relations. Lambert and Finch (1999) point to research that indicates that interpersonal problems are the most commonly addressed in therapy. The IR items measure marriage, family, friendship, and life relationships.

The nine items on the Social Role (SR) scale assess "a patient's level of dissatisfaction, conflict, distress, and inadequacy in tasks related to their employment, family roles, and leisure" (Lambert & Finch, 1999, p. 833). Inclusion of these types of items demonstrates a recognition of the importance of measuring how intrapsychic problems can affect a patient's ability to perform both personal tasks (e.g., leisure activities) and societal tasks (e.g., work).

Each of the 45 items on the OQ-45 includes five Likert-type response choices that the patient uses to indicate the degree or frequency (*Never* to *Almost always*) at which the content of the item has been present during the previous week. Each of the five response choices is weighted so that the score for each of the three scales is computed by summing the weights of the response choices selected for the items on that scale. A Total scale score also is calculated by summing response weights from all 45 items. An important feature of the OQ-45 is the normative data that are available for use with scored results. Lambert et al. (1996) report individual sets of normative data for community, employment assistance program (EAP), university counseling center, community mental health, and inpatient psychiatric samples, as well as for three samples of undergraduate students.

The availability of different norm sets increases the applicability and utility of the instrument. However, the interpretation of the results is based on the use of the community sample norms. A Total scale raw score of 63 (approximately 1 standard deviation from the mean of the community sample) or greater makes it more likely that the respondent belongs to a patient sample than a community (nonpatient) sample (Lambert et al., 1996). For the subscales, similar interpretations are made using cutoff scores of 30 for the SD subscale, 15 for the IR subscale, and 15 for the SR scale (Lambert & Finch,

1999). Elevated subscale scores can provide clues as to what aspects of functioning are particularly problematic for the patient when the Total scale score is 63 or greater. Individual item analysis also will enable a more specific determination. In general, an elevated Total scale score suggests problems in one or more of the general areas associated with the subscales. An elevated SD score suggests that the patient is bothered by symptoms associated with anxiety, affective, adjustment, and stress-related disorders. A high IR score suggests loneliness and problems in the patient's relationships with spouse, family, or others, whereas a high SR score points to problems in the patient's role as worker, homemaker, or student.

The OQ-45 was developed not only as an outcomes instrument to be administered at the beginning and end of treatment, but also as an instrument that can be used to monitor the progress of patients during the course of treatment. To assist in the monitoring of patient status over time, Lambert et al. (1996) provide the reliable change index (RCI) values for the Total scale and each of the three subscales. Based on the work of Jacobson and Truax (1991), the RCI values are 14 for the Total scale, 10 for SD, 8 for IR, and 7 for SR. Thus, a change in the Total scale score or any of the subscale scores between any two points in time by at least their respective RCI values is considered a reliable change. Improvement is indicated if the difference value is reliable and reflects a decrease in the Total or subscale score from one point in time to another. If the difference value is reliable and reflects an increase in the score from one point in time to another, a worsening of the patient's condition is indicated.

The OQ-45 was designed to meet the needs of MBHOs and other behavioral health care providers and organizations. It has been shown to be a valid and reliable instrument that lends itself to one or more readministrations during the course of an episode of care. The Total scale score represents a combination of items designed to measure three dimensions of patient functioning that are thought to be important in the conceptualization of mental disorders (American Psychiatric Association, 1994). Support for the independence of the subscales that measure these dimensions (SD, IR, SR) has not been strong. However, as Mueller, Lambert, and Burlingame (1998) state,

Whereas the domains of symptom distress, interpersonal relationships, and social role functioning, as measured with the OQ, appear at the present time to be so highly correlated that they effectively represent a single factor, they also represent distinct and important psychological constructs that merit concern and investigation by researchers and practitioners alike. Thus, clinical use of the OQ may continue to utilize the scales that have been developed. . . . [T]he content groupings of these subscales may provide clinicians with valuable information regarding various aspects of their patients' lives in a manner clinicians can readily incorporate into treatment. (p. 260)

Umphress, Lambert, Smart, Barlow, and Clouse (1997) see the OQ-45 as a measure of psychological distress with interrelated domains that allow for a more complete picture of a patient's overall functioning. This view is consistent with those of Mueller et al. (1998) and Lambert, Hansen, Umphress, et al. (1996) in recommending the use of only the Total scale score for monitoring statistically and clinically significant change (see chapter 6).

Behavior and Symptom Identification Scale (BASIS-32)

Another instrument that is gaining acceptance as an outcomes measure is the Behavior and Symptom Identification Scale, or BASIS-32 (Eisen, 1996; Eisen & Culhane, 1999; Eisen, Dill, & Grob, 1994). It can be distinguished from most other outcomes measures from three perspectives: It was developed on an inpatient psychiatric sample; it includes an assessment of problematic symptoms and functioning; and its content reflects the patient's perspective— that is, it addresses problems that are meaningful to the patient. Like the OQ-45, this is a brief, inexpensive instrument that provides for a measure of multiple domains of patient functioning.

The BASIS-32 was initially constructed as a clinician-administered interview (Eisen et al., 1994). Development of this instrument began with evaluation of the reports of 354 psychiatric inpatients concerning the problems that led them to inpatient treatment. The 897 identified problems were categorized and then further reduced by cluster analysis, resulting in the derivation of the final 32 items. Factor analysis of the data obtained during the clinician interviews at the time of admission yielded five factors that became the BASIS-32 scales: Relation to Self and Others, Daily Living and Role Functioning, Depression and Anxiety, Impulsive and Addictive Behavior, and Psychosis. Patients respond to the 32 BASIS items by indicating how much they have been bothered by the each of the 32 listed problems during the past week, using a Likert-type scale of 0 *(No difficulty)* to 4 *(Extreme difficulty)*. The score for each scale is computed by averaging all rating values assigned to each of the items contained in the given scale. In addition to the average rating for the five scales, an overall mean response score is computed.

There are no specific guidelines for interpreting the BASIS-32 results. As with the OQ-45 and many other multiscale instruments, however, interpretation can take place on the item, subscale, and overall severity or impairment level. At each of these levels, one can establish a rating criterion for determining the presence of problems that one considers significant and that require intervention (or at the least further investigation). Alternately, one can use normative data to guide decisions about the severity of problems or the necessity of attending to them. In this way, the BASIS-32 can serve as a useful source of information for treatment-planning purposes.

Originally, the BASIS-32 was developed for use in inpatient settings. As part of their development efforts, Eisen, Dill, et al. (1994) published inpatient normative data based on the 387 patients who completed the BASIS-32 (via interview) at or about the time of admission. Since then, the use of the BASIS-32 in outpatient settings has been investigated, resulting in the availability of outpatient normative data (Eisen, Wilcox, Leff, Schaefer, & Culhane, 1999; Eisen, Wilcox, Schaefer, Culhane, & Leff, 1997).

The BASIS-32 has the advantage of yielding not only symptom-related information, but also information related to social and day-to-day functioning. It has a large range of applicability, having been originally designed for use with psychiatric inpatients, but now also having empirical backing and gaining wide acceptance for use in outpatient and partial-hospital programs. Research to this point generally supports its use in outpatient settings as a measure of outcomes in a variety of important symptomatic and functional domains. The overall scale mean is particularly useful as a summary measure in both clinical and research applications. The psychometric properties of the Psychosis subscale and the Impulsive and Addictive Behavior subscale frequently have been shown to be relatively weak in various analyses, perhaps warranting more caution in their use as clinical or research measures. Due to the findings of Hoffman, Capelli, and Mastrianni (1997), one should also exercise caution when using the BASIS-32 with adolescents.

Brief Psychiatric Rating Scale (BPRS)

Unlike the other instruments presented here, the Brief Psychiatric Rating Scale (BPRS; Overall & Gorham, 1962, 1988) is a clinician-completed instrument. It has been used in numerous studies of the severely mentally ill (e.g., schizophrenic patients) and the effectiveness of pharmacological interventions for these types of populations. It was originally developed for use with psychiatric inpatients, but it also has demonstrated its usefulness in a variety of settings.

Overall and Gorham (1962) indicated that the purpose of designing the BPRS was to make available "a highly efficient, rapid evaluation procedure for use in assessing treatment change in psychiatric patients while at the same time yielding a rather comprehensive description of major symptom characteristics. It is recommended for use where efficiency, speed, and economy are important considerations" (p. 799). They later reported that it was developed to meet the needs of psychopharmacological research (Overall & Gorham, 1988). The 18 BPRS symptom constructs that are rated by the clinician are Somatic Concerns, Anxiety, Emotional Withdrawal, Conceptual Disorganization, Guilt Feelings, Tension, Mannerisms and Posturing, Grandiosity, Depressive Mood, Hostility, Suspiciousness, Hallucinatory Behavior, Motor Retardation, Uncooperativeness, Unusual Thought Content, Blunted Affect, Excitement, and Disorientation. Each of the constructs is rated on a 7-point Likert scale, with rating options ranging from *Not present* to *Extremely severe*. An anchored version of the BPRS, the BPRS-A (Lachar, Bailley, Rhoades, Espadas, Aponte, Cowan, Gummattira, Kopecky, & Wassef, 2001; Woerner, Mannuzza, & Kane, 1988), was developed to provide a description of the expected problems and symptoms for each of the 7 rating points along each of the 18 symptom dimensions.

Overall and Klett (1972) proposed an additional source of organizing BPRS data based on the results of factor analyses that had been conducted. They identified four factor dimensions, each of which is scored by summing the unweighted ratings for the three rating constructs that comprise the dimension. The four dimensions include Thought Disturbance, Withdrawal-Retardation, Hostile-Suspiciousness, and Anxious Depression.

Generally, interpretation of the scores is based on a comparison of current rating to the baseline ratings with regard to individual rating constructs, factor dimensions, or the total score (i.e., the sum of all 18 construct numerical ratings). Lachar, Bailley, Rhoades, and Varner (1999) have indicated that a BPRS percent change score (PCS) is often used to determine the effects of medication. This same approach can be used for monitoring change occurring from one point in time to another, regardless of the type of intervention that has occurred (medication, psychotherapy, electroconvulsive therapy, etc.). The PCS is calculated by subtracting the score from the latest BPRS rating from the previous score, dividing the difference by the score from that previous rating, and multiplying the result by 100.

The need for a rating scale like the BPRS will not occur very frequently in outpatient settings. In most cases, patient self-report measures will be more than adequate to meet the type of evaluation demands that most clinicians are likely to have. Self-report measures will also be more cost effective because they require little clinician time to obtain the results. However, there are situations in which a clinician-rating scale will provide information that might not otherwise be obtained (e.g., from patients who cannot read or are too disturbed to complete self-report measures). There also are times when clinician ratings are desired *in addition to* patient self-report information. This is not uncommon in some systems of outcomes management. In these cases, the BPRS is among the best available options.

SF-36 Health Survey (SF-36)

The SF-36 Health Survey (SF-36; Ware, Snow, et al., 1993) contains 36 items that comprise a total of eight independent scales—four having to do with the patient's physical health and its effects on role functioning, and four having to do with the patient's mental health and its effects on role functioning. Two component summary scales also can be derived to present an overall summary of the patient's responses on each of the constructs measured by the two sets of four scales.

Comprehensive yet brief overviews of the development of the SF-36 are presented in Ware (1999b) and Wetzler, Lum, and Bush (2000). In summary of these works, development of the SF-36 can be said to have its origins in two large-scale studies. One was the Health Insurance Experiment (HIE), which investigated issues related to health care financing. The other was the often-referenced Medical Outcomes Study (MOS), which investigated physician practice patterns and consequent patient outcomes. Both required the use of brief measures of functional and health status. The MOS investigators used a

149-item questionnaire that made use of items from other commonly used instruments, including those used in the HIE. It is from this questionnaire that 36 items were selected to represent the eight health concepts that were considered to be most affected by disease and treatment, and that were also the most widely measured concepts in other instruments. The following scales represent these eight health concepts: Physical Function (PF), Role Physical (RP), Bodily Pain (BP), General Health (GH), Vitality (VT), Social Function (SF), Role Emotional (RE), and Mental Health (MH). Each of the scales is composed of 2 to 10 of the items, and each of the 35 scale-related items (the one GH item is not a scale item) scores on only one of the scales.

Factor-analytic work on SF-36 findings from several sources revealed that 80%–85% of the instrument's reliable variance could be accounted for by the physical and mental health factors referred to earlier. These factors led to the development of the Physical Component Summary (PCS) and Mental Component Summary (MCS) scales (Ware, Kosinski, & Keller, 1994). The transformed z scores of all eight scales contribute to the computation of the T scores for both summary scales. However, the PF, RP, GH, and BP z scores are multiplied by positively weighted factor coefficients in the computation of the PCS scale. The MH, RE, and SF z scores are multiplied by positively weighted factor coefficients in the computation of the MCS scale. The VT scale contributes to both summary scales through positive factor weightings. The SF-12 (Ware, Kosinski, & Keller, 1995) was later developed as a means of predicting MCS and PCS scores from only 12 items (discussed in the next section).

Version 2 of the SF-36 was developed in 1996 (see QualityMetric, Inc., 2000). Enhancements in this version include improved formatting and presentation of the items and instructions, wording changes to improve objectivity and understandability, increased measurement precision through expanded item response choices, norms-based standardized scoring (i.e., T scores), and the development of norms for Version 1 that enable direct comparison with Version-2 results.

Patient-level interpretive information is unavailable. However, consistent with the recommendations of Ware, Snow, et al. (1993), one can probably feel safe in interpreting SF-36 scale and summary scale scores (original transformed scores or T scores) that are less than 1 standard deviation below the mean of the appropriate age and gender general population norms as indicating limitations in the construct purported to be measured by the scale in question. Similarly, a score that is 1 standard deviation above the mean for a scale or summary scale suggests that the patient is reporting functioning in the area that is generally better than that of the normative comparison group. Scores that are based on specific disease or disorder norms are interpreted *relative* to the comparison group's functioning and should not be used to make statements regarding the patient's general level of functioning.

The SF-36 provides an excellent means of gathering data on both physical and mental health status, economically and with minimum burden on both patient and clinician. Its value for this purpose has been recognized for several years now, and it is likely to grow considerably as integrated general and behavioral health care moves toward becoming the norm. It has a large, solid research base that continues to grow and will likely lead to further innovations in the measurement of health status.

The SF-36 was originally developed as a population- or group-based measure. However, many practitioners use the instrument alone or as part of clinical assessments of individual patients. There are those who contend that the psychometric properties of the instrument are not adequate for use of the instrument in individual assessments. For example, McHorney and Tarlov (1995) argue that the SF-36 does not meet all of their six criteria for individual patient applications. The two criteria on which they felt the SF-36 fell short were those for ceiling effects and reliability (internal consistency and test-retest). One could (and should) note that their reliability requirements are too stringent. By McHorney and Tarlov's standards, the MMPI-2 would not be considered appropriate for individual testing purposes (see Tables D-1 through D-9 in Butcher, Dahlstrom, et al., 1989). As for the ceiling effects, Ware (1999a) would argue that there is more of a problem with floor effects, and that these occur more frequently with the more severely ill patients. One also might rightly argue that the required "practical features" come only with some sacrifice of other required features, whether in the form of lowered validity or reliability or of limitations in the breadth or depth of measurement. In short, this author as well as others in the field would argue that the SF-36 is certainly more than adequate for individual assessment of general health status, especially in light of the demands (e.g., economy, brevity, ease of use) that managed and other health care systems place on such instruments if they are to be incorporated into the daily work flow of individual clinicians and provider organizations.

As a final note, the issues raised by McHorney and Tarlov (1995) may be adequately dealt with if basic interpretation of the individual patient's results is initially limited to those pertaining to the PCS and MCS scales. Refinement of this initial interpretation of the component summary scales can come through examination of those health concept scales that are associated with a PCS or an MCS score that falls outside the average range. In such cases, this approach can provide insight into those aspects of the patient's physical or emotional functioning that may be especially problematic.

SF-12 Health Survey (SF-12)

In their investigations of the SF-36, Ware and his colleagues came across two important findings. One was that physical and mental factors accounted for 80–85% of the variance in the SF-36's eight health concept scales; the other was that the PCS and MCS scales were almost always sensitive to hypothesized differences in independent mental and physical criterion variables (Ware et al., 1995). Together, these findings suggested that the SF-36 could be shortened without losing a substantial amount of information, and subsequently led to the development of the SF-12 Health Survey (SF-12).

Using regression methods, the desired abbreviated summary measures were derived from 10 items representing six of the SF-36 health concept scales. Two additional items were added to allow for representation from all eight of the health concept scales. The results from the 12 items yield scores on two scales, the PCS-12 and MCS-12, that represent estimates of the T scores that would have been obtained for the PCS and MCS scales had the full SF-36 been administered. As noted by Ware et al. (1995), "the high degree of correspondence between SF-36 PCS and MCS summary scores estimated using SF-12 items suggests that PSC-12 and MCS-12 scores will have much the same interpretation as scores estimated using the full SF-36" (p. 18). Thus, this author recommends interpreting T scores of 40 or less as suggestive of significant impairment, and T scores of 60 or greater as suggestive of better than average functioning.

Using only 12 items from the SF-36, the SF-12 provides a very quick estimate of the Physical and Mental Component Summary scales. When should one use the SF-12 instead of the SF-36, and vice versa? Keller and Ware (1996) offer the following recommendations:

In the cases where only the summary measures are of interest the choice of whether to use the 36-item or 12-item short form is largely a practical choice, because the 12-item survey reproduces the summary scales (PCS and MCS) based on the SF-36 as well. . . . When more information is sought regarding why there is a physical or mental health effect or the specific nature of that effect, all eight scales of the SF-36 should be evaluated. . . . When there is interest in examining all eight scales, it is recommended that the 36-item survey be used, as the SF-12 lacks the precision required for this level of analysis. (p. 3)

Thus, the SF-12 is best suited for situations in which brevity is a must and the finer level of discrimination and interpretation offered by the SF-36's eight scales is not required. An excellent example is the use of the PCS-12 and MCS-12 variables for treatment-monitoring purposes.

Visit-Specific Satisfaction Questionnaire (VSQ)

There are several patient satisfaction surveys that are available. However, one that can be of assistance in treatment monitoring is the nine-item, visit-specific questionnaire that was derived from the Group Health Association of America's (GHAA's) Consumer Satisfaction Survey (Davies & Ware, 1991). Unlike most other satisfaction instruments, the Visit-Specific Satisfaction Questionnaire (VSQ; Davies & Ware, 1991; Radosevich, Werni, & Cords, 1994; Rubin et al., 1993; Ware & Hays, 1988) measures aspects of satisfaction that were experienced during a *specific office visit,* measured at the end of that visit. This is in contrast to most other instruments that survey the patient's perceptions of multiple aspects of service during an *episode of care,* measured at the end of that episode.

The VSQ was adapted from the Patient Satisfaction Questionnaire–III (Hays, Davies, & Ware, 1987) and developed for use as part of the MOS (see Davies & Ware, 1991). It contains nine items taken from the questions related to access to care (appointment wait, office location, telephone access, office wait) and quality of care (time with doctor, explanation of care, technical skills, personal manner, overall care). Each of these aspects of the office visit are rated on a 5-point scale (*Excellent* to *Poor*) and each item is treated as a separate scale unto itself.

Davies and Ware (1991) present the number and percentage of the 18,118 MOS respondents who gave answers to each of the five response choices for each of the nine items. How the findings for a given patient are interpreted will depend on the situation and what one considers to be important. For instance, in Rubin et al.'s (1993) investigation of the ratings given by patients seen in different types of medical practice with different payment plans, the authors chose to classify a patient's response as either *excellent* or not excellent (i.e., *poor, fair, good,* or *very good*) because "current theories of quality management and improvement recommend comparisons to best practices rather than to minimum standards" (p. 836). However, one could choose another convention, such as including *very good* with the *excellent* response or even grouping the *good* response with these two highest levels of satisfaction.

The VSQ enables a clinician to determine *immediately* whether a single patient or sample of patients perceives any problems related to their care, and thus allows these problems to be handled sooner. The obvious limitation with the VSQ is the lack of validity and reliability data, as well as the lack of behavioral-health normative data. It is hoped that large-scale investigations into the use of this instrument in MBHOs will take place in the near future. Regardless, it is a face-valid instrument that clinicians can use to quickly obtain important information about their specific performance and areas of service that require improvement. Moreover, with regular use of the instrument, clinicians can begin to develop their own internal standards for comparison.

CAGE-AID

Numerous brief substance abuse-screening instruments are currently available. Many of these have been developed for the purpose of screening for alcoholism only; they do not include questions about the use of other drugs. With the prevalence of abuse of multiple substances, it becomes important to ensure that one screens for *all* types of substance abuse. One instrument that has been developed for this purpose is the CAGE-AID (Brown & Rounds, 1995).

The original CAGE consisted of four yes-no items inquiring about the need to *Cut* down drinking, feeling *Annoyed* by others' criticism of their drinking, *Guilt* over drinking, and needing a drink as an *Eye-opener* in the morning; thus the CAGE acronym. Subsequently, Brown and Rounds (1995) identified the need for an instrument like the CAGE that would screen for both alcohol and other drugs (also see Brown, 1992). They subsequently developed and tested a version of the CAGE questions that were *Adapted to Include Drugs* (CAGE-AID) on a group of 124 primary care patients using various cutoff scores for the modified instrument

The research suggests that employing a cutoff of one or more affirmative responses to the CAGE-AID questions should be used in situations that seek to maximize sensitivity, whereas a cutoff of two or more affirmative responses is appropriate for maximizing specificity or optimizing both sensitivity and specificity. As with any type of screening, it is this author's preference to optimize both sensitivity and specificity, and for this reason the general recommendation is to use the two or more affirmative responses as the criterion for whether the individual should undergo further evaluation for a substance abuse problem. One may wish to increase the cutoff score to 3 or more when screening women, given that the CAGE-AID may be less sensitive to substance-abusing women than substance-abusing men.

SUMMARY

Psychological testing can serve as an important source of clinical information. The standardized manner in which test data are gathered, along with the validity, reliability, and normative data that support the conclusions drawn from test administration, can provide a value-added dimension to clinical assessment. Together with information obtained during the clinical interview and from other sources, test-based information can assist in various aspects of the treatment-planning process, including problem identification and clarification, identification of important patient characteristics that can facilitate or hinder treatment, and monitoring treatment progress.

Unfortunately, in the age of managed care, the importance of psychological testing for traditional purposes has become secondary to other purposes. MBHOs place more value on testing for gathering population-based data for process and outcomes measurement and program development than on that for gathering individual patient data for the purpose of problem identification or clarification, diagnosis, or treatment planning. This situation is the result of several factors, including the health care industry's ongoing efforts to streamline services and contain costs; its less than positive attitude toward testing that

Putting It Into Practice

Case Study of Mary Smith (*continued*)

RESULTS OF PSYCHOLOGICAL TESTING

Mary Smith

In order to clarify the nature and severity of her problems, Ms. Smith was administered the MMPI-2. In addition, the OQ-45 was administered to obtain an objective baseline measure of her psychological status against which the results of readministrations of this same instrument at various points during the course of treatment can be compared. Such comparisons will enable the monitoring of changes in Ms. Smith's status as the result of the planned psychotherapeutic interventions. The results of both instruments, along with the findings from the clinical interviews with her and her husband, will also be used to develop the case formulation for the patient. The results of the testing are presented in Table 3.1.

The MMPI-2 results are generally quite consistent with the impressions formed from the assessment interview information. This is not surprising, given that the MMPI-2 is a self-report instrument that asks for many of the same types of information that are obtained through clinical interviews. Examination of the MMPI-2 validity scales indicates that Ms. Smith was open and honest in responding to the items of the inventory. The pattern of scores for the basic clinical scales reveals clinically significant elevations on Depression (*D*) and Psychasthenia (*Pt*). The prototypical 2–7 codetype is indicative of anxious depression and is characterized by anxiety, depression, guilt, self-devaluation, tension, and proneness to worry (Friedman et al., 2001). Ruminations are present and are frequently accompanied by insomnia, feelings of inadequacy, and a reduction in work efficiency. Individuals with this profile tend to overreact to minor stress with anxious preoccupations and somatic concerns. Also, they may become meticulous, compulsive, and perfectionistic. They have a strong sense of right and wrong, and they tend to focus on their deficiencies, even though they have experienced many personal achievements in their lives. Often these achievements are attained out of a sense of responsibility and accomplished in a compulsive manner.

The MMPI-2 results also are indicative of people who tend to be dependent and lack assertiveness, resulting in their taking on increased responsibilities. This can lead to their becoming overwhelmed and, consequently, more anxious and depressed. When things go wrong, they tend to see themselves as being responsible. For people with this profile, suicidal ideation is common, with actual attempts being a realistic possibility. Historical information and direct questioning indicate that Ms. Smith is not a suicidal risk.

Ms. Smith's responses to the MMPI-2 also revealed a pattern of clinically significant elevations on several MMPI-2 content scales—Anxiety (*ANX*), Obsessiveness (*OBS*), Depression (*DEP*), Low Self-Esteem (*LSE*), Family Problems (*FAM*), and Work Interference (*WRK*)—that is consistent with her history and presentation. Again, anxiety, depression, worry, obsessive ruminations, concentration problems, difficulty completing tasks, low self-esteem, giving in to the needs of others, family discord, and not being able to work as well as she used to are all indicated (Greene & Clopton, 1999). Moreover, the scores on the Anxiety and Repression factor scales suggests the presence of general distress and maladjustment. This, along with the elevated score on the Ego Strength (Es) scale and the low score on the Negative Treatment Indicators (TRT) content scale, are positive indications that Ms. Smith is likely to become easily engaged and to remain in treatment.

Ms. Smith's OQ-45 Total scale raw score (≥ 63) indicates the presence of significant psychological distress or disturbance that is characteristic of a patient population. This is reflected most notably in symptoms of anxiety and depression (Symptom Distress [SD] raw score ≥ 30) and disruption in her role as law student (Social Role [SR] raw score ≥ 15). The score on the Interpersonal Relations (IR) scale suggests the presence of some impairment in her interpersonal relations, but not so much as to be considered significant (raw score ≤ 15).

Table 3.1 Summary of Ms. Smith's MMPI-2 and OQ-45 Test Results

MMPI-2 Clinical and Supplemental Scales		MMPI-2 Content Scales		OQ-45 Scales	
Scale	T Score	Scale	T Score	Scale	Raw Score
L	52	ANX	66	Total	87
F	72	FRS	59	SD	53
K	54	OBS	87	IR	13
Hs	59	DEP	67	SR	21
D	77	HEA	57		
Hy	63	BIZ	52		
Pd	58	ANG	50		
Mf	45	CYN	46		
Pa	59	ASP	49		
Pt	86	TPA	64		
Sc	63	LSE	70		
Ma	53	SOD	57		
Si	62	FAM	68		
A	71	WRK	67		
R	65	TRT	46		
Es	66				

has resulted from several factors (e.g., past misuse of testing, lack of empirical demonstration of value); and the use of medications to assist in the diagnosis of certain conditions. This is not to say that the status of psychological testing will remain as it is today. However, it is unlikely to improve until the psychological or other behavioral health professions are able to empirically demonstrate the direct effects, and thus the value, of psychological testing in the treatment of mental health and substance abuse disorders.

Regardless of the status of testing in the eyes of the health care industry, it is fortunate that there are a number of available psychological measures that can assist in patient assessment. Selecting the best among the available options should be based on several important factors, including the instrument's length, psychometric properties (especially test-retest reliability when used for treatment monitoring), available normative data, cost, content, required reading level, ease of use, and comprehensibility of results, as well as the clinician's desire for a self-report versus an observer-completed instrument. Examples of useful instruments for gathering clinical assessment data were presented earlier.

✎ TEST YOURSELF ✎

1. **MBHOs are *most* interested in the use of testing for which of the following purposes?**
   (a) To answer diagnostic questions
   (b) To assist in program evaluation
   (c) To assist in treatment planning
   (d) To meet demands for outcomes information
   (e) Both a and c
   (f) Both b and d

2. **Which of the following is *not* a reason for the decline in authorization for psychological testing by MBHOs?**
   (a) Lobbying efforts by the American Psychiatric Association
   (b) The movement to contain health care costs
   (c) A lack of empirical demonstration of cost effectiveness
   (d) Inappropriate use of testing in the past

3. **Which of the following is a way in which testing can contribute to the treatment-planning process?**

   (a) Identification of important patient characteristics

   (b) Problem clarification

   (c) Treatment-progress monitoring

   (d) All of the above

4. **A particularly important psychometric property for treatment monitoring is**

   (a) content validity.

   (b) internal consistency.

   (c) test-retest reliability.

   (d) concurrent validity.

   (e) face validity.

5. **Because of the amount of clinician time involved, which of the following instruments would an MBHO be *least* likely authorize?**

   (a) BSI

   (b) Rorschach

   (c) MMPI-2

   (d) SCL-90-R

   (e) SA-45

6. **What are some of the justifications one can provide to increase the likelihood that psychological testing for treatment planning will be authorized for reimbursement?** _____

   _____

7. **What might you do if you felt that testing were required to develop an appropriate treatment plan for a patient, but the patient's health plan would not authorize reimbursement for it?** _____

   _____

8. **What circumstances, or the need for what type of treatment-planning information, would lead you to choose the administration of the MMPI-2 over the SCL-90-R or BSI?** _____

   _____

9. **Why would the OQ-45 be considered a good instrument to use for treatment-planning purposes?** _____

   _____

(continued)

10. What are some of the types of important assessment information discussed in chapter 2 that the MMPI-2 could help gather? _____
_____

Answers: 1. f; 2. a; 3. d; 4. c; 5. b; 6. Use can provide data for outcomes measurement, program development, assistance in diagnosing difficult cases, problem identification and clarification, monitoring treatment progress, and identifying patient strengths that could be used in treatment; 7. Utilize low- or no-cost instruments that require little in terms of clinician time, then demonstrate to the health plan the value of the obtained information in providing high-quality, low-cost care; 8. cases in which more in-depth, detailed information about multiple aspects of functioning are required, and as a means of determining the validity of the results; 9. It addresses problems seen across various disorders, has norms developed for many different populations, can easily be used for treatment monitoring, is relatively brief, and is low cost; 10. presenting problems, level of subjective distress, potential to resist therapeutic influence, coping styles, mental status, motivation to change.

Four

CASE FORMULATION

Having gathered the necessary clinical assessment information, the clinician is now in the position to begin the next important step leading to the development of a treatment plan. This is the *case formulation*. It is a task that some clinicians formally complete as part of the assessment process, particularly when patients are referred for comprehensive evaluation by other clinicians or another third party requiring detailed feedback (e.g., the court system). In such cases, the referring party frequently asks for a case formulation and expects to receive a detailed written or oral report of that formulation. In the more typical case, the assessing clinician is also the treating clinician, and the formulation is informal. That is, only the most salient aspects of the patient assessment are attended to, with no attempt to account for or integrate information that is not obviously related to the presenting problem(s). Moreover, documentation or reporting of the formulation is likely to be relatively broad or sketchy. Overall, the more informal case formulations may be a reflection of how thoroughly the patient was assessed, the need to prepare such a formulation (e.g., for patients being seen for brief, problem-focused therapy), or the value placed on this clinical work product by the treating clinician or party responsible for the payment of treatment.

Regardless of how its value and utility are perceived by individual providers or third-party payers, the case formulation remains an integral part of the mental health and substance abuse treatment process. For this reason, this chapter is devoted to its development in daily clinical practice.

WHAT IS A CASE FORMULATION?

Any discussion of how to develop a case formulation requires an understanding of what a case formulation is and why it is so important for planning the treatment of behavioral health patients. This section provides the grounding necessary to proceed to a discussion of case formulation development.

Case Formulation Defined

According to Tompkins (1999),

> a case formulation is a hypothesis about the underlying psychological mechanisms that drive or maintain a client's problems. A case formulation is generally theory driven; that is, problems or psychopathology are explained on the basis of structures and processes of a particular psychological theory. Case formulations are used by therapists to guide and focus therapy, and are particularly useful when a client's difficulties are numerous and complex, or when a client is not responding to treatment. (p. 318)

Makover (1992) further clarifies the nature and importance of the case formulation, describing it as

> a model of the patient, a tentative, partial representation that must be revised as new data are acquired. Arriving at a formulation is, from the standpoint of treatment planning, the primary objective of the [clinical assessment], because the hypotheses that the therapist generates from it will form the basis of a proposed therapeutic contract with the patient. (p. 339)

DON'T FORGET

Key Aspects of Case Formulations

- Primary objective of the clinical assessment
- Model or representation of the patient
- Theory-based hypothesis about the patient and the patient's problems
- Basis of the treatment plan
- Requires revision as new information about the patient is acquired

Note. From Makover (1992) and Tompkins (1999).

In their definitions, Tompkins (1999) and Makover (1992) have identified several key aspects of case formulations. First, a case formulation is the *primary objective of the clinical assessment.* It is a *model* or representation of the patient and how that patient functions in the world. It provides a *hypothesis* about the patient's problems that are *based on the theory of psychopathology* that guides clinicians' understanding and treatment of such problems. As such, it serves as the *basis of the treatment plan.* Moreover, the case formulation is *not a static product.* As with any hypothesis, the hypotheses about the patient, and thus the treatment plan, should be revised as new information about the patient is acquired. This latter point is particularly important and, as is discussed in chapter 6, provides further justification for the clinicians' efforts to monitor patient progress during the course of treatment.

The Role of Case Formulations

The time and effort required to arrive at a case formulation can yield benefits that make this sometimes tedious endeavor worthwhile. The benefits derived from having a well thought-out case formulation can be seen in the multiple roles it serves during the patient's episode of care. As Persons (1989) notes, its most important role is to serve as the basis of the treatment plan. It does so by providing many different types of information and assisting in therapeutic decision making, thus serving several subordinate roles both before and during the course of treatment. As summarized in Rapid Reference 4.1, Persons has identified nine such roles, or ways in which case formulations can assist clinicians.

Understanding relationships among problems. An important function of the case formulation is to tie together or clarify the relationships of all the patient's

≡Rapid Reference 4.1

Key Roles of Case Formulations

Case formulations assist the clinician in each of the following:
- Understanding relationships among problems
- Choosing a treatment modality
- Choosing an intervention strategy
- Choosing an intervention point
- Predicting behavior
- Understanding and managing treatment noncompliance
- Understanding and working on relationship difficulties
- Making decisions about extratherapy issues
- Redirecting an unsuccessful treatment

Note. From Persons (1989).

problems (Persons, 1989). In a sense, it attempts to find a common thread that brings these problems together and thus provide insight into the source or meaning of what the patient is experiencing. Related to this, it allows the clinician to determine whether one or a subset of the patient's problems can be successfully treated without attempting interventions for other problems that might exist. For example, is it possible to successfully treat a dually diagnosed patient for major depressive disorder without also treating a comorbid alcohol dependence problem? Knowing the relationship between the two problems can help answer this question.

Choosing a treatment modality. Knowing the source or real cause of the patient's problems can have implications in selecting a treatment modality that will best suit the patient's needs and increase the likelihood of a positive therapeutic outcome. Persons (1989) relates an example of a woman presenting with panic attacks and a high level of anxiety. Although the initial inclination was to treat this woman's problem with relaxation training, the case formulation suggested a different tack would be most beneficial. Through this formulation, it was revealed that this woman's problems involved issues related to her assuming a great amount of responsibility for tending to the needs of others while receiving no assistance from her husband. A similar pattern was noted in previous relationships with males, including her father. Thus, marital therapy was determined to be a better way to proceed than individual, relaxation-oriented treatment.

Similarly, case formulations also may be helpful in making higher levels of decisions. For example, they may be useful in determining the appropriate level of care (e.g., partial hospitalization vs. outpatient treatment).

Choosing an intervention strategy. Related to the selection of treatment modality is the selection of the intervention strategy within that modality (Persons, 1989). On the surface, there may be multiple strategies for effectively treating the patient's problems. However, the case formulation may reveal the nature of the problem to be such that one option is better than others in terms of effecting lasting change in multiple problem areas or in improving overall coping capabilities.

Choosing an intervention point. As Persons (1989) points out, it is unrealistic to try to eliminate all of the patient's problems. (This is particularly true in the era of managed behavioral health care.) With an understanding of the relationships among all of the patient's problems (discussed earlier), the clinician can determine which are most related to the central difficulties and focus the patient's efforts on them. The assumption here is that ameliorating the core problem or issue will yield positive effects for the other related problems.

Predicting behavior. The case formulation provides an organized conceptualization of how the patient views, lives in, and reacts to the environment. With this knowledge in hand, it becomes relatively easy for the trained clinician to make predictions about how the patient will behave in any number of circumstances (Persons, 1989). Knowing how the patient is likely to act can be invaluable in planning treatment, whether it be in the selection of the general therapeutic approach or the specific intervention.

Understanding and managing treatment noncompliance. Similar to assisting in the prediction of behavior, the case formulation can help the clinician (and the patient) gain insight into noncompliance with the prescribed treatment regimen (Persons, 1989). This same insight can provide the clinician with direction as to how to modify or otherwise proceed with the planned treatment.

Understanding and working on relationship difficulties. Persons (1989) suggests that the case formulation can be particularly helpful in understanding and ameliorating interpersonal relationship problems. This likely stems from the level of complexity at which the case formulation tries to explain how the patient interacts with the environment.

Making decisions about extratherapy issues. Here, Persons (1989) is referring to issues related to the nontherapeutic aspects of the clinician-patient relationship. In the example she provides, the clinician's acceptable solution to a patient's difficulty in paying for treatment is linked to what the patient's case formulation suggests is therapeutic.

Redirecting an unsuccessful treatment. Other things being equal, the failure of treatment may be viewed as an indication of a faulty case formulation (Persons, 1989). A new formulation and new interventions are required in such cases. Support for the accuracy of the revised case formulation either will or will not be demonstrated in the effectiveness of the new interventions. Although further revisions may be required, such efforts will be facilitated by the fact that the case formulation allows the clinician to proceed systematically through this process.

Direct Benefits of Sharing the Case Formulation With the Patient

The roles that case formulations may serve can greatly assist the clinician in providing the best patient care. As a consequence, the patient benefits from the end product or outcomes of a well thought-out, useful case formulation. However, the benefits of the case formulation extend beyond the therapeutic decision-making aids to ones that have a more direct effect on the patient.

Bergner (1998) has identified four benefits that can accrue from sharing case formulations with patients. First, it can provide patients with a schema or organized manner in which to view their problems. They are presented with a central maintaining factor, which helps to reduce or eliminate any confusion or erroneous conceptions about their current circumstances. Second, this central factor provides patients with direction as to where to focus their energies for change in order to obtain the most bang for the buck, so to speak. Third, identification of the problem in terms of something that is comprehensible and controllable can have an empowering effect on patients. Finally, the feeling of empowerment can help diminish the fear, helplessness, or hopelessness that can accompany those patients who think of themselves as being crazy or unable to cope with their problems.

CASE FORMULATION DEVELOPMENT

There are several ways in which a clinician could develop a case formulation. One that has applicability across many theoretical approaches to the understanding and treatment of behavioral health problems is what Bergner (1998) refers to as the *linchpin approach*. According to Bergner,

> Clinical assessment would ideally culminate in the construction of an empirically grounded, comprehensive case formulation that organizes all of the key facts of a case around a "linchpin." That is to say, it would organize them around some factor that not only integrates all of the information obtained, but in doing so also identifies the core state of affairs from which all of the [patient's] difficulties issue. Further, it would do so in such a way that this formulation becomes highly usable by the clinician and the [patient] in matters such as their selection of a therapeutic focus, identification of an optimum therapeutic goal, and generation of effective forms of intervention. Most importantly, the existence of such a formulation would allow the clinician to focus therapeutically on that one factor whose improvement would have the greatest positive impact on the [patient's] overall problem or problems. (p. 287)

To further clarify, Bergner adds that

> the concept of a "linchpin" is not that of a single cause or influence acting in isolation. Rather, it is a concept having to do with what is at the center of multiple states of affairs—a "common pathway" as it were between prior influences and current consequences. A linchpin, as the metaphor implies, is what holds these together; it is what, if it be removed, may cause them (most importantly, the destructive consequences) to fall apart. (p. 290)

The linchpin approach, at least as described by Bergner (1998), is a general approach that is quite similar to or even reflective of other approaches espoused by various theoretical orientations. Simply put, the procedures involved include (a) determining the facts of the case, (b) developing the facts into an explanatory account, and (c) checking, implementing, and revising the formulation if indicated. A more detailed variant of this approach to case formulation, based on the work of Mumma (1998), Persons (1989), and Tompkins (1999), is presented in the next section. These authors approach the task from a cognitive therapy orientation, but from this author's perspective, the steps involved have widespread applicability. For this reason, the following approach to the development of a case formulation is recommended, regardless of the clinician's theoretical orientation.

Steps to Developing a Case Formulation

Clinicians should find the following stepwise approach to facilitate the development of case formulations, regardless of their theoretical orientation, the problems that the patient presents, or the setting in which treatment will be rendered.

　　1. Develop a comprehensive problem list. A thorough assessment (as described in the chapter 2) should provide a good psychological picture of the patient—where the patient came from, where the patient currently is, and where the patient is likely to be in the future—and thus enable the clinician to easily construct a list of the patient's problems. This, of course, would include the patient's *stated* problems. Indeed, the patient's verbatim chief complaint or reason for seeking behavioral health treatment can be quite revealing (Persons, 1989). This list also would include problems that the patient denies or is unaware of, but that are apparent to the clinician. It may also include problems identified by third parties (e.g., family, courts, schools).

Clinicians employing a cognitive approach to conceptualizing and treating mental health and substance abuse problems would describe such problems in terms of cognitions, moods, and behaviors (Persons, 1989; Tompkins, 1999). Not inconsistent with the cognitive view is a more atheoretical conceptualization that the reader should find useful in developing a problem list, regardless of the clinician's approach to understanding and treating psychopathology. Essentially, it reflects the recommended assessment content presented in chapter 2. Thus, the problem list would include any difficulties related to the following: generalized level of distress, sense of well-being, specific signs and symptoms of psychopathology, risk of harm to self or others, physical health, family and other interpersonal relationships, functioning at work or school, patient-identified goals, third party-identified goals, and motivation to engage in treatment.

At this point, it also may be useful to identify the degree to which each identified problem is clinically significant (Mumma, 1998). This should not have a bearing on the development of the case formulation per se, but it can be useful later on when determining which problems merit directed efforts toward therapeutic intervention.

2. Determine the nature of each problem. To fully understand an identified problem one must also understand the nature of that problem. Three types of information are important here. First, what is the *origin* of the problem? (When did the problem begin, and what was going on in the patient's life at that time?) Second, what are the current *precipitants* of the problem? (What triggers the appearance of the problem, or if the problem is always present to some degree, what exacerbates its presentation or the patient's experience of it?) Finally, what are the *consequences* of the problem that maintain or (in behavioral terms) reinforce its continued presence? (Why does the problem continue? How does the patient benefit from its existence? What would happen (or not happen) if the problem disappeared?) Knowing the origins, precipitants, and consequences of the identified problems is critical for the completion of the next step of the case-formulation development process.

3. Identify patterns among the problems. Having answered the questions related to their nature, one must now begin to examine regularities within and connections among the identified problems. The purpose of this task is to determine patterns or commonalties that emerge across problems. These might be reflected in the origins, precipitants, or consequences of the problems. Mumma (1998) indicates that an analysis of the data using a temporal (horizontal) or a theoretical (vertical) approach may be used to explore and reveal commonalities among the problems. Another potentially fruitful approach that might be used separately or in conjunction with the horizontal and vertical approaches is one that involves content analysis. The goal here would be to discern whether there are any common symbols or themes that seem to underlie the problems.

What is revealed as a result of this analysis depends on the particular circumstances of the patient. For one patient, the commonalities that become readily apparent might be related to the circumstances under which the problems surface or under which they grow in intensity (e.g., whenever the patient perceives that performance on a given task falls short of adequate in the eyes of an authority figure). For another, it might be the time or circumstances under which the problems began (e.g., difficulties began shortly after the patient's marriage). In yet another case, what happens as a result of the presence of any of the problems may be a common thread (e.g., the patient's spouse becomes more attentive to the patient's needs).

4. Develop a working hypothesis to explain the problems. The next step in case formulation development represents the ultimate goal of the clinician's information-gathering (i.e., assessment) and analysis efforts. Persons (1989) equates the hypothesis of the underlying mechanism or central problem with the case formulation itself. It is at this point that the clinician brings together all the information obtained about the patient in an attempt to develop an organized, comprehensive picture and explanation of the patient's problems.

This explanatory hypothesis stems from the products of the first three steps in this process. As recommended by Mumma (1998), one may first want to generate a number of hypotheses to avoid prematurely eliminating all possibilities for the pursuit of a single, possibly incorrect formulation. All other things being equal, having several possibilities also allows the clinician to determine the most parsimonious explanation among the more plausible hypotheses being considered. Based on explanatory coherence, precision, and simplicity, a single hypothesis then can be selected for the more rigorous exploration described in the next step.

5. *Validate and refine the hypothesis.* Once the clinician is satisfied with the hypothesis about the central problem, it is necessary to validate that hypothesis. This is a critical step in development of a case formulation. Persons (1989) recommends several means of testing the accuracy of the hypothesis that can be implemented before the final acceptance of the case formulation and the beginning of treatment. As summarized in Rapid Reference 4.2, the first is that the hypothesized underlying mechanism accounts for all identified problems. Second, the reported events leading to the current episode are easily understood in terms of the hypothesis. Third, hypothesis-based predictions are tested against the information available at the time and found to be accurate. Fourth, the patient agrees with the hypothesis.

It is important for the clinician to recognize that failure of any of these tests may require modification or perhaps complete revision of the mechanism hypothesized to underlie the patient's problems. Failure to do so may only lead to the development of a treatment plan that yields less than maximum (if any) benefits to the patient. Of course, information obtained during the treatment process may later prove the case formulation to be less than accurate. Those circumstances are dealt with in the next step of case formulation development. At the point of planning a course of treatment, however, one must be as confident as possible that the resulting treatment plan is based on the most accurate assessment of the patient that is available to the clinician *at that time*. Submit-

Rapid Reference 4.2

Tests of Case Formulation Validity

1. The hypothesized underlying mechanism accounts for all identified problems.

2. The reported events leading to the current episode are easily understood in terms of the hypothesis.

3. Hypothesis-based predictions are tested and found to be accurate.

4. The patient agrees with the hypothesis.

5. Treatment based on the hypothesized underlying mechanism yields positive outcomes.

Note. From Persons (1989).

ting the case formulation to Persons' (1989) tests will help provide this needed assurance.

6. Test and revise the hypothesis during treatment. Validation of the hypothesized underlying mechanism does not end when treatment begins. It is an ongoing process. Based on the case formulation, the clinician should be able to make and test predictions about the patient both during and outside the treatment sessions. Responding to aspects of both treatment and nontreatment situations in a manner that is not predicted by the case formulation should be cause for a careful review of the hypothesized underlying mechanism (Mumma, 1998).

In addition, another of Persons' (1989) tests of the validity of the central problem hypothesis is whether treatment yields positive outcomes. Patients receiving treatment that is based on the hypothesized underlying mechanism should show improvement in the problems that led them to seek treatment in the first place as well as in other aspects of their lives. Lack of improvement after a sufficient amount of time should lead the clinician to reconsider and revise the initial case formulation.

In all, this last step in case formulation might be considered an ongoing, recursive process (Tompkins, 1999). The sequential elements of this process include the development or revision of a case formulation, planning and implementing an intervention based on that formulation, monitoring and evaluating the outcomes of the intervention, and revising the formulation based on that evaluation. Thereafter, the cycle begins again. In essence, this last step represents a continuous quality improvement (CQI) process.

A brief review of the steps involved in developing a case formulation are presented in Rapid Reference 4.3.

Rapid Reference 4.3

Steps to Developing a Case Formulation

1. Develop a comprehensive problem list.

2. Determine the nature of each problem.

3. Identify patterns among the problems.

4. Develop a hypothesis to explain the problems.

5. Validate and refine the hypothesis.

6. Test the hypothesis during treatment and revise as necessary.

CAUTION

- Case formulations should always be based on a thorough assessment of the patient.
- Treatment should never be delayed due to difficulties in obtaining information needed to complete the case formulation.
- Case formulations should never be considered carved in stone.

Limitations

Proceeding through the process just described and arriving at a well thought-out, valid case formulation is an ideal or a goal that one strives to achieve. Achieving it, of course, is not always possible. For instance, there will be times when all of the pieces of the patient puzzle do not fit well together for any number of reasons. For example, there may be inadequate information about the patient. This type of situation would not be uncommon with patients who are being treated through MBHOs. For managed care patients, health plan benefit restrictions and the expectations for providers set by the MBHOs frequently do not allow the clinician the luxury of spending unlimited amounts of time in information-gathering activities. It is at these times that it may not be possible to develop a valid case formulation, at least not as described here.

In cases in which it is not possible to gather all the information needed to develop a solid case formulation, treatment should not be delayed. Persons (1989) recommends that for these patients, treatment should begin with a symptom focus. Howard and his colleagues (Howard, Lueger, Maling, & Martinovich, 1993) would suggest that, if necessary, this be preceded by dealing with any feelings of demoralization patients may be experiencing as a result of their problems. Regardless of whether this approach has a significant impact on the patient's status, it can at least yield more information that will be useful in the development of a valid case formulation as treatment progresses.

SUMMARY

The case formulation occupies a unique position in the mental health and substance abuse treatment process. It not only represents the end product of a thorough clinical assessment, but it also serves as the basis for the treatment plan. As a hypothesis about the patient and the patient's way of viewing and dealing with the environment, the case formulation can assist the clinician in understanding

Putting It Into Practice

Case Study of Mary Smith (*continued*)

CASE FORMULATION

Mary Smith

Mary Smith is a young woman experiencing difficulty in coping with the demands being placed on her by her marriage, her family, and law school. This is evident in the multiple problems she is experiencing and that interfere with her successfully fulfilling her roles as wife, daughter, sister, and law student. Prominent among these problems are obsessions and concomitant compulsive behaviors that have their origins in early adolescence. The expectations set for Mary's behavior by her devoutly religious parents often were in conflict with what is generally considered normal for adolescent girls. The underlying resentment and anger that developed as a result of not being allowed to be "like everyone else" and for having to assume responsibility for being caregiver to her younger siblings could not be expressed: Doing so would have been contrary to being the perfect, dutiful daughter. Instead, unrealistic fears of accidentally hurting others began to occur and, consequently, controls were implemented in order to keep these fears and unacceptable feelings in check. These maladaptive coping mechanisms were well established by the end of her adolescence and became further ingrained during her years in college, often appearing in other circumstances in which great demands or expectations were made of her. It would appear that her husband's subtle pressure for them to start a family is the most recently imposed expectation or demand.

There were a number of attempts to ignore her obsessions or not give in to the accompanying compulsions to act on them. At times, Mary experienced success from these efforts, but the anxiety and guilt that eventually emerged, as well as her inability to express angry feelings appropriately, have always caused these successes to be rather short-lived. As a consequence, she has found herself giving in to the needs and expectations of others, including assuming responsibility for the care of her ailing father and even attending law school in order to meet her husband's expectations to "live up to her potential."

All of this has taken a toll on Ms. Smith. Over the past few years, she has described herself as generally not getting much pleasure out of life. This has been accompanied by periods of sleep difficulties, poor appetite, and more recently, by irritability, general fatigue, and difficulty concentrating on her studies and other activities. Also, she is currently experiencing a high level of distress. As a result of her current condition, her relationships with her husband and family have been strained and her performance in school has suffered. Overall, Ms. Smith feels sad, is critical of herself, and feels hopeless about ever "ridding myself of those crazy things I do" or experiencing true happiness and contentment in her life.

the relationships among the patient's problems; selecting the best modality, strategy, and intervention point for treatment; dealing effectively with relationship and extratherapy issues; predicting behavior; and understanding noncompliance and redirecting treatment as necessary. Moreover, sharing the case formulation with the patient can have positive therapeutic effects by itself.

The recommended process for case formulation proceeds through the following sequential stages: (a) identifying problems, (b) determining the nature of those problems, (c) determining patterns among the problems, (d) hypothesis development, (e) hypothesis validation, and (f) further hypothesis testing during treatment. For any number of reasons, there are patients for which case formulations cannot be finalized prior to the initiation of treatment. In these cases, the recommendation is first to assure that the patient is sufficiently confident in his or her ability to profit from treatment, and then to focus on symptom alleviation. This will likely result in additional information that can assist in arriving at a valid formulation of the case.

TEST YOURSELF

1. **Which of the following is *not* a key aspect of case formulations?**
    (a) It is the main reason for conducting a clinical assessment.
    (b) It can be revised with the attainment of new information.
    (c) It is atheoretical.
    (d) It is the basis of the treatment plan.
    (e) It explains how and why the patient functions in the world.

2. **A case formulation can help the clinician in all but which one of the following activities?**
    (a) Understanding how problems are interrelated
    (b) Predicting behavior
    (c) Understanding noncompliance with treatment
    (d) Selecting the best approach to intervention
    (e) Revising the treatment plan when therapeutic progress is not being made
    (f) None of the above

3. **In which of the following would MBHOs likely find the greatest benefit from a case formulation?**
   (a) Understanding relationship difficulties
   (b) Choosing an intervention point
   (c) Making decisions about issues that are not directly related to treatment
   (d) Understanding the link between problems
   (e) Providing patients with a schema with which to make sense of their problems

4. **Treatment of a patient should not begin until a valid case formulation is obtained.** True or False?

5. **A formal case formulation is *least* likely to be requested in which of the following conditions?**
   (a) Patients being seen for routine outpatient treatment through an MBHO
   (b) Presentencing evaluation of convicted criminals
   (c) Child custody cases
   (d) Assignment of subjects to either cognitive-behavioral or psychodynamic treatment groups in a controlled study of treatment effectiveness

6. **List some of the circumstances in which a "formal" case formulation is necessary in a forensic setting.** _____
   _____

7. **For what types of patients do you think MBHOs would most likely value a case formulation?** _____
   _____

8. **What are some situations or conditions in which a patient's disagreement with the clinician's case formulation would be less disconcerting than others?** _____
   _____

Answers: 1. c; 2. f; 3. b; 4. False; 5. a; 6. child custody cases (parents and children), cases in which one party is being sued for psychological or emotional distress, cases in which psychiatric treatment is being considered as an alternative to incarceration for a convicted individual, or cases in which a military veteran is suing the government for service-related mental health benefits; 7. patients who either have been resistant to treatment or have had multiple episodes of care, or those whose illness is chronic in nature (e.g., schizophrenics); 8. child patients and patients who either are psychotic, have been forced into treatment against their will, or may have an ulterior motive for seeking treatment (e.g., in child custody cases).

Five

DEVELOPING A TREATMENT PLAN

With the completion of a working version of the case formulation, the clinician is ready to develop the patient's treatment plan. It is during this process that one begins to appreciate the importance of the information gained during the assessment and case formulation process, and to see the value in taking the time to complete these sometimes-tedious preliminary treatment-related activities.

There are many ways in which one can develop a treatment plan. The approach described herein represents a continuation of the same process that began with the clinical assessment and case formulation approaches described in the previous three chapters. Essentially, it is an atheoretical, generic process, one that is meant to have applicability across most approaches to conceptualizing and treating mental health and substance abuse disorders and problems. Consequently, an effort is made to avoid recommendations that would not be well suited for the more commonly employed therapeutic approaches.

PRELIMINARY CONSIDERATIONS

Before beginning a discussion of the actual planning for the treatment for a specific patient, we must first consider a number of issues that the clinician must keep in mind regardless of the particular patient and associated problems. Losing sight of these matters can result in a technically appropriate document that will be of limited usefulness because the clinician was unable to see the forest for the trees.

Purposes of the Treatment Plan

When developing a treatment plan, the clinician should always be cognizant of the *purpose* of the plan. This might seem to be a rather common-sense recommendation that some would feel should go without saying. The fact is that a treatment plan can serve any of several purposes—and it likely will serve multiple purposes. Those for which it is developed should therefore dictate various aspects of the plan, including its content, tenor, and overall desired goal. The most common potential purposes of the treatment plan include the initial planning of treatment for the individual patient, the support of requests for specific or additional treatment, and the fulfillment of requirements set by accrediting bodies or state or federal regulatory agencies.

To Plan Treatment

The most common purpose of the treatment plan is, of course, to plan treatment. The information gathered during the clinical assessment, along with the picture of the patient and the patient's problems that is painted by the case formulation, helps chart the patient's and the clinician's course through the episode of care. As with any journey, successfully navigating through treatment requires knowing where one is and where one wants to go, determining the most efficient way to get there, identifying likely obstacles to arriving at the final destination, and determining an estimated time of arrival. The treatment plan provides a means of organizing and documenting this critical information and serves as a map to which the clinician and the patient can refer to guide individual sessions or at times when they appear to be lost. Also, the therapeutic process can come up against unexpected hazards and delays that require detours and rerouting. Thus, reviewing and (as necessary) revising the treatment plan to reflect new strategies for overcoming unexpected obstacles to treatment is quite appropriate. (This matter is discussed in chapter 6.)

To Support Requests for Continued Services

At times, initial and updated versions of treatment plans are required by third-party payers (e.g., MBHOs, insurance companies) before any treatment is authorized, or before requests for treatment beyond what was initially authorized are considered. How these third parties actually use this information varies from one organization to another. For example, one MBHO may carefully scrutinize a treatment plan submitted by a provider to ensure that the planned course of action is consistent with and appropriate to the problems for which the patient is seeking help. If the planned intervention seems reasonable and appropriate, the requested amount of treatment (e.g., hospital days, outpatient visits) is authorized; otherwise, the request for authorized services is denied or (more commonly) is granted in some modified form (e.g., with only 6 of the 10 requested outpatient sessions authorized).

For other third parties, submission of a treatment plan is nothing more than a formality. It serves as means of formally requesting services and documenting that request, but it is never really evaluated for appropriateness of what is being requested. In these cases, the requested services are authorized, and the treatment plan is then rubber-stamped (so to speak) and filed away. Under circumstances as described in the first example, the value of a clear, carefully detailed treatment plan will be apparent: These treatment plans are much more likely to result in the authorization of requested services. In the second example, however, it probably will make little difference how well thought-out the document is, since the end result (i.e., approval) will always be the same.

To Meet Accreditation or Regulatory Requirements

Similar to practitioners in the situation just described, clinicians may find themselves developing treatment plans to meet requirements set by state or federal regulatory agencies or by accreditation organizations such as JCAHO or NCQA. The degree to which extensive treatment planning must be completed or documented will depend on the particular regulatory or accrediting body and the criteria against which that body audits treatment plans. In some instances, all that may be required is that there is some form of documented treatment plan. In cases of MBHO provider networks, it may be that the MBHO conducts the actual on-site auditing and checks the plan for thoroughness, completeness, and utility.

Rapid Reference 5.1 lists other purposes that treatment plans can serve, as identified by one large MBHO (UBS, 1994).

≡Rapid Reference 5.1

Potential Purposes of Treatment Plans

- Clarification of treatment focus
- Provision of a standard against which to judge treatment progress
- Clarification of realistic treatment expectations for the patient
- Communication with the patient's other care providers
- Communication with external reviewers
- Provision of a record for quality assurance purposes

Note. From UBS (1994).

Intended Users of the Treatment Plan

Notwithstanding the issues related to "Will anyone even look at it?" one must assume that the treatment plan will be read and indeed be meaningful to various stakeholders in the patient's treatment. The question then becomes, "Who will be the audience for the document that will reflect the intended course of treatment?" At the minimum, one must consider the treating clinician (who in most circumstances develops the plan), the patient, and relevant third parties. Each will likely have a unique interest in and view of the plan, so it behooves the clinician to develop the plan in such a way that all potential stakeholders' needs are met.

The Treating Clinician

In reality, the clinician should be considered the primary audience for the written treatment plan. As indicated earlier, it will (or at least should) serve as a map or guide for conducting the patient's treatment (Seligman, 1993), and thus is something that the clinician should refer to regularly in order to ensure that the treatment is on track. As such, it can be viewed as a tool for the clinician to facilitate the process of therapeutic intervention. In most cases, the clinician will refer to or make use of it more frequently than anyone else.

In most cases, the clinician who develops the treatment plan for a patient will also be the clinician who assumes primary responsibility for that patient. The treatment plan therefore should be developed in a way that organizes the assessing clinician's understanding of the patient and the patient's therapeutic needs. In cases in which the assessing clinician is not the treating clinician, clear and complete communication of this information is very important. In its absence, misunderstandings can occur and may result in less than maximum therapeutic efficiency and benefit for the patient.

The Patient

As with the case formulation, the treatment plan should be developed and shared with the patient. The patient needs to agree with the identified problems, treatment goals, and interventions indicated in the plan prior to the initiation of treatment. The patient's so-called buy-in is critical to achieving the stated goals of treatment.

In one sense, the treatment plan serves as a contract between the clinician and the patient, something that the patient can refer to when questions about the who, what, when, and why of some aspect of the therapeutic process arises during the course of treatment. As such, it can be a source of reassurance to the patient. It also can serve as a means of holding both the clinician and the patient accountable for the roles and responsibilities they had mutually agreed upon prior to the initiation of treatment. Here again, the clarity and completeness of the plan are important.

Insurers

As discussed earlier, there are times when MBHOs and other insurers require the submission of a treatment plan more as a formality than as a means of ensuring quality of care. Assuming this is not the case, the treatment plan can be a means of conveying to the insurer that appropriate, adequate care is or will be provided to its health plan member. Perhaps more importantly, it can provide evidence that the treatment is medically necessary and thus is covered by the patient's behavioral health plan benefits. Being able to describe the patient's problems, proposed treatment, and therapeutic goals in a manner that is consistent with medical-necessity guidelines established by the insurer can facilitate the approval of requested services and thus the initiation of treatment.

The same focus is important when updated treatment plans are submitted to the insurer in support of requests for additional authorized services. Here, it also is important to document progress (if any) that has been made during the most recent period of authorized services, as well as the need for continued behavioral health services. When progress has not been made, the clinician will also have to provide justification for either continuation of the same therapeutic strategy or the implementation of a new strategy or approach.

Other Third-Party Stakeholders

Depending on the particular circumstances, there may be other parties with a stake in the patient's treatment. In many of these cases, the interested party requires a treatment plan. This will likely necessitate a focus in the written plan that differs from the clinician's standard treatment plan. Such a focus may be reflected in a special emphasis on content determined to be important for that party's needs, or in use of terminology or language that is consistent with that party's way of communicating to internal and external individuals and organizations. The third party may also require an estimate of how much recovery can be expected from the planned intervention.

For example, a patient receiving assessment and treatment services through a state vocational rehabilitation agency would probably want to ensure that the plan includes goals directly related to the amelioration of problems that are keeping the patient from engaging in gainful employment. The agency would also be interested in knowing about psychological strengths and deficits, as well as other aspects of the patient's functioning that would have a bearing on the type of employment that the patient may be best suited for. In a forensic setting, the court may want to know whether the convicted sex offender is treatable at all; and if so, would society's interests be best served if the patient received that treatment in prison, in a hospital for the criminally insane, or through a halfway house. Issues pertaining to dangerousness to others as well as the patient's ability to benefit significantly from treatment would probably be the foremost concerns and thus would need to be addressed adequately in the treatment plan. Other examples of potential third parties with special interests include organizations or agencies overseeing law enforcement officers and others in high-risk or high-stress occupations (e.g., air traffic controllers, fire fighters), the military, the clergy, and students being evaluated for special education services.

Patient Involvement in Treatment Planning

The changes in health care delivery systems that have taken and will continue to take place have led to changes in the roles that patients will assume in numerous aspects of their treatment, including their participation in the planning for that treatment (Tickle-Degnen, 1998). A more collaborative effort between clinician and patient, based on two-way communication and sharing of information, is called for. As has always been the case, patient information is communicated during the clinical assessment. Based on that information, the clinician must then communicate information to the patient about treatment options and associated outcomes in a manner that will enable the patient to make an informed decision about how to proceed.

The need for and benefits of a collaborative effort also are discussed by Frank, Eisenthal, and Lazare (1978), who state that

in seeking and weighing the merits of various treatment alternatives, therapists need to be encouraged to begin where the patient is. By this we mean that therapists should elicit and respond to what kinds of help the patient wants and thinks he needs. By encouraging the patient to voice his treatment preferences, the therapist not only promotes the patient's sense of autonomy and self-esteem, but cements the formation of a therapeutic alliance, and learns what treatment the patients will be most likely to accept . . . and benefit from. (p. 68)

As Tickle-Degnen (1998) noted, "In a truly collaborative environment, the [patient] has the option to either pursue or decline participation in treatment. The collaborative choice is at the heart of the transformation of the health care system into a consumer-driven one" (p. 526).

The patient's involvement in treatment planning and responsibility for treatment raise numerous issues. Among them are each party's expectations for treatment. Most patients come to treatment with some expectations. These expectations—what will be required of the patient, what the clinician will be responsible for, the likely outcome, the time it will take to achieve that outcome, the limits to the clinician-patient relationship—will vary, based on any number of factors. These factors might include such things as the patient's personality characteristics, previous experience with behavioral health care treatment, information obtained from others or through the media, and whether the patient is seeking treatment voluntarily. Knowing these expectations can have a significant bearing on the various types and aspects of treatment that the clinician may propose to the patient. It also is important in facilitating the patient-clinician alliance (Beutler, 1991). Thus, an exploration of the patient's expectations becomes a critical part of the collaborative treatment-planning process.

At the same time, it is important for the clinician to convey the expectations for the one or more type of treatment that are being proposed to the patient. This becomes an important part of obtaining *informed consent* from the patient. Chambless et al. (1996) have noted that

as part of the informed consent process, clinicians should make sure that [patients] understand what the treatment can be reasonably expected to accomplish and in what period of time, what any negative effects of the treatment might be, what other treatments might be considered, and whether these would be expected to be more or less helpful and more or less costly. (p. 10)

Issues such as these are particularly important, regardless of whether what is being proposed is brief or short-term therapy (Budman & Gurman, 1988) or long-term therapy (Wenning, 1993). Chambless et al. go on to add that "clinicians who remain uninformed about the research literature are ill equipped to discuss these issues with [patients] and thus to discharge their ethical obligation" (pp. 10–11).

The matter of informed consent must always be attended to. From a legal standpoint, failure to obtain informed consent could result in disastrous financial and professional consequences for the clinician. More importantly, however, beginning treatment without informed patient consent runs contrary to professional ethics. The APA (1992) provides standards for obtaining informed consent from patients who seek therapy services through its *Ethical Principles of Psychologists and Code of Conduct*. Although these standards may not protect the clinician from a legal standpoint, they will provide assurance that professional standards for entering into a therapeutic relationship with the patient are being met.

DON'T FORGET

APA Ethical Standards for Informed Consent to Therapy

1. Psychologists obtain appropriate informed consent to therapy or related procedures, using language that is reasonably understandable to participants. The content of informed consent will vary depending on many circumstances; however, informed consent generally implies that the person (a) has the capacity to consent, (b) has been informed of significant information concerning the procedure, (c) has freely and without undue influence expressed consent, and (d) consent has been appropriately documented.

2. When persons are legally incapable of giving informed consent, psychologists obtain informed permission from a legally authorized person, if such substitute consent is permitted by law.

3. In addition, psychologists (a) inform those persons who are legally incapable of giving informed consent about the proposed interventions in a manner commensurate with the persons' psychological capacities, (b) seek their assent to those interventions, and (c) consider such persons' preferences and best interests.

Note. Adapted from APA (1992, p. 1605).

Based on the communication of the patient's initial expectations and those conveyed by the clinician for the proposed treatment options, the two parties must move toward arriving at a plan that both view as realistic, worthwhile, and acceptable. Aside from the obvious legal and ethical problems that might arise, lack of agreement on either the treatment plan or the expectations for the process or outcomes of that plan will inevitably result in problems later on.

Common Elements in Treatment Planning

The manner in which a treatment plan may be developed can vary greatly. In the section that follows, one approach to treatment plan development is presented. Chances are that the reader can refer to other works that address the topic of treatment planning and find approaches that differ in varying degrees from the one presented here. Regardless of the extent to which the structure and content of treatment plans may differ, most if not all share common elements (e.g., see Beutler, 1991; Jongsma & Peterson, 1999; Makover, 1992; Mumma, 1998; UBS, 1994). These include an identification of the problems that will be addressed through treatment, the aims and goals of that treatment, and the intervention strategies and tactics that will be employed to achieve those aims and goals. In addition, an element of flexibility in the plan during the course of treatment is usually implied.

Problem Identification

Jongsma and Peterson (1999) discuss two important aspects of problem identification. First, with the likelihood of the patient's presenting with multiple problems, both clinician and patient must work to identify and prioritize the most significant problems to work on during treatment. As they note, "An effective treatment plan can only deal with a few selected problems or treatment will lose its direction" (p. 4). Second, the problem must be defined in a manner that indicates how the problem exhibits itself in the patient. This will not only help the clinician and patient maintain the focus of treatment but will also help to establish criteria for successful completion of that treatment.

Aims and Goals

Treatment must always be directed to achieving something for the patient. This something is usually referred to as the *goals* of treatment. In Makover's (1992) *hierarchical treatment-planning* structure, goals actually are conceptualized as being subordinate to the aim of treatment. He defines an *aim* as the single overall desired outcome of a period of therapy. Achieving it should resolve the distress that brought the patient to the therapist and allow further progress, growth, and development. . . . As the single desired outcome, the aim will often involve the restoration of function in, or successful resolution of, one of several broad problem areas. (p. 343)

Aims should be specific, achievable, and require an economy of effort to achieve.

A *goal,* on the other hand, is "a subsidiary objective or end point of therapeutic work that is one of the components needed to realize the aim" (Makover, 1992, p. 344). Multiple goals may need to be achieved in order to achieve the aim of treatment. Makover suggests that the identification of appropriate goals of treatment can be facilitated if the clinician asks, "What different things have to happen for the patient to achieve the aim of the therapy?"

It would seem that what Makover refers to as *aims* and *goals* are essentially what most others would refer to as *goals* and *objectives,* respectively. These latter terms will be used from this point on because of the audience's greater familiarity with them. In addition, the use of this terminology avoids the implication that there is a single overall desired outcome of treatment, a conceptualization that many clinicians would not agree with.

Strategies and Tactics

Planned interventions in the hierarchical treatment planning scheme are conceptualized in terms of strategies and tactics. According to Makover (1992), a *strategy* refers to the general process or approach that the clinician will use to move the patient toward an objective. In other words, it is the therapeutic modality selected to attain an objective that is necessary to achieve in order to accomplish the goal of the treatment. A *tactic* is a specific task that is undertaken or technique that is used within the context of the strategy to help meet the objective. Multiple strategies can be used to achieve an objective; similarly, multiple tactics can be employed within each strategy.

As an example, a clinician may opt to employ a combination of cognitive-behavioral therapy and psychopharmacological strategies for treating a patient's depression. The tactics that will be used within these approaches may include initiating a regimen of a specific antidepressant medication, teaching the patient to challenge irrational thoughts, and establishing a behavior modification system that rewards involvement in positive social activities.

CAUTION

Like case formulations, treatment plans should not be carved in stone. They should be modified as additional information about the patient is obtained.

Flexibility

Even when manualized treatments are employed, most experts would espouse a flexible approach to treatment planning. Thus, a change in the case formulation based on additional information or a lack of responsiveness to an existing course of treatment should prompt the evaluation and possible modification of the patient's treatment plan. Failing to do so may result in less than the desired outcome of treatment, an unnecessary extension of the episode of care, or exacerbation of the problems for which the patient is seeking help.

WHAT TO INCLUDE IN THE TREATMENT PLAN

Armed with an assessment-based case formulation and being mindful of the general considerations just discussed, the clinician is prepared to develop a formal plan for treatment of the patient. In this context, *formal plan* refers to a written document of specific areas of patient-related information that serves multiple purposes. The potential uses of the formal treatment plan range from being a therapeutic contract for ensuring that both the clinician and patient agree on particulars such as the what, how, and duration of treatment; to serving as a road map to be referred to when the direction of treatment becomes unclear; to being a vehicle for requesting authorization for services from the patient's insurer; to protecting the clinician from unwarranted litigation that may be brought against him or her at a later date.

Following is a discussion of the recommended content for a formal treatment plan (also see Rapid Reference 5.2). The content indicated here probably should be considered the ideal for a formal plan. Some clinicians may not find it necessary to develop a written treatment plan to include all of the same content described, opting instead for an abbreviated or otherwise modified version of it. Other clinicians may never develop such a formalized document at all, either as described here or in some modified form. This may be because they see no real need for such a document (e.g., the clinician sees all patients only two to three times for crisis resolution); they feel that that they can develop and maintain a treatment plan in their heads, so to speak; third-party

Rapid Reference 5.2

Recommended Content for Formal Treatment Plans

- Referral Source and Reason for Referral
- Presenting Problem
- Problem List
- Diagnosis
- Goals and Objectives
- Treatment
- Patient Strengths
- Potential Barriers to Treatment
- Referral for Evaluation
- Criteria for Treatment Termination or Transfer
- Responsible Staff
- Treatment Plan Review Date

payers do not require it; or, frankly, the clinicians do not provide good clinical care. Regardless, having a written treatment plan of some form that is mutually agreeable to both the patient and the clinician should be considered a standard of care for all behavioral health care professions.

Referral Source and Reason for Referral

Identifying the person or organization that referred the patient for treatment and the reason for that referral can communicate important information. In some instances, patients are self-referred, having recognized that they need help in coping with their problems and taken the initiative to identify and contact a behavioral health care provider. In other instances, others in whom they have confided their problems make the referral. Common examples here include friends who have undergone treatment themselves, ministers, physicians, emergency room and crisis intervention workers, and EAPs. Referrals can also come from courts, school systems, employers, parents, and other parties that have identified a problem with the patient and that are in a position to require the patient to engage in treatment.

Presenting Problem

Next, the treatment plan should include a statement about the problem for which the patient is seeking treatment. As was discussed earlier, the presenting problem or complaint should always be indicated in the patient's own words. The patient's own problem description frequently can convey more information about the patient, the intensity of the problems for which treatment is being sought, and how those problems affect the patient's life than the clinician could ever hope to communicate. Note the following example of the presenting problem of a patient seeking help for his depression: "My wife asked me to come here. Life has become a struggle. I just can't get going and I don't know that I want to even try. Nothing seems worthwhile anymore." Compare this to the clinician's indicating instead that "The patient is suffering from depression." Obviously, quite a bit gets lost in the translation.

Here as in other parts of the treatment plan, it is important to remember that one of the purposes of the written plan is to serve as a vehicle for communicating with others. Thus, when the patient's statement is not sufficiently clear or informative, the clinician can always provide clarification of what the patient actually meant to convey or what was implied in the patient's response to the question about the reason for seeking treatment.

Problem List

A thorough assessment of the patient can reveal any number of problems. By the same token, it may reveal no significant problems requiring behavioral health intervention (although this type of situation is relatively rare for patients seen in behavioral health care settings). Problems that are judged by any of the potential referring parties to (a) have a significant impact on the patient's ability to function appropriately and adequately in any sphere of life (e.g., family, social, work, school) and to (b) be amenable to behavioral health care intervention should be listed here. The latter point is especially important to keep in mind, given the limitations that are imposed by the therapeutic relationship.

Recognizing again the treatment plan as a communication tool, the identified problems also should be stated in clear and unambiguous language. For example, "problems in school" could mean a lot of things for a given patient; instead, "academic underachievement," "disruptive behavior during class," or "aggressive behavior outside of the classroom" provides a better description of the problem(s) that will be the focus of the intervention.

Patient-Identified Problems

With the possible exception of those entering treatment involuntarily, patients should be able to indicate one or more problems that they would like to work on in treatment. It may be necessary for the clinician to help the patient verbalize exactly what those problems are, based on the information obtained during the assessment. In these instances, clinicians should always seek their patients' validation of any interpretation of what they are trying to convey.

Referral Source-Identified Problems

In most cases, the source of the patient's referral to the clinician will have one or more specific problems that the referring person thinks require the attention of a behavioral health care professional. Similar to patient-report problems, these too may require clarification and verification.

Other-Identified Problems

Frequently, there will be problems that neither the patient nor the referring party has identified, but which the clinician has noted and judged to be having a significant impact on the patient's functioning. Severe psychiatric symptomatology (e.g., hallucinations, delusions, clinical depression), substance abuse or dependence, extensive use of a particular defense mechanism (e.g., denial), and impaired marital functioning are a few examples of behaviors that patients or their referral sources may not be aware of as existing or as being problematic.

Prioritization of Problems

The length of the problem list can vary considerably from one patient to another. Once the list is compiled, it then becomes important to verify that all of the problems (a) are understood and conveyed in clear language, (b) significantly impair the patient's ability to function in some important sphere of life, and (c) are amenable to psychological, psychiatric, or related intervention. This being confirmed, the clinician must then prioritize the problems. Prioritization will provide a guide as to which problems should be addressed by the treatment first.

How should the final list of problems be prioritized? A number of factors need to be considered. One is the degree and extent to which they impact the patient's life. This will have special significance at the beginning of treatment when taking steps toward reduction in symptom-intensity level is important. However, one must not lose sight of the case formulation and how the identified problems relate to a broader picture of the patient's functioning. That is, the clinician must consider the central problem or underlying mechanism that has been identified and determine which problems must be dealt with first in order to achieve a resolution of the problem to which many or all of the identified problems are tied. In addition, the clinician must identify those problems that can be dealt with relatively easily. Quick resolution of one or more of these problems in the early phases of treatment can provide the patient with a sense of accomplishment and mastery that will reinforce those early efforts, instill a sense of hope, and encourage continued effort in working on the more difficult problems.

Regardless of the relative importance of other-identified problems, one should always give special consideration to those problems identified by the patient. This will acknowledge the patient's importance in the treatment-planning process and will help ensure the patient's involvement in the actual treatment.

Rapid Reference 5.3 provides a set of questions that can facilitate the clini-

≡ Rapid Reference 5.3

Questions to Consider When Prioritizing Problems

- What problems does the patient identify as being most troublesome or the primary reason for seeking help?
- Which of the identified problems are having the greatest impact on the patient's life?
- Which of the problems must be dealt with first in order to resolve the central problem identified in the case formulation?
- Which problems can provide the patient with an opportunity to easily and quickly experience a sense of success and mastery early in the therapeutic process?
- If the patient had only one treatment session available and could work on only one problem during that session, which problem would you (i.e., the clinician) choose?
- If the patient had only one treatment session available and could work on only one problem during that session, which problem would the patient choose?

cian's efforts to prioritize the patient's problems. It is important to keep in mind that problem prioritization, like all aspects of treatment planning, is a collaborative effort. Thus, the patient's involvement in this task is critical.

Limiting the Length of the Problem List

At times, clinicians will encounter patients who have a plethora of problems. Resolution of all of these

DON'T FORGET

- Report the patient's presenting problem or complaint verbatim.
- List all problems that are identified by relevant stakeholders in the patient's treatment and that are appropriate for inclusion in the treatment plan's problem list.
- Give special consideration to patient-identified problems in prioritizing the problem list.

problems in a timely manner may be impossible due to limitations imposed by the patient's health plan benefits, the probability of keeping the patient engaged in treatment over an extended period of time, a planned relocation outside the local geographical area, the patient's reluctance to work on all identified problems, or any of a number of other patient variables. Clinician variables such as an impending closing of the clinician's practice, cutting back on practice hours, or other factors that lead to limited accessibility may also come into play and limit what can reasonably be expected to be accomplished during the episode of care. Under such circumstances, the clinician should consider limiting the stated problem list to include only the more highly prioritized problems that can be fully and effectively treated under the imposed limitations. Doing so keeps the treatment plan grounded in reality, and is consistent with setting realistic expectations for the patient.

Diagnosis

Which diagnostic classification system should be used? That, of course, may be dictated by the payer of the treatment. In most cases, the *DSM-IV-TR* is required or is acceptable. In other cases, the *ICD-9* or *ICD-10* may be required. As suggested in chapter 2, if one is given the choice, the *DSM-IV-TR* system is recommended, given its widespread use and familiarity among members of various behavioral health care professions as well as its incorporation of multiaxial diagnostic information. It is also the system that is likely to be taught in graduate school courses, practicums, internships and residencies. Whenever possible, providing information on all five *DSM-IV-TR* axes is recommended (see chapter 2).

Goals and Objectives

At this point, the clinician should be able to work with the patient in arriving at a clear set of goals and objectives for the treatment that will be rendered. Earlier, the concepts of aims and goals were presented within the context of Makover's (1992) hierarchical treatment-planning structure. Here, the associated concepts of goals and objectives deserve additional clarification.

Jongsma and Peterson (1999) discuss "setting broad goals for the resolution of the target problem. These need not be crafted in measurable terms but can be global, long-term goals that indicate a desired positive outcome to the treatment procedure" (p. 5). Objectives, on the other hand,

> must be stated in behaviorally measurable language. It must be clear when the [patient] has achieved the established objectives; therefore, vague, subjective objectives are not acceptable. . . . Each objective should be developed as a step toward attaining the broad treatment goal. In essence, objectives can be thought of as a series of steps that, when completed, will result in the achievement of the long-term goal. There should be at least two objectives for each problem, but the clinician may construct as many as are necessary for goal achievement. (p. 5)

They add that each objective should be accompanied by a projected time line in which it should be accomplished. When all necessary objectives are met (including those that have been added during the course of treatment), the associated goal should successfully be accomplished and the associated target problem resolved.

Important Characteristics of Goals and Objectives
It may be natural for the clinical graduate student or novice clinician to think that establishing goals and objectives is a relatively easy part of the treatment planning process. The patient has a specific problem, the goal of treatment is to alleviate that problem, and the objectives are obvious once the goal is identified, right? Unfortunately, as any experienced clinician knows, nothing can be

further from the truth. Selecting, developing, and implementing treatment goals and objectives require careful consideration of several factors that can come into play and influence the eventual outcome of the episode of care.

Achievable. Among the most important things that must be determined in considering a potential treatment goal is whether the goal is achievable. In other words, given the resources and circumstances, is this something that the patient is capable of accomplishing? If so, is the patient capable of accomplishing it within a reasonable time line? Occasionally, the clinician may be faced with patients seeking help to change their lives or realize some other goal in manner that simply is not possible. For example, for a patient diagnosed with chronic undifferentiated schizophrenia who has been hospitalized periodically over the course of several years, a goal of eventually securing a high-pressure position in a stock brokerage firm probably is not achievable. And although smoking cessation is an achievable goal, it is highly unlikely that this goal can be achieved within a period of two weeks.

Unachievable goals, objectives, or time lines for completion should always be avoided, regardless of any pressure that the clinician may receive from the patient or a third-party stakeholder (e.g., courts, families). Giving in to such pressures is setting the patient up for failure and the possibility of premature treatment termination.

Realistic. Having determined that the patient can indeed achieve a goal or objective during a specified period of time, the next question is how realistic that goal, objective, or time line is. Does the patient have the motivation to do the work that is required? Does the patient have the support of significant others? Are all of the requisite external factors (e.g., opportunities for desired employment, willingness of a spouse to engage in conjoint marital therapy) currently present? Is the patient's insurance company willing to pay for treatment to meet these particular goals or objectives? Regardless of the patient's ability to achieve a goal or objective within a certain time period, the reality of the situation must be taken into consideration when determining whether it should become a part of the treatment plan. Again, as with achievability, inclusion of an unrealistic goal, objective, or time line can only result in negative consequences.

Measurable. Jongsma and Peterson (1999) indicated that objectives, but not necessarily goals, need to be measurable. It is this author's contention that whenever possible, goals should also be stated in measurable terms. In order to be measurable, goals and objectives and the steps thereto should be quantifiable, specific (see Munich, Hurley, & Delaney, 1990), and easily understood by the patient and relevant stakeholders in the patient's treatment.

Measurability is important from several perspectives. It allows for the tracking or monitoring of patient progress through the episode of care, and thus provides information about whether the treatment plan is effective. This information may then be used by the clinician to make any necessary adjustments to the patient's treatment, or to help the clinician decide whether treatment should be continued or is no longer warranted. In addition, having this information allows patients to see for themselves where they were at the beginning of treatment and what they have accomplished, thus providing an incentive for continued participation in treatment, if warranted. This information can also support requests to insurers for authorization for initial or continued treatment.

Stated in the positive. A review of treatment plans from various settings would probably reveal that goals and objectives are stated in both positive terms (e.g., "Increase the patient's level of self-esteem") and negative terms (e.g., "Decrease the patient's level of anxiety in social situations"). Even general goals and objectives are commonly stated as both something that the patient will seek to gain and something that the patient will seek to be rid of. For example, UBH (2000) lists the following as general treatment goals for the patients it serves: education of the patient and the patient's support system, obtaining informed consent, reduction in the frequency or intensity of core symptoms, reduction of dysfunctional behaviors, restoration of the patient to the baseline level of functioning, and the prevention of relapse.

Whenever possible, goals and objectives should be stated in the positive rather that in the negative. This conveys an effort to move toward improvement in the patient's life rather than to move away from something that is having a negative effect. Consequently, it reinforces the idea that the patient is striving to gain something rather than lose something. Because it is often difficult to attain a positive goal without eliminating or reducing one or more types of behaviors (e.g., physically acting out

CAUTION

• Do not report problems that either have no impact on the patient's functioning or are not amenable to treatment.

• Setting unrealistic or unattainable goals can result in negative, demoralizing experiences for the patient.

against others), emotions (e.g., severe depression or anxiety), or cognitions (e.g., feeling that others are undermining the patient's efforts to succeed on the job), it is appropriate to state objectives in the negative.

Development of goals and objectives should be a collaborative effort between patient and clinician. Rapid Reference 5.4 presents several questions that the clinician can pose to the patient to facilitate this process. These questions reflect many of the important issues that were raised in the preceding discussion. Discussions stemming from these questions should reinforce the collaborative relationship, as well as help set expectations for the patient's involvement in treatment and the outcomes of that treatment.

Prioritization of Goals and Objectives

The importance of prioritizing the patient's problems was discussed earlier. Just as important is the prioritization of the goals and objectives for treatment. In general, the priority given to the goals and objectives should mirror the priority assigned to the problems. Note that regardless of the goals' various priority levels, one can work toward achievement of two or more goals simultaneously. Consequently, objectives tied to two or more goals also can be

---

≡Rapid Reference 5.4

Questions for Patients to Consider When Setting Goals and Objectives

- What do you see as your biggest problem?
- Do you think there is an immediate crisis that needs to be addressed?
- What do you see as your biggest goal in therapy?
- How will you know if you have achieved your goal?
- Does the goal involve changing things about yourself?
- Does the goal involve changing things about other people?
- What problems do you anticipate in reaching that goal?
- How will you be different after reaching that goal? What positive things will you be doing? What negative things will no longer be present?
- What skills will help you attain that goal?

Note. Adapted from UBS (1994, p. 11).

> **DON'T FORGET**
> ....
> • Involve the patient in setting the goals and objectives for treatment.
> • Prioritize goals and objectives so that the patient can experience some quick wins.

addressed simultaneously. In fact, taking this approach represents the most efficient use of the patient's and therapist's time.

There are instances in which focusing on a single goal or on a single objective for a particular goal is called for. This may be the case particularly at the beginning of treatment, when symptom reduction or alleviation may be required before treatment can proceed any further. Similarly, there may be instances in which a particular objective needs to be addressed first in order to engage the patient in the treatment process. This is likely to be the case when the patient is being forced into treatment by a third party (e.g., parent, spouse, the court system). With cases such as these, active participation in treatment becomes an objective in itself. The clinician will find that helping the reluctant patient achieve something that is important to him or her—no matter how unrelated to the patient's real problems it may seem—can result in greater participation in the treatment process.

Treatment

Following the listing of the patient's problems, goals, and objectives is the plan for how the clinician will help the patient resolve those problems and consequently achieve those goals and objectives. For clinicians who are strict adherents to a single therapeutic approach (e.g., cognitive-behavioral therapy), the intervention will generally be the same for all patients, regardless of what the problems are. The selection of the intervention to be used becomes more of a challenge for those clinicians who are more eclectic in their treatment orientations. One broad approach (i.e., single-theory vs. eclectic) is not necessarily better than another; however, it is for the those clinicians who are open to employing different therapeutic approaches with different types of patients presenting with different types of problems that the remainder of this section is intended.

Clinical Practice Guidelines

The appearance of clinical practice guidelines is a relatively new development in the field of medical and behavioral health care. Nathan (1998) attributes this to several factors, but he identifies two as being the most influential. The first has to do with the effectiveness of methods to change behavior and measure the outcomes of that change during the past 25 years. The second has to do with the identification of more empirically supported treatments and with the greater demands being placed on clinicians to use these treatments and demonstrate the efficacy of their use.

Berg, Atkins, and Tierney (1997) have attributed this growing interest to other circumstances. These include an interest in replacing older guidelines with ones that have greater promise of validity and reliability; clinicians' need for a means of keeping up with and making sense of the vast amount of health care information on a given topic; patients' growing demands to understand the links of benefits and harms with outcomes so that they can be more involved in health care decisions; and the cost variability in health care practices. Also, the proliferation of clinical practice guidelines has been to linked to several health care–related effects, including improved health care quality and access, both the empowerment and limiting of clinician autonomy, and limited medical liability (Hayes, 1994).

Moreover, the need to reduce practice variation and associated costs has been identified (e.g., Abrahamson, 1999; Citrome, 1998; Clinton, McCormick, & Besteman, 1994; Hayes, 1994). Referring to observations of others, Hayes sees the major cause of practice variation as being a lack of professional consensus about what constitutes best practices for specific problems occurring under specific conditions. Although their success as cost-control measures (see APA, 1995; Stricker et al., 1999) and perhaps some of these other purported effects may be debatable among informed parties, the contributions of clinical practice guidelines toward improving the quality of care is much more evident. By their nature, guidelines represent the consensus of experts about what is best for a given patient under specific conditions. As such, they provide the type of guidance that, if followed, should lead to both the provision of consistent types of treatment and consequent cost savings.

Definition. The Institute of Medicine (IOM) has defined *clinical practice guidelines* as "systematically developed statements to assist practitioner and patient decisions about appropriate health care for specific clinical circumstances" (Field & Lohr, 1990, p. 38). As Berg et al. (1997) point out, the term is frequently used interchangeably with such other terms as *practice parameters, clinical pathways, algorithms, practice policy,* and *clinical guidelines.* The APA's Template Implementation Work Group (2000) makes a distinction between guidelines and standards. Whereas standards are considered as expressing some type of mandatory behavior or treatment, guidelines are viewed as only supporting certain actions or approaches. However, as Nathan (1998) points out,

> Despite prefatory statements to the AHCPR guidelines and the psychiatric guidelines . . . affirming that differences among patients require detailed knowledge of each patient's needs and the exercise of clinical judgment before a treatment plan is developed, each guideline endorses specific treatments for specific conditions. Like it or not, practice guidelines do establish a standard of practice from which clinicians will not try to stray. (p. 297)

The Template Implementation Work Group (APA, 2000, p. 1) also makes a distinction between practice guidelines and *treatment guidelines,* citing the former as consisting of "recommendations to professionals concerning their conduct and to the issues to be considered in particular areas of practice, rather than on patient outcomes or recommendations for specific treatments or specific clinical procedures at the patient level." However, from a practical standpoint, the distinction that is drawn between the two remains unclear to this author and adds further to the confusion that comes with the use of different terminology. Because a large portion of the professional literature appears to address clinical practice guidelines as they are defined by the IOM, the remainder of this section will take this same approach, and will simply use the term *guidelines* in doing so.

Purpose. Guidelines can serve several purposes. In addition to improving the quality of care (Berg et al., 1997; Clinton et al., 1994; Stricker et al., 1999), probably the most important role performed by guidelines is providing assistance to clinicians in making informed practice decisions (Berg et al.; Clinton et al.; Hayes, 1994; McIntyre, 1996). Related to this is their ability to assist clinicians in identifying the most effective treatments and reducing practice variation (to be discussed shortly), and to help patients take active roles in treatment decisions by informing them of their health care options (Clinton et al.; Hayes; Stricker et al.). Some have also pointed to guidelines' ability to provide means of reducing health care costs and ascertaining deficiencies in clinical knowledge (Clinton et al.).

There also are other, less altruistic purposes that guidelines may serve. Berg et al. (1997) have noted that guidelines can be used by clinicians to justify their actions when malpractice cases are brought against them. Conversely, patients suffering from adverse treatment outcomes can use the guidelines to back claims of malpractice. They might also be used by some clinicians and professional groups when turf issues arise. Guidelines are not developed for such purposes, but as Berg et al. caution, clinicians should be prepared to see them used in unintended ways.

Differences and desirable attributes. Guidelines may differ in several ways. As noted by Hayes (1994), they can vary according to their *clinical orientation* (i.e., the focus being on a specific process or technology), *clinical purpose* (i.e., for screening, prevention, evaluation, diagnosis, or treatment), *complexity, format* (e.g., presented algorithms vs. narrative text), and *intended users* (i.e., clinicians, patients, or other users). Regardless of the variability in how and what is addressed, the IOM (1990) has identified attributes that might be considered ideal for all guidelines and may thus be used to guide their development. These include

- *Validity,* evidenced by their leading to the health or cost outcomes they are purported to achieve.
- *Reliability or reproducibility,* in terms of both their content (i.e., if two sets of experts would develop the same guideline independently) and of their interpretation and application (i.e., across clinicians).
- *Clinical applicability,* in terms of including appropriately defined patient populations and explicitly stating to whom the guidelines apply.
- *Clinical flexibility,* in terms of identifying exceptions to recommendations and how to consider patient preferences. Flexibility is an attribute that is emphasized by many other experts (e.g., APA, 2000; Nathan, 1998; Stricker et al., 1999).
- *Clarity,* in terms of how they are presented.
- *Multidisciplinary process,* in terms of representation by members of key affected groups in the development and review of the guidelines.
- *Scheduled review* of the guidelines, to determine whether new evidence warrants a revision.
- *Documentation* of the guideline development process, the evidence considered, the assumptions and rationales that were used, the analyses performed, and the participants in the process.

Two other guideline attributes have been identified by the APA (2000) as important dimensions that should be considered in evaluating guidelines. The first dimension is *clinical efficacy,* which refers to

> a valid ascertainment of the effects of a given intervention as compared to an alternative intervention, or to no treatment, in a controlled clinical context. The fundamental question in evaluating efficacy is whether a beneficial effect of treatment can be demonstrated scientifically. . . . Without evidence of efficacy, health care professionals are forced to rely exclusively on their direct experience of the effects of different treatment interventions—an approach that risks erroneous conclusions. (pp. 4–5)

The other dimension is *clinical utility,* which

> addresses (1) the ability of health care professionals to use, and of patients to accept, the treatment under consideration, and (2) the range of applicability of that treatment. This dimension reflects the extent to which the intervention will be effective in the practice setting where it is to be applied, regardless of the efficacy that may have been demonstrated in the clinical research setting. The evaluation of clinical utility involves the assessment of interventions as they are delivered in real-world clinical settings. (p. 10)

APA's identification of these two dimensions as important considerations when evaluating guidelines recognizes the fact that even the most scientifically sound intervention will be of limited or no value if it is not accepted by clinicians and patients, has limited applicability, or is not easily implemented. Conversely, well-accepted and easily implemented guidelines with apparent application to a wide variety of patients will be virtually useless if there is no empirical backing for their apparent effectiveness. Of course, it is unlikely that any guideline will be found to be 100% clinically efficacious and 100% clinically useful. Clinicians will therefore have to settle for more realistic criterion levels—perhaps ones that are quite adequate for their specific needs—and proceed accordingly.

Treatment Manuals

Clinicians will find that some of their patients may be candidates for interventions that are prescribed through *treatment manuals.* Strosahl (1998) describes treatment manuals as "the implementation arm of clinical practice guidelines" (p. 382). According to Kazdin and Kendall (1998),

> Manuals specify guidelines, session foci, and content; the progression of treatment; and when and how to continue particular practices, tasks, sessions, and themes. . . . [They] can encompass all aspects of treatment that can be documented. Some of the information may seem relatively trivial, such as the materials used in a session, instructions to explain treatment, and forms used to document the sessions. (p. 220)

Havik and VandenBos (1996) add that psychotherapy manuals

> are either broad and complex descriptions of a specific treatment approach to a specific clinical problem or narrow and highly detailed descriptions of a particular technique that can be utilized in addressing a specific, generally low prevalence, clinical symptom. . . . Most [manualized approaches] exist within the context of brief, highly technical, methodological journal articles . . . [the majority of which] do not represent psychotherapies as much as detailed clinical techniques within a more general approach to psychotherapy. (p. 265)

Manualized treatment is frequently used in research in which standardization of procedures is a key requirement. In fact, the impetus for manual development began as the result of the methodological weaknesses that were noted in psychotherapy research (Havik & VandenBos, 1996). A prime example is research investigating the effectiveness or efficacy of one form of treatment (e.g., cognitive-behavioral) over another (e.g., psychoanalytic) for a specific type of problem (e.g., panic disorder, agoraphobia). In general, clinicians' attitudes toward treatment manuals have been found to vary (Addis & Krasnow, 2000; Najavits, Weiss, Shaw, & Dierberger, 2000).

The use of treatment manuals compares to the more individualized treatment intervention plans that stem from the development of a comprehensive case formulation, as described in chapter 4 and recommended throughout this book. Mumma (1998) particularly advocates the use of the formulation-based treatment in specific instances, such as with patients who have not responded to treatment, present with substantial comorbidity, or exhibit complex symptomatology, or with patients for whose psychopathology no empirically based, standardized treatment exists.

Manualized treatments do have a number of advantages, not the least of which is the empirical backing that typically accompanies the procedures dictated therein. As well, they may address a number of different but related problems that might not otherwise be considered (Eifert, Evans, & McKendrick, 1990). However, most experts would likely agree that complete adherence to manuals may not be necessary, and that some flexibility and individualization is required for the clinical application of manualized treatments (see Chambless et al., 1996; Kazdin & Kendall, 1998). A summary of some of the reported criticisms or concerns and advantages of treatment manuals is presented in Rapid Reference 5.5.

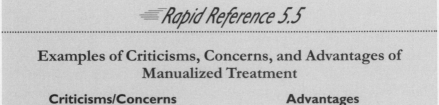

Examples of Criticisms, Concerns, and Advantages of Manualized Treatment

Criticisms/Concerns	Advantages
• Generalizability of findings to clinical settings is limited	• Structured, time-limited nature yields more highly focused treatment
• Holds actuarial decision making as superior to clinical judgment	• Facilitates patient involvement in treatment
• Has mechanical (inflexible, insensitive, nonintuitive, etc.) implementation	• Facilitates clinical training, supervision, and auditing
• Requires considerable training	• Increases dissemination of treatment to clinicians
• Impedes innovative clinical strategies	• Need not be rigidly applied
• Impacts the therapeutic relationship	• Reduces practice variability
• Limits the clinician to what needs to be done	• Provides common framework for patients and clinicians to understand and discuss the therapeutic process
• May not meet patient needs	
• Feasibility of training, implementation, and patient acceptance	• Identifies when to refer to or collaborate with other specialties
	• Provides clearer indication of when effective therapeutic dose has been provided

Note. From Addis, Wade, and Hatgis (1999), Heimberg (1998), Lambert (1998), Marques (1998), Parloff (1998), and Wilson (1998).

Perhaps the ideal approach is the one expressed by Eifert et al. (1990) when they stated,

> What we need are individually tailored treatment [manuals] based on a comprehensive framework model of abnormal behavior which allow us to identify and conceptualize the specific problems of a [patient] within the framework. In addition, we need to develop a system of rules of *how* that conceptualization can be translated into a specific program that includes those components necessary for a given [patient], but excludes others that are not necessary. (p. 166)

Empirically Supported Treatments

Obviously, only treatments that have been found to yield positive outcomes should be considered for inclusion in the patient's treatment plan. At issue here are the criteria that should be used to determine the appropriateness of a specific treatment for a specific problem. In many (if not most) instances, clinicians will rely on their past training and clinical experience with similar patients presenting similar types of problems, in determining the best course of action for the patient being considered. Hopefully, somewhere in their training or experience clinicians have considered the empirical evidence supporting the use of the treatment, but this is not always the case.

In the past several years, the work of task forces formed by APA's Division 12 (Clinical Psychology) have yielded information that has brought the importance of *empirically supported treatments* (*ESTs;* also referred to as *empirically validated treatments,* or *EVTs*) to the attention of clinical psychologists and those involved in their graduate education. ESTs are defined as "clearly specified psychological treatments shown to be efficacious in controlled research with a delineated population" (Chambless & Hollon, 1998, Introduction, para. 1), and they tend to be based on treatment manuals (Wilson, 1998). Beginning with the work of the Task Force on Promotion and Dissemination of Psychological Procedures (1995) and continuing with the work of the Task Force on Psychological Interventions (Chambless et al., 1996; Chambless et al., 1997), a number of ESTs have been identified and disseminated.

The APA reports have yielded interesting debates over issues related to ESTs. The reader is referred to the positions taken by Chambless (1996) and Garfield (1996) as well as those of several others in a series of articles and commentaries that were published in *Clinical Psychology: Science and Practice* (vol. 3, no. 3) for a good overview of these issues. Regardless, this author feels that the findings of these APA task forces must be examined in light of two important considerations. The first is the fact that the treatments that were considered were judged on the basis of their efficacy, without regard to their effectiveness or efficiency. A treatment's *efficacy* refers to the benefits it yields under well-controlled conditions. *Effectiveness* refers the treatment's utility under actual clinical conditions, whereas *efficiency* refers to its cost effectiveness. In today's health care market, it is both difficult and unwise to consider any one of these characteristics in the absence of the other two.

The second important factor that must be considered consists of the criteria by which the APA task forces or any other party judge whether a treatment is efficacious. Application of different sets of criteria would probably result in different sets of identified treatments. For example, Chambless and Hollon (1998) have developed a modified version of the criteria used by APA (see Rapid Reference 5.6). Beutler (1998) argues that the Chambless and Hollon criteria are more supportive of long-term treatment than the APA task force criteria; at the same time, neither would support psychoanalytic therapy.

Related to this second factor is an interesting point made by Nathan (1998). He observed that behavioral treatments are prominent among those identified by the Division 12 task forces. He attributes this to several factors, including the fact that they have been shown to be effective with a number of disorders, induce distinct behavioral changes that are detectable by outcomes measures, are well suited to manualized programs, are borne out of a tradition of experimental validation, and produce changes that occur within the constraints of time-limited outcomes studies.

What are the implications of the work carried out by the APA task forces? As Chambless et al. (1996) note, first the clinician should never use a treatment identified by EST criteria as a substitute for his or her own judgment. One must take into consideration the empirical evidence in light of its relevance to a particular patient for a particular purpose under particular circumstances. In addition, ESTs may not be available for all disorders or problems. Second, the clinician must stay current with the published literature both in his or her own area of interest (e.g., behavior therapy) and in other areas (e.g., cognitive therapy) in order be aware of any innovations or advancements in treatment that yield more efficacious, effective, or efficient results. Third, based on EST findings, the clinician must include information about what the patient can expect from treatment as part of the informed consent process.

The debate over the usefulness of ESTs in clinical practice is likely to con-

≡ Rapid Reference 5.6

Criteria for Empirically Supported Psychological Therapies

- Comparison with a no-treatment control group, alternative treatment group, or placebo (a) in a randomized control trial, controlled single case experiment, or equivalent time-samples design (b) in which the EST is statistically significantly superior to no treatment, placebo, or alternative treatments or in which the EST is equivalent to a treatment already established in efficacy, and power is sufficient to detect moderate differences.
- These studies must have been conducted with (a) a treatment manual or its logical equivalent; (b) a population, treated for specified problems, for whom inclusion criteria have been delineated in a reliable, valid manner; (c) reliable and valid outcome assessment measures, at minimum tapping the problems targeted for change; and (d) appropriate data analysis.
- For a designation of efficacious, the superiority of the EST must have been shown in at least two independent research settings (sample size of 3 or more at each site in the case of single case experiments). If there is conflicting evidence, the preponderance of the well-controlled data must support the EST's efficacy.
- For a designation of possibly efficacious, one study (sample size of 3 or more in the case of single case experiments) suffices in the absence of conflicting evidence.
- For a designation of efficacious and specific, the EST must have been shown to be statistically significantly superior to pill or psychological placebo or to an alternative bona fide treatment in at least two independent research settings. If there is conflicting evidence, the preponderance of the well-controlled data must support the EST's efficacy and specificity.

Note. From Chambless and Hollon (1998, appendix A).

tinue for quite some time. As the arguments continue, it may be helpful to keep in mind Nathan's (1998) observation about the issue. As later summarized by Wolfe (1999, p. 448), "Empirically supported treatments in mental health are not ideal, but they represent essential steps toward reaching two overarching health care goals: enhanced clinical effectiveness and improved accountability."

Other Considerations

Regardless of the patient or the reasons for seeking treatment, there are several issues that the clinician should consider in deciding upon the optimal intervention.

The patient's stage of readiness for change. The degree to which patients are prepared to engage actively in treatment varies considerably. Over the years, theorists, researchers, and clinicians have expressed the importance of considering the patient's readiness for change in selecting the one or more optimal interventions. The assertion here is that the most appropriate focus of or approach to treatment will vary as a function of where the patient is in terms of the patient's considering, deciding on, and committing to making positive life changes.

One theory of change that has gained much attention and acceptance during the past 20 years is that developed by Prochaska and his colleagues (DiClemente & Hughes, 1990; McConnaughy, et al., 1983; Prochaska, 1995; Prochaska & DiClemente, 1982, 1992; Prochaska et al., 1992; Prochaska, et al., 1988; see additional references in chapter 2). Their *transtheoretical model of change* has important implications for the therapeutic approach or the specific type of intervention or technique that might be initiated at various points in the treatment process. Core features of this model include the following:

1. Five stages of change: *precontemplation, contemplation, preparation, action,* and *maintenance* (a description of each of these stages is presented in chapter 2). Patients beginning treatment may be at any one of these motivational and temporal aspects of change, a fact that has implications for the types of processes that will be most helpful in moving the patient from one stage of change to the next. Movement through these stages tends to be cyclical rather than linear.

2. Ten processes of change: *consciousness raising, self-liberation, social liberation, counterconditioning, stimulus control, self-reevaluation, environmental reevaluation, contingency management, dramatic relief,* and *helping relationships.* These are activities that are used by people to change the way they think, behave, and feel. According to Prochaska et al. (1992), "The processes were selected by examining recommended change techniques across different theories, which explains the term *transtheoretical.* At least 10 subsequent principal component analyses on the processes of change items . . . have yielded similar patterns" (p. 1107).

3. Five levels of change: *symptom or situational problems, maladaptive cognitions, current interpersonal conflicts, family systems conflicts,* and *intrapersonal conflicts.* This represents a hierarchy of problems that psychotherapy can address. These types of problems are interrelated, such that a

change at one level will likely result in a change at other levels. Intervention may begin at any level, but the recommendation is to begin at the highest level that is clinically advisable.

As explained by McConnaughy et al. (1983), the transtheoretical model would predict

1) that particular processes of change are most effective with [patients] working in particular stages of change; 2) that resistance to therapy increases if the therapist is working on a different stage of change than what the [patient] is in; 3) that resistance to change occurs if spouses and family members are involved in different stages of change; 4) that the premature termination and/or length of therapy is related to which stages of change [patients] are in at the beginning of therapy; and 5) by matching the [patient's] stage profile with the appropriate processes of change, progress in psychotherapy can be optimized. (p. 375)

The transtheoretical model is mentioned here both because of its espousal of an eclectic approach to treatment and because of the empirical support that it has garnered. Elements of this model also have been incorporated into other approaches to treatment planning (e.g., see Beutler et al., 1999); thus it provides important considerations in the selection of treatment in day-to-day practice.

Another popular theory of change has been espoused by Howard and his colleagues through their *phase model of psychotherapy* (Howard, Lueger, Maling, & Martinovich, 1993; Howard, Moras, Brill, Martinovich, & Lutz, 1996). The phase model proposes a standard patient progression through distinct phases of psychotherapy that occur in a consistent sequence. The successful accomplishment of one phase permits the patient to move to the next phase and, consequently, to move efficiently and effectively through the entire therapeutic process.

The first phase identified by Howard and colleagues (Howard, Lueger, et al., 1993; Howard et al., 1996) is *remoralization*. Patients begin treatment demoralized, seeing themselves as failures in terms of meeting their or others' expectations of them, unable to cope with problems, stuck in a situation that they feel incapable of changing. The therapist's establishing a sense of trust with patients, helping them identify their problem, instilling a sense of hope, and thus increasing their sense of well-being are key at this phase of treatment. Not all patients enter treatment with the sense of demoralization described here. For them, initiation of treatment may begin at the second phase.

This second phase of psychotherapy is *remediation* (Howard, Lueger, et al., 1993; Howard et al., 1996). Having helped patients acquire confidence in their ability to cope, therapy can begin to focus patients on overcoming the symptoms that led to their sense of demoralization. As suggested earlier, some patients also may not require the type of interventions typically presented in this phase, in which case the treatment begins by focusing on the tasks generally reserved for the third and last stage of therapy.

Feeling better about themselves and their capabilities, and with their symptomatology improving, patients can move into the last stage of therapy, the *rehabilitation* phase (Howard, Leuger et al., 1993; Howard et al., 1996). Here, the focus is on improving those aspects of functioning that are impaired. These may be related to functioning within the family or social groups, on the job or at school, or in some other life role.

What are the implications of this model? As Howard, Lueger, et al. (1993) point out,

> From a psychotherapy practice standpoint, the phase model suggests that different change processes (and thus certain classes of interventions) will be appropriate for different phases of therapy and that certain tasks may have to be accomplished before others are undertaken. It also suggests that different therapeutic processes may characterize each phase. Therapeutic interventions are likely to be most effective when they focus on changing phase-specific problems when those problems are most accessible to change. (p. 684)

Furthermore, Howard et al. (1996) assert that

> to the extent that these three phases are distinct, they imply different treatment goals and, thus, the selection and assessment of different outcome variables to measure progress in each phase. (p. 1061).

Rapid Reference 5.7 provides a brief summary of the key aspects of both models of change. Regardless of whether one is an advocate of Howard's, Prochaska's, or a similar theory that identifies distinct phases in the treatment process, the ongoing monitoring of treatment is extremely important as one considers the implications of moving from one phase of treatment to another. This issue is discussed further in chapter 6.

≡Rapid Reference 5.7

Implications of Stages or Phases of Treatment According to Prochaska's and Howard's Models

Model	Stage or Phase	Processes or Tasks Necessary for Movement to Next Stage or Phase
Transtheoretical	Precontemplation	Consciousness raising
		Dramatic relief
		Environmental reevaluation
	Contemplation	Self-reevaluation
	Preparation	Self-liberation
	Action	Reinforcement management
		Helping relationships
		Counterconditioning
		Stimulus control
	Maintenance	Building on all previous processes
		Assessment of conditions likely to cause a relapse
		Development of alternative coping strategies
Phase	Remoralization	Increase in sense of hope and well-being
	Remediation	Alleviation of symptoms
	Rehabilitation	Improvement in role functioning

Note. Transtheoretical (Prochaska and colleagues); Phase (Howard and colleagues).

Comorbid medical or psychiatric disorders. Treating patients with one or more co-morbid psychiatric disorders (i.e., those for which the patient is not seeking treatment) or medical disorders can present difficult challenges for the clinician. The deeply ingrained, maladaptive patterns of thinking, behaving, or coping of personality-disordered individuals, or the cognitive impairment exhibited by brain-impaired patients, are only a few examples of the types of barriers that the clinician might experience in treating patients for unrelated but commonly seen psychiatric disorders, such as major depression or a specific phobia. Especially when faced with time or session limitations imposed by health plans, comorbid problems such as these and the barriers they can impose must be considered when developing an effective plan of treatment.

Comorbid medical (physical) disorders, particularly those that are frequently accompanied by depression, anxiety, or other psychiatric symptomatology (e.g., diabetes, asthma, congestive heart failure) also may require special attention during treatment plan development. At the minimum, interventions may require close coordination of clinician's efforts with those of the patient's medical care provider, whether it be a specialist or the patient's PCP. Beyond that, it is important to consider carefully the physical and psychological symptoms that accompany the disease or disorder and that potentially could interfere with the type of treatment that would otherwise be prescribed for the patient. For example, for a stroke patient, the ability to use proven behavioral techniques may be significantly affected by the resulting limitations in mobility resulting from the patient's paralysis. For another patient, a stroke may have resulted in speech deficits that will lead one to question the viability of employing therapeutic techniques that rely heavily on verbal expression. For the patient with limited physical endurance accompanying severe emphysema, briefer but more frequent therapy sessions may be more beneficial than the standard treatment regimen of weekly 50-minute sessions.

Physicians and others practicing in the nonpsychiatric medical professions (e.g., clinical nurse practitioners, physician assistants) are becoming more sensitive to the presence of psychiatric problems in their patients. They are also becoming more willing to refer these patients to behavioral health care providers. As a result, clinicians are more likely to see these types of patients than they had been in the past. Consequently, considering comorbid medical disorders in the planning of psychological treatment is becoming more important. Thus, it behooves clinicians to become familiar with some of the more prevalent physical diseases and disorders and the ways in which they may impact the planned behavioral health interventions.

Patient-therapist-treatment interactions. One issue raised in the Chambless et al. (1996) report had to do with the importance of considering not only the patient's problems but also characteristics of the patient (e.g., gender, coping style) that may bear upon the effectiveness of an EST. Beyond considering the interaction of patient and treatment variables, or what is referred to as Aptitude X Treatment Interactions (ATIs; Shoham-Salomon & Hannah, 1991; Smith & Sechrest, 1991), Beutler (1991) also points out the role that therapist variables (e.g., training, facilitative skill) may play in the differential effects of the treatment being considered. The interaction among patient, treatment, and therapist variables (and possibly others) may have significant implications for evaluating treatment-effectiveness research for the purpose of clinical applications.

Some established approaches to treatment planning take a number of patient, treatment, or clinician variables into consideration. The transtheoretical model and Beutler's systematic treatment selection (Beutler, 1991; Beutler & Clarkin, 1990; Beutler et al., 1999) are good examples. However, not adhering to such approaches should not keep clinicians from taking these types of variables into consideration. Even if relevant research is lacking, clinicians should be able to draw upon their knowledge of related research or personal clinical experience to arrive at rationally based hypotheses regarding how and by whom the patient's problems should be treated (if there are indeed such options) in order to maximize the potential for positive outcomes.

Validation of the intervention-selection decision. Once tentative intervention decisions are made, there are several questions that clinicians should ask themselves about these decisions. These questions, presented in Rapid Reference 5.8, provide clinicians with an opportunity to validate their decisions before proceeding with the development of the remainder of the treatment plan, and

≡ Rapid Reference 5.8

Some Questions for Validating Intervention Selection Decision

- Will the planned intervention enable the patient to meet all or most of the selected goals?
- Does the treating clinician have the skills necessary for implementing the planned intervention?
- Is what the patient will be expected to do realistic?
- Is what the clinician will be expected to do realistic?
- Will the clinician be able to know within a reasonable amount of time if the intervention is working?
- Could a different type of intervention yield the same outcomes? If so, why was it not selected?

certainly before actually initiating treatment with their patients. Answering these questions honestly and modifying the decision as appropriate will help ensure that patients receive the best possible care that has the greatest chance for achieving the desired treatment outcomes.

Appropriate Level of Care

One of the first considerations in planning for the treatment of a patient is the level of care (LOC) that is most appropriate, given the patient's particular circumstances. In general, the factors that should play into a decision about LOC are the severity of the problems that the patient is experiencing at the time of assessment, the type of treatment that is effective and most appropriate for the problem intensity level, and the availability of that treatment. There are several LOCs at which a patient can receive treatment. The more restrictive levels are typically used to stabilize the patient or to help ensure the safety of the patient or others, or both. Health plans will vary in the number and types of LOCs they reimburse for; however, there generally is a large overlap in the LOCs that are offered and their associated medical necessity criteria. Among the commonly offered LOCs are 23-hour bed, inpatient, partial hospitalization, intensive outpatient (IOP), and outpatient care for mental health treatment. Similar but separate LOCs and medical necessity criteria are established for substance abuse treatment and sometimes for child and adolescent patients.

Following is a broad overview of the more common LOCs for adult mental health patients. Because it is likely that most patients will be covered under a managed care plan, the descriptions presented are based on the medical necessity criteria that are found in the guidelines for UBH (2001) and CIGNA (1999), two large, nationwide MBHOs. Note that accompanying the determination of the most appropriate LOC for a given patient are the assumptions that (a) there is a *DSM-IV-TR* Axis I disorder present, (b) the assigned LOC can provide the type of treatment the patient needs at that point in time, and (c) it is the least restrictive LOC for the patient to receive that treatment.

- *Inpatient.* Precertification for admission into an inpatient unit typically requires that the patient's symptoms present a serious and imminent risk of harm to self or others; have caused a severe disturbance in the patient's affect, behavior, judgment, or thought processes; or are serious and accompanied by acute deterioration in functioning. In these cases, appropriate treatment requires the type of daily oversight and close monitoring and supervision that an inpatient stay provides and that are not available through less restrictive LOCs.

- *Partial hospitalization or day treatment.* Generally, this LOC is intended for patients who are experiencing symptoms or deterioration in functioning at a level of severity that requires regular monitoring that cannot be provided at lower LOCs; however, they do not require the same level of monitoring and intervention that is offered through the inpatient LOC (e.g., the patient can contract for safety while not physically attending the program). In cases such as these, the patient might attend a hospital-based or free-standing partial hospitalization or day treatment program 5 hours a day, 4 or 5 days a week until changes in the patient's condition warrant transfer to a lower LOC.

- *Intensive outpatient.* This LOC is similar to but less intense than partial hospitalization, with the patient attending the intensive inpatient program perhaps only 3 days a week, 3 hours a day. It is appropriate when more structure, monitoring, and intervention are required than can be offered through standard outpatient services, but the intensity of intervention that is needed is less than that found in a partial hospitalization program.

- *Outpatient.* Outpatient treatment is appropriate and warranted if the patient exhibits clinical symptoms or behaviors along with impairment or deterioration in functioning. Treatment at this level is appropriate when there is no serious risk of harm to self or others; there are clear, focused, and objective treatment goals; and there is linkage with some form of community support.

MBHOs and other third-party insurers may also cover treatment offered through other mental health and substance abuse LOCs, depending on the contracts they have with specific employers or health plans. Examples may include inpatient detoxification, substance abuse halfway houses, home health care services, custodial care, and residential care of children and adolescents.

Type or Mode of Intervention

There are several possible modes of behavioral health intervention that might be considered for the patient. What is considered optimal for the individual patient will depend on a number of factors, some of which were discussed earlier (e.g., availability of desired services, ability of patient to meet LOC medical necessity criteria, benefits included in the patient's health plan). However, all other things being equal, there are a few considerations to bear in mind when deciding upon treatment modality.

Psychotherapeutic. For the vast majority of individuals seeking help for mental health or substance abuse problems, so-called talk therapy will be the first line of treatment. Typically, a number of psychotherapeutic modality options—individual, group, marital, family—are available to patients. For some, the best plan will be to see the patient in individual sessions; for others, another mode will yield the best results. For example, conjoint marital therapy will likely yield the maximum benefit for a couple seeking help with their sexual problems. On the other hand, a patient whose primary problem is an inability to relate well and make friends with others may be best served through group therapy. There are yet others for whom a combination of modalities (e.g., individual and group psychotherapy) or a succession of modalities (e.g., 5 sessions of individual psychotherapy followed by 10 sessions of group psychotherapy) may be determined to be the best approach to treatment.

In some instances, the LOC determined to be the most appropriate for the patient will dictate the format of the interventions that are provided. For example, for the patient being hospitalized for stabilization after a drug overdose, individual and family psychotherapy is warranted but may not be practical to initiate during a 2–3 day inpatient stay.

Psychopharmacologic. The symptoms presented by the patient may be such that psychopharmacologic intervention is warranted. For some disorders, this option is obvious given that medication has been found to be an effective therapeutic agent, either alone or as an adjunct. Examples of good candidates for psychopharmacologic intervention include patients suffering from major depression, psychotic symptoms, or hyperactivity. In other cases, the decision about whether to use medication is not so clear-cut and will depend on a number of variables. Among others, these include the ability to treat the patient's problems efficiently and effectively without the use of medication, the effectiveness of medication for the symptoms in question, the patient's motivation and ability to participate actively in a regimen of psychopharmacotherapy, the presence of other physical or mental conditions that contraindicate the use of otherwise safe and effective medications, and financial burden. The issue frequently involves weighing the potential benefits against the potential costs of implementing this type of intervention—an issue that at the minimum requires a referral to a psychiatrist or other knowledgeable medical specialist (to be discussed in the *Medical* section).

Psychopharmacologic treatment may be the sole treatment for a patient, or may be used in conjunction with other forms of treatment (discussed later). UBH (2000) has cautioned that when it is the only type of treatment the patient is receiving, it be administered in the context of *clinical management*. This would involve education of the patient about the treatment, periodic assessment of the patient during the course of treatment, and involvement of social supports, as necessary.

Medical. As with psychopharmacologic treatment, other types of pharmacological treatment, as well as more drastic types of medical interventions, may be suggested. These types of treatment will, of course, require a referral to a specialist in psychiatry or another area of medicine. At times, drastic procedures such as electroconvulsive therapy (ECT) treatments or neurosurgical procedures (e.g., removal of a tumor) may result in improved patient functioning. Looking beyond these obvious examples, however, the clinician may find that other types of medical interventions for physical conditions (e.g., plastic surgery for burn or mastectomy patients, control of diabetes through insulin) also can go a long way in helping the patient achieve the desired treatment goals. Appropriate referral for these types of interventions makes it incumbent upon the clinician to acquire the knowledge necessary for sensitivity to the potential presence of medical conditions and issues.

Some would argue that in general, it is appropriate to recommend the most economical forms of treatment first. Tillett (1996) states that most medical treatments (including the use of psychopharmacologic agents) would fall into this category because they require much less time and may have the same efficacy as other forms of treatment. He supports this recommendation by noting that "recommending a trial of medical treatment does not preclude the possibility of a psychotherapeutic approach concurrently or at a later date" (p. 13). While this is true, one must be careful in adopting a view that may result in the delay of the best treatment for a given patient at a given point of time. Consequences that may result include unnecessary continuation of psychological suffering and distress, deterioration of the patient's condition, and treatment dropout due to lack of progress.

Educational. There are a number of useful educational activities that can be utilized as adjuncts to the interventions offered by the treating clinician. These include opportunities offered through books on relevant topics, interactive Internet Web sites, workshops, college courses, and other means of educating patients about their disorder and techniques for dealing with the conditions. The knowledge gained in these manners can facilitate the work that is done during face-to-face interventions, thus making treatment a much more efficient process.

Other modes of intervention. Other types of interventions may be appropriate for the patient. Among these are community self-help and support groups (e.g., Alcoholics Anonymous), retreats and encounter groups focused on specific topics (e.g., improving marital relationships), standardized treatment offered through interactive Web sites, and bibliotherapy. Although incorporating activities such as these into the overall plan of treatment may significantly and positively affect outcomes, they should never be employed as the primary treatment modality for any patient.

Multimodal or eclectic approach. As was just suggested, a multimodal approach to treatment certainly can be recommended. The most frequent example of this is treatment using a combination of psychotherapeutic and psychopharmacologic interventions. However, the clinician might also employ a combination of different modes of psychotherapy. Combining individual psychotherapy with group therapy or marital therapy is a common practice in treating a patient for whom marital problems and general interpersonal problems, respectively, significantly limit the patient's functioning.

Similarly, different approaches of one mode of treatment may be prescribed for the patient. For example, a clinician may simultaneously treat a patient using two or more different psychotherapeutic approaches. For a phobic patient, the combination of behavioral therapy (e.g., desensitization, implosion) and cognitive therapy (e.g., rational emotive therapy) can greatly facilitate the amelioration of the phobic response. Or the clinician may find it advantageous to use one approach to treatment at the beginning of therapy and another approach at some point later in treatment. In their transtheoretical model of therapy, Prochaska and DiClemente (1992) have noted that while behavior therapy will play an important role in dealing with symptoms or situations when the patient is in the action stage of change, cognitive therapy will play an important role in dealing with maladaptive cognitions during both the contemplation and action stages.

Thus, the choice of the type of approach or mode of treatment may vary according to a number of factors. The degree to which the clinician is flexible and open to all options for approaching the patient's problems and efficiently working toward achieving the stated goals of treatment may have a significant bearing on the final outcomes of the episode of care.

Strategies and Tactics

In Makover's (1992) hierarchical treatment planning schema, the type or mode of intervention and the general approach within that mode (e.g., a cognitive approach to psychotherapy) represent what he would describe as the *strategies* for arriving at specific goals and objectives. Recall that *tactics* are the specific techniques that are used to implement the strategy. For example, eye movement desensitization and reprocessing (EMDR) and desensitization are techniques that might be employed within a behavior therapy approach (strategy) to treat a patient suffering from posttraumatic stress disorder (PTSD). Free association, dream interpretation, and analysis of transference could be used with a depressed patient undergoing psychoanalytic psychotherapy. As much as possible, the techniques that the clinician plans to employ should be specified in the treatment plan. This will help ensure that the patient and relevant third parties (e.g., MBHOs) clearly understand what the treatment will involve and thus eliminate any unrealistic expectations for what will go on during the course of treatment. Moreover, it will facilitate obtaining informed consent.

One tactic that should be (and usually is) considered for every patient is the assignment of homework to be completed outside the treatment setting. This would usually involve having the patient perform some type of behavior, such as keeping a log of the days, dates, and times the patient feels or thinks a certain way; reading a book provided by the clinician that is relevant to the patient's problems; performing some duties at school, work, or home in a timely manner; or engaging in some social activity. Homework assignments help the patient try out or complement what has been learned in treatment. They also reinforce the notions that the patient is responsible for problem resolution, and that working on change must continue outside the treatment setting.

Intent of the Interventions

There are times when written treatment plans include listings of multiple interventions for the patient's problems. Accompanying the statement of whatever types of intervention the clinician has selected, there should also be an indication of the target and intended effect of each intervention (Mumma, 1998) and of how and when the intended effect will be measured—all of which should serve as criteria for termination, which will be presented later in the treatment plan.

Frequency and Duration of Treatment

Treatment plans should indicate the frequency at and duration for which the patient will be seen in treatment. In some cases, statements regarding frequency and (especially) duration may be nothing more than guesses based on the clinician's experience with similar patients, problems, and treatment goals. The projected duration may be relatively long (e.g., weekly outpatient sessions for 1 year) or even open ended, with the stated duration actually reflecting a case review date. Generally, this should be avoided except in cases for which long-term or continuous treatment is quite appropriate (e.g., with schizophrenics or other patients with chronic mental disorders). In most cases, one should try to provide a very specific and accurate determination of frequency and duration. This is probably easiest to do when the intent is for planned short-term or brief therapy.

Planned brief therapy (Budman & Gurman, 1988) and *planned short-term therapy* (Bloom, 1992) are two terms describing essentially the same process. According to Bloom,

> the word *planned* is important—planned short-term treatment is intended to accomplish a set of therapeutic objectives within a sharply limited time frame. Planned short-term psychotherapy is short-term by design and should be distinguished from what might be called *unplanned short-term therapy,* that is, services that are brief because treatment is terminated unilaterally by the [patient]. (p. 158)

The current attention to and interest in planned brief therapy (Budman & Gurman, 1988) or planned short-term therapy (Bloom, 1992) is reflective of several factors. These include (a) growing consumer education and demand for fast, efficient, and cost-effective treatment; (b) changes in practice, such that there is more focus on patient strengths, greater utilization of crisis intervention and behavior modification techniques, and greater attention to precipitating rather than predisposing circumstances; and (c) realization of the effectiveness of planned short-term treatment. This last point is very important. It reflects Bloom's conclusion that "virtually without exception, empirical evaluations of short-term outpatient psychotherapy or short-term inpatient psychiatric care have found that planned short-term psychotherapies are essentially equally effective and are, in general, as effective as time unlimited psychotherapy, regardless of diagnosis, treatment orientation, or duration of treatment" (p. 158). Supporting this conclusion is Budman and Gurman's assertion that "the enormous body of research on the outcomes of various individual psychotherapies ... taken collectively, constitutes research on time-unlimited brief therapy" (p. 7).

What is considered *brief* or *short?* This can vary depending on a number of factors. Bloom (1992) indicates that short-term therapy can range from 1 to 20 sessions, with the average being 6 sessions. Interestingly, Budman and Gurman (1988), citing the work of Garfield, indicate that most patients expect to stay in treatment for about 6 to 10 sessions and actually do stay in treatment for 6 to 8 sessions. Bloom's 6-session average is consistent with the duration typically found for patients being seen through at least one large MBHO (Maruish, 2002).

An issue related to the determination of duration of treatment is how much therapy is enough. There appear to be two components to this issue. The first has to do with the argument that as far as therapy is concerned, more is better. Budman and Gurman (1988) point to published literature reviews and the work of Howard and his colleagues (Howard, Kopta, Krause, & Orlinsky, 1986) that supports this contention—up to a point. That is, there appears to be a point after which more therapy begins to yield diminishing returns. It is at this time that a cost-benefit analysis would be called for to determine the wisdom of continuing treatment.

The other component of the issue has more to do with the question of supply and demand of therapy services. After first pointing out the large, underserved population of people with mental health problems and the long-term costs of providing inadequate, too-short treatment to those who do receive services, Kiesler (2000) offers the following for consideration:

If one accepts the notion that the population of untreated patients is substantial, one quickly gets to the concept of *good enough treatment.* This concept implies that (a) the treatment is not ideal, (b) perhaps with more substantial treatment better outcomes could be obtained, but (c) with the pressures of the payer's requirements, the press of untreated cases, and the capitation level, treatment sufficient to avoid relapse and return is good enough under the circumstances. (p. 485)

This concept may have particular appeal and warrant special consideration not only in MBHOs but also in any type of setting in which the demand for services is greater than the resources that are available to meet that demand.

Overall, the reported findings and the recommendations of Bloom (1992), Gurman and Budman (1988), and Tillett (1996) lead this author to conclude that all patients (excluding those with chronic conditions) should be considered for planned short-term therapy. Failing successful completion of treatment by this approach, other options are always available. As Budman and Gurman succinctly summarize,

> Our recommendations in patient selection are to monitor the patient's response to treatment on a trial basis [i.e., one to three therapy or pretherapy "trial" sessions]; to be prepared to make creative modifications as necessary (two such modifications may involve the patient's seeing another therapist or including the patient's family); and to be prepared to use various alternatives, including longer and more open-ended treatment. (p. 25)

As a final note, the prescription of planned short-term therapy assumes the availability of a clinician who can provide this type of treatment. Budman and Gurman (1988) have pointed out differences in the value systems of long- and short-term therapists. In their view, long-term therapists view the patient's presenting problems as indicating more basic psychopathology, and they seek to change the patient's basic behavior. They believe that change will not take place in day-to-day life. When change does occur, long-term therapists want to be there and thus are willing to wait for it. In most cases, therapy is viewed as being benign, useful, and the most important part of the patient's life. On an unconscious basis, such therapists recognize the value of maintaining a long-term relationship with the patient. In contrast, short-term therapists do not believe in a so-called cure. Instead, they tend to emphasize the patient's resources and prefer a pragmatic and parsimonious approach to treatment. Significant change is viewed as being inevitable from a developmental perspective, and in many cases these changes will not be observed by the therapist. Psychotherapy is sometimes useful, sometimes harmful, and not necessarily timeless. Regardless, being in therapy is not as important as being in the world.

For short-term therapists, fiscal issues often are not very prominent. One will note that overall, the values and attitudes of the short-term therapist are generally consistent with those held by MBHOs.

Bloom (1992) points out that short-term planned treatment should be undertaken by a clinician who is experienced in provision of long-term psychotherapy. However, with greater current emphasis on training graduate students specifically in delivering short-term therapy, experience in long-term treatment may not be as critical now as it was at the beginning of the last decade. Perhaps more important than the number of years of long-term therapy experience are the clinician's attitudes and values with regard to the practice of psychotherapy.

In general, taking a short-term planned approach to treatment would appear to be the best approach from the perspectives of the patient, clinician, payer, and other third parties with a stake in the patient's health. However, it is not an approach that is befitting for everyone seeking behavioral health care services. Even beyond those with chronic conditions, there are individuals for whom a plan for short-term treatment would be inappropriate. This will likely be the case with a patient whose plan includes multiple goals and objectives, or whose goals or objectives by their very nature will require relatively long periods of time to accomplish. Overall, good clinical judgment is called for here.

CAUTION

- Recommending an LOC that is inappropriate to the patient's needs may result in no change or in a worsening of the patient's condition.
- Failure to coordinate treatment with the patient's PCP can impede the patient's progress.
- Planned brief therapy is not appropriate for all patients.

DON'T FORGET

- Be sure to assess the patient's readiness for change, comorbid physical problems, and patient-therapist interaction variables when determining the best course of treatment for the patient.
- Determine whether the patient would benefit from either a manualized or an empirically supported treatment, or from a treatment for which guidelines have been developed.
- The type and amount of treatment may be more limited for MBHO patients than for patients with other forms of insurance.

Patient Strengths

The importance of the including the patient's strengths or assets identified during the clinical assessment cannot be stressed enough. Documentation of the resources for coping that are available to the patient, and when they are available (Lehnhoff, 1991), is essential for communicating to both the patient and relevant third parties the coping skills, personality characteristics, and other assets the patient can draw upon during the course of treatment and thereafter. Consequently, it also can help determine the best strategies and tactics for the interventions that will be employed.

Consistent with Lehnhoff's (1991) view, patient strengths should be described in terms of "external, specific observable variables rather than inferred, internal processes" (p. 12). In other words, an operational definition of each strength is recommended. For example, instead of indicating that one patient has "perseverance," it may be appropriate to indicate the patient's "ability to continue on task despite occasional setbacks and failures," or that the patient "continues assigned tasks until their completion." Similarly, the patient's "self-sufficiency" can be described as the "ability to meet all the needs for daily living without the assistance of others" or as "the ability to be financially independent." Expressing strengths in this manner helps the clinician be clear to him- or herself and others (including the patient) about those aspects of the patient's functioning that can be used in the service of the intervention.

Potential Barriers to Treatment

Any barriers to the implementation of any part of the treatment plan—either existing or potential—that might arise during the episode of care should be noted. These should be accompanied by suggested ways to surmount these barriers. Being aware of and prepared for obstacles to recovery can help the clinician overcome them and proceed with treatment with as little disruption of the treatment process as possible.

Patient Barriers

Some of the most troublesome hindrances to successful treatment can emanate from the patients themselves. Aside from the challenges that patients commonly present in daily practice (e.g., the psychological defense system, transference, difficulty establishing rapport), there are other problems that may appear. Probably the most common of these barriers has to do with the patient's level of motivation. This is to be expected with those patients who are "forced" into treatment by others (e.g., parents, spouses, courts). In these cases, motivation may be low or nonexistent. Motivation to participate in treatment also may be an issue for those who seek treatment services on their own volition. Here, the required level of motivation to come to treatment may present, but it may not be adequate for the patient to work effectively toward making life changes.

Environmental Barriers

Elements in the patient's social and physical environment also can operate in a manner that undermines treatment efforts. Lack of support from family members, friends, the school system, or the employer can present huge stumbling blocks in the patient's efforts to obtain help. This might be evidenced by such things as an employer not providing the patient with time off from work to attend treatment sessions; parents' unwillingness to establish and follow a behavior modification program (e.g., a token economy) for a child patient at home; or a spouse's reluctance to participate in marital therapy with the patient who is being treated for depression that stems from problems in the marital relationship. These and other types of environmental barriers frequently are beyond the patient's (and certainly the clinician's) control. Consequently, the clinician will sometimes need to find creative ways to work around them.

Resource Limitations

Perhaps among the greatest potential obstacles to patients seeking mental health or substance abuse treatment are their available resources. These can range from what the patient's health plan will pay for, to what is available and accessible to the patient. Although the behavioral health parity laws that are being enacted throughout the United States and the standards of NCQA, JCAHO and other accrediting bodies are helping to ameliorate these concerns, such obstacles will continue into at least the foreseeable future.

Health plan coverage considerations. The patient's behavioral health care benefits often will dictate (and restrict) the type and amount of services that patient realistically can engage in. Issues here include the types of services that are covered by the health plan, maximum annual payment limits, copayments that the patient is responsible for, and the requirement that the patient's condition meet the health plan's medical necessity criteria. Generally, medical necessity requires that symptoms supporting or potentially supporting an Axis I diagnosis be present, and that the symptoms or diagnosis be amenable to treatment.

As discussed earlier, the LOC that the MBHO or other insurer authorizes for the patient is determined by the symptoms that the patient is experiencing at the time of the request, the type of treatment that is effective and most appropriate for the patient's symptom intensity level, and the availability of that treatment (see the next paragraph). There are several levels of care that may be available to the patient. The more restrictive levels are used for stabilization of the patient or to help ensure the safety of the patient or others. Health plans will vary in the number and types of LOCs they cover, based on the needs of the particular health plan membership that they serve.

Availability and accessibility of appropriate services. Having adequate coverage for the types of services that the patient requires is no guarantee that those services are either available to or accessible for the patient. *Availability* refers to whether the services that are required are indeed available to the patient. For example, does the provider network of the patient's health plan include Spanish-speaking clinicians for Spanish-speaking patients? Does it include a residential treatment facility for substance abusers needing such care? Does it include providers who specialize in treating eating disorders for patients diagnosed with anorexia nervosa or bulimia? Availability also has to do with the number of sessions that the health plan authorizes or that the patient can pay for.

Accessibility refers to the ability of the patient to receive needed treatment that is available. In other words, do the clinician's office hours allow the patient to make appointments that are convenient to the patient's work schedule? Is there a psychiatrist on the HMO provider panel who can schedule the ADHD patient for monthly medication follow-up visits? Does the depressed patient with suicidal ideation have the means of getting to an emergency room or 24-hour crisis intervention drop-in center in time?

Generally, issues related to availability and accessibility of services arise infrequently. However, when they are present, they can be quite problematic. It is at these times that the clinician should carefully explore other options for treatment (e.g., through state- or federally funded programs) with the patient.

Referral for Evaluation of Other Psychiatric, Psychological, or Medical Problems and Issues

Occasionally, the clinical assessment will indicate the need for referral to one or more other professionals. Generally, this will be for evaluation or treatment of problems that (a) appear to be directly related to the reason for the patient's seeking services, or (b) are not directly related to the patient's problems but whose resolution would facilitate the patient's treatment.

Psychiatric and Medical. Referral for evaluation by a psychiatrist or other medical practitioner (e.g., the patient's PCP) is called for under a few general conditions. The most common is when the patient appears to be a good candidate for psychopharmacologic intervention, either alone or in conjunction with psychotherapy or other mode of intervention.

Psychiatric and medical referrals are also appropriate when there is a question about whether the patient's problems are part of the manifestation of a physical disease or disorder. For example, the sudden onset of impaired memory and concentration, visual hallucinations, violent outbursts, and impulsive behavior in a 45-year-old male with no history of mental health or substance abuse problems should lead one to suspect the presence of an organically based problem. In this case, referral to a neurologist—either directly or through a psychiatrist—would be appropriate, particularly if other symptoms (e.g., speech and gait disturbances) have also been observed. Referrals also are appropriate whenever the patient's history is suggestive of significant physical diseases or disorders that have gone unevaluated or untreated, or for which treatment has been inappropriately discontinued.

Neuropsychological. Neuropsychological evaluation by either a neuropsychologist or other qualified clinician can be extremely useful in clarifying the functional deficits (and assets) of patients with a history of known brain dysfunction (e.g., stroke victims, patients with closed head injuries). Not only can this type of information help identify the types of therapeutic approaches or techniques patients can benefit from, it also may help determine what can realistically be achieved in and out of treatment sessions, given their limitations. Arranging for regularly scheduled (e.g., annual) reevaluations of neuropsychological functioning would also be called for with patients suffering from dementing diseases.

Social services. A referral to any number of social service agencies may be beneficial for many patients. For those in the lower socioeconomic classes, ensuring that they have been evaluated by the state or county welfare agency for eligibility for benefits (e.g., health care, food stamps, job training) would be extremely important. Other social services agencies (e.g., Family Services, Catholic Charities, Planned Parenthood) may also provide evaluation and informational services that will benefit patients and support the behavioral health care treatment efforts.

> ### CAUTION
> ....
>
> - Failure to refer patients to other professionals for evaluation when appropriate may ultimately lessen the effectiveness of the prescribed behavioral health intervention.
> - Referrals for evaluations should be made only to those qualified by education, training, or experience to perform such evaluations.

Educational. Referrals for educational evaluations are appropriate for patients with a suspected developmental or learning disability. Generally, this type of evaluation is the responsibility of the local school system, but such services may not be available for older teens or adults. In these latter cases, a referral to an independent educational specialist would be called for.

Vocational or career interest. People do not generally turn to a clinician because they do not know what they want to do with their lives. However, uncertainty about one's career path or dissatisfaction with one's current profession can figure prominently in problems that can lead a person to seek psychological treatment. For this reason, patients for whom either of these concerns cause or exacerbate their behavioral health problems would benefit from a referral to a career counselor or professional trained in conducting vocational interest assessment (e.g., a counseling psychologist).

Other. Any number of other types of evaluation for specific problems may be appropriate for a given patient. Depending on the patient, the types of services offered by speech pathologists, occupational therapists, pastoral counselors, attorneys, dieticians, and other professionals whose work focuses on improving people's ability to function, their quality of life, or their sense of well-being can be useful for the patient both within and outside the therapy session.

Criteria for Treatment Transfer or Termination

No treatment plan would be complete without an indication of the criteria for successful treatment. Both the clinician and the patient must have an agreed-upon point at which treatment or a portion thereof is considered complete and the services being offered to the patient are terminated or transferred to a more appropriate LOC. In general, the criteria employed should be objective and measurable and should reflect the stated goals and objectives. Vague, unspecified, or no criteria can lead to the provision of treatment with no clearly defined endpoint—a circumstance that can result in unfocused therapeutic efforts that lead one to question the goals of treatment.

The criteria for treatment termination should be different for patients being seen at different LOCs. Whereas the criteria for termination (i.e., discharge) from a mental health inpatient unit may include things such as symptom control, initiation of a medication regimen, and no longer being dangerous to self or others, termination of outpatient services will be quite different. Here, the criteria may include things such as the elimination of significant psychiatric symptomatology, return to gainful employment, resolution of marital conflict, or involvement in an organized group for socialization. Again, the criteria should be objective and measurable. Examples of how the inpatient and outpatient termination criteria noted here can be presented in objective, measurable terms are presented in Rapid Reference 5.9.

≡Rapid Reference 5.9

Examples of Objective, Measurable Treatment Termination Criteria

Termination Criterion	Objective, Measurable Criterion
Symptom control	Patient eats at least two meals each day and sleeps 7–8 hours each night.
Initiation of a medication regimen	Patient was begun on and is able to tolerate a regimen of SSRI antidepressants for 1 week.
No longer dangerous to self or others	Patient expresses no suicidal or homicidal ideation for 48 hours.
Elimination of significant symptomatology	Patient scores 60T or lower on all scales of the Brief Symptom Inventory.
Return to gainful employment	Patient has worked for 2 months without any absences.
Resolution of marital conflict	Patient and spouse have reported the resolution of 10 conflictual issues without resorting to verbal or physical aggression.
Involvement in a service or fraternal organization	Patient has joined and has attended regular meetings of the American Legion during the past 6 months.

Similarly, criteria can be established for transferring the patient from one LOC to another, across the entire continuum of care, during the entire episode of care. For example, one of the goals for patients admitted for inpatient treatment will most often be to stabilize the patient to the point that they can be transferred or *stepped down* to a lower LOC, such as to a partial hospitalization, intensive outpatient, or outpatient program. In these cases, the criteria would not reflect the accomplishment of problem resolution; rather, they would be indicative of the patient's achieving an improvement in psychological status that would indicate the need for continued treatment through a less restrictive LOC. For instance, one criterion for inpatient treatment listed in the LOC guidelines employed by UBH (2001) indicates that the patient's level of disturbance requires 24-hour management and supervision. Stepping the treatment of the patient down to partial hospitalization care would not necessitate that the patient's functioning is no longer inadequate, but only that it no longer requires 24-hour supervision.

Responsible Staff

Having indicated the patient's problems, goals, objectives, and interventions, it is now necessary to indicate who will be responsible for overseeing and providing the care the patient will receive. The number of people involved in the treatment of the patient will vary according to the LOC at which the treatment is delivered, the patient's individual needs, and the available resources, including the types of services that are covered by the patient's health plan.

Primary Provider

The primary provider that is identified should be the clinician who will have the ultimate responsibility for the care that has been prescribed in the treatment plan. In the higher, more restrictive LOCs there may be little choice as to who will be the patient's primary provider. On an inpatient unit, this will usually be the attending psychiatrist. However, once the patient is discharged to a lower LOC (e.g., partial hospitalization, outpatient), the responsibility will commonly shift to another clinician who will be providing or overseeing the care in that setting.

The most common scenario involves the patient who is seen for outpatient treatment. The clinician who conducts the clinical assessment and develops the case formulation and treatment plan typically provides the psychotherapeutic services and is identified as the primary provider. However, in a clinic, group practice, or other situation in which care could be provided by any of a number of clinicians, one should consider the options that are available. Especially in cases involving high-risk problems, every effort should be made to match a patient's problem (e.g., bulimia) with a clinician skilled in treating that type of problem (e.g., a psychologist with specialized training and experience in treating eating disorders). Other considerations should come into play as well. For instance, Beutler (1991) identified the importance of looking at the similarities and differences between the patient and the clinician to determine whether there is good fit. He noted that

> a good match ... is one in which there are sufficient similarities to establish a common bond and sufficient differences to induce cognitive dissonance and to motivate change. A working position is to encourage therapist-patient pairs that share demographic similarity, but which hold quite different attitudes around those belief systems that are implicated in the patient's problems. These differences usually revolve around perspectives of emotional and social attachments. (pp. 459–460)

Of course, the earlier discussion of the importance of considering the interaction of patient, clinician, and type of treatment is relevant here.

Other Care Providers

Other health care and social services providers frequently are involved in the patient's overall mental health or substance abuse treatment. Common examples inlcude psychiatrists or PCPs providing psychopharmacotherapy, social workers, vocational rehabilitation counselors, and clergy. Because coordination among all providers is necessary to ensure quality care, the name of all providers (individual, facility, or organization) or the types of adjunctive service (if any) also should be indicated.

Care Manager or Coordinator

At times, the patient's third-party insurer will assign a specific person to oversee or manage the care of the patient to ensure that the patient is receiving quality treatment. In instances in which this information is known, it should also be noted in the treatment plan.

Treatment Plan Review Date

There should always be a time indicated for treatment plan to be reviewed. When this should occur will depend on a number of factors, including the severity and chronicity of the patient's problems, the timelines that were indicated for the completion of goals and objectives, the requirements of the patient's insurer for periodic treatment plan review, and expectations for time of recovery. For example, for a patient undergoing short-term planned treatment, the clinician may wish to schedule the review date to coincide with the projected date of treatment completion. On the other hand, the clinician might want to review the treatment plan of another patient being seen for uncomplicated major depression 6 months from the time of treatment initiation. However, annual review of the treatment plan may be quite appropriate for a chronic schizophrenic patient whose condition has remained stable for 2 years.

WRITING TREATMENT PLANS FOR MBHOS

The treatment plan content and format that have been recommended up to this point might be considered ideal from this author's perspective. Some behavioral health care groups or organizations have a standard treatment-plan template developed specifically for use within the group or organization. These templates usually elicit the minimum information that is required for the group or organization to make treatment authorization decisions and meet specific accreditation (e.g., NCQA, JCAHO) or regulatory (e.g., state, federal) requirements. Of particular note are the treatment plans that MBHOs require their provider panels to submit.

MBHOs often have a standard treatment-plan form that they require providers to complete and submit for authorization to provide initial or continued patient services. Actually, these forms are not strictly treatment planning forms because they are used to elicit information for a variety of purposes (e.g., determination of medical necessity, report of patient progress, report of the clinician's adherence to the MBHO's particular expectations for providers). Typically, the clinician is asked in a page or two to provide basic information related to current problems and symptomatology (usually via rating scales), previous treatment, assessment of risk, diagnosis, current medications, treatment goals, planned interventions, and type and amount of services requested. Frequently, the clinician will also be asked to indicate whether the patient has been screened for substance abuse, and whether the patient's PCP has been notified about the patient's receiving behavioral health care services. When continued services are being requested, the clinician is usually asked to provide a report of the patient's progress up to that point, as well.

In writing treatment plans for MBHOs, it is helpful for the clinician to keep in mind the orientation or philosophy of managed care as it pertains to the treatment of behavioral health care patients. In general, MBHOs are oriented to providing brief therapeutic interventions that are focused on symptom alleviation of patients meeting medical necessity criteria. Thus, plans that include lengthy treatment (except with chronic conditions such as schizophrenia), that are focused on characterological or personality changes, or that are intended to help the patient reach some nebulous state such as self-actualization or self-realization are not going to be well received by MBHO care managers who are charged with reviewing and approving treatment plans.

One large MBHO has offered useful suggestions for writing the goals, interventions, and outcomes criteria sections of treatment plans (UBS, 1994). These are presented in Rapid Reference 5.10. Note the consistency of these recommendations with those that were describe earlier for treatment plans in

≡Rapid Reference 5.10

Recommendations for Writing Initial Treatment Plans for MBHOs

Treatment Plan Section	Recommendations
Goals	• Relate to symptom alleviation
	• State in behavioral terms
	• Ensure achievability
Interventions	• Indicate in behavioral terms what the clinician will do
	• Indicate in behavioral terms what the patient will do
Outcomes	• Indicate in behaviorally specific terms what the patient will be doing differently
	• Indicate in behaviorally specific terms what the criteria for goal attainment are

Note. From UBS (1994).

general. For treatment plans that are submitted in support of or as requests for continuing treatment, the MBHO recommends (a) documenting the progress made thus far, (b) describing current symptoms in specific, measurable terms, (c) relating goals to symptom alleviation, and (d) establishing criteria for treatment termination.

SUMMARY

The development of the treatment plan represents the end product of the clinician's efforts to understand the patient, the patient's problems, and the patient's consequent needs. It is a document that is intended for the use of not only the therapist, but also the patient and those responsible for the payment of the services the patient receives. It organizes and conveys the plan of action for the therapeutic intervention and thus can help ensure consistency between patient and therapist expectations. It also can help ensure that the patient has realistic expectations for the outcomes of treatment. Moreover, it can serve to support the therapist's requests for continued services and to help meet provider accreditation requirements.

The content of treatment plans will differ, varying by the clinician who develops the plan, the expectations of the setting in which the services will be offered to the patient, and the demands of payers and other third parties with a vested interest in the patient's care. However, at the minimum, it is recommended that the treatment plan state the patient's presenting problem, source of and reason for referral, problem list, and diagnoses. Realistic goals that are both achievable by the patient and measurable in terms of being able to determine objectively any progress made toward them must be clearly indicated. These goals should be prioritized based on the seriousness or severity of the identified problems. At the same time, one may need to ensure that the patient is provided with the opportunity to be reinforced for efforts early in the treatment process in order to establish an adequate level of motivation and engagement in the therapy.

The treatment plan should thoroughly document all planned interventions, including the LOC in which they will be offered, the mode(s) of intervention (including both strategies and tactics), and the frequency and duration of treatment. The selected intervention should take into consideration the unique aspects of the patient and the clinician in relation to the type of treatment that

Putting It Into Practice

Case Study of Mary Smith (*continued*)

TREATMENT PLAN

Name: Mary Smith

Date: October 12, 2001

Referral Source and Reason for Referral

Mary Smith is a 28-year-old Caucasian, married female who is a second-year student at the Acme University School of Law. She was referred to this clinic by the school's counseling center after it was determined that Ms. Smith is experiencing psychological problems that the counseling center would not be able to treat effectively.

Presenting Problem

According to Ms. Smith, "I can't get these thoughts out of my head. I can't concentrate. It's getting worse and it's affecting my ability to study. I don't know what I'll do if I flunk out of school."

Problem List

Based on interviews with her and her husband, as well as the results of psychological testing, Ms. Smith is currently experiencing the following problems:

- Long-standing obsessions and compulsive behaviors that have recently intensified and have resulted in significant impairment in her ability to concentrate on her schoolwork and other tasks.
- Depressed mood and accompanying symptoms of depression (sleep and appetite disturbance).
- Significant, generalized psychological distress.
- Inability to decline responsibility for meeting the needs and expectations of those close to her.
- Inability to express anger in an appropriate, effective manner.

Diagnosis

Ms. Smith meets the criteria for the following *DSM-IV-TR* diagnoses:

Axis I   300.3 Obsessive-compulsive disorder
           300.4 Dysthymic disorder
Axis II   Rule out 301.4 Obsessive-compulsive personality disorder
Axis III   None
Axis IV   Academic problems; stress from familial demands
Axis V   GAF = 70 (current)

Goals and Objectives

The goals and objectives of Ms. Smith's treatment will include the following:

- Return of concentration ability to premorbid level within 1 month.
- Improvement in mood, appetite, and ability to sleep within 1 month.

(continued)

- Development of effective means of reducing or eliminating obsessions and compulsions and their effects on Ms. Smith's functioning within 6 months.
- Development of the ability to recognize and effectively implement limits of her responsibility and duty to others within 6 months.

Treatment

Treatment will consist of weekly outpatient psychotherapy sessions over a course of at least 6 months. The following will be employed to attain the stated goals and objectives:

- As appropriate, psychopharmacological treatment of symptoms of anxiety and depression, including her impaired concentration.
- Insight-oriented approach to instilling an understanding of the nature of both her long-standing and her current problems.
- A cognitive-behavioral psychotherapeutic approach to reducing or eliminating obsessions and compulsions. Relaxation training, thought-stopping, and self-monitoring are among the techniques that will be employed.
- Assertiveness training to assist Ms. Smith in expressing anger in an appropriate manner, as well as in saying no to requests and demands for her to assume more responsibility for others than is reasonable, especially given the demands that she currently contends with.
- Conjoint marital therapy to increase Mr. Smith's awareness of all of the demands that are being placed on his wife as well as what she views as important for her future in the way of family and career goals.
- Monitoring of treatment progress every other treatment session on the following measures: OQ-45 Total, SD, IR, and SR raw scores; average number of obsessions and compulsions that occur during the course of a day; and self-rating of concentration ability on a 7-point Likert scale.

Patient Strengths

Following are characteristics or other aspects that should assist Ms. Smith in benefiting from psychological intervention:

- High level of intellectual functioning
- Ability to gain insight into her problems
- Motivation to change
- Ability to tolerate high levels of stress

Potential Barriers to Treatment

- Husband's questionable willingness to engage in treatment and otherwise support his wife in her therapeutic efforts. This will be addressed in conjoint marital therapy, assuming that he displays at least some degree of cooperation with the therapeutic endeavor.

Referral for Evaluation

Ms. Smith will be referred to Dr. John Jones, staff psychiatrist, for evaluation for appropriateness of psychopharmacotherapy for symptoms of anxiety and depression.

Criteria for Treatment Termination

Treatment will be terminated when the following criteria are met:

- Ability to concentrate is reported to have returned to premorbid levels.
- Occurrence of both self-monitored obsessions and compulsions decreases to less than 50% of baseline levels.
- OQ-45 Total scale score is less than 63.
- OQ-45 SD scale score is less than 30.
- OQ-45 SR scale score is less than 15.

Treatment Plan Review Date

The treatment plan will be reviewed in 3 months, by which time significant improvement is expected.

Responsible Staff

Mark Maruish, PhD, staff psychologist, will be Ms. Smith's primary therapist and will assume responsibility for the management and coordination of all care provided to Ms. Smith. Dr. Jones will manage her psychopharmacotherapy if Ms. Smith is found likely to benefit from a regimen of antidepressant or other medications.

appears most appropriate. Only treatments that have been shown to yield positive outcomes should be considered. However, as Sechrest (2001, p. 17) has noted, "Establishing an evidence base does not necessarily mean that practice must be limited to a few manualized treatments. Evidence can be developed for strategies and principles as well as for specific treatment maneuvers, but the evidence must be there and be persuasive."

With regard to how often and for how long the treatment will take place, all but those patients suffering from chronic disorders should be considered for a course of short-term planned therapy. However, this may depend on several factors, not the least of which is the patient's ability to achieve all the stated goals within a reasonable amount of time. Referral to other professionals or service agencies for evaluation or adjunctive services may be necessary in order to ensure that other needs that are either directly or indirectly related to those for which the patient is seeking behavioral health care services are also met.

A listing of anticipated barriers to the patient's receiving maximum benefit from treatment should be presented, along with potential solutions to avoiding or overcoming these barriers. Depending on the patient's problems and the LOC in which treatment initially is being provided, criteria for continued treatment, transfer to a lower LOC, or termination should be clearly stated.

This should be accompanied by a date or time frame for reviewing the plan and the patient's progress toward meeting the goals of treatment. Finally, identification of the clinician with primary responsibility for the patient's care as well as all other care providers involved in the treatment of the patient is a key component of the treatment plan.

Treatment plans developed for MBHOs frequently serve multiple purposes. Consequently, MBHOs usually require the use of a standard form that elicits all the information that the managed care company is interested in. In developing treatment plans for patients covered by this type of behavioral health care, the wise clinician will provide all of the requested information and present (as appropriate) a plan for a brief, problem-oriented intervention. Failure to do so may result in a denial of payment for the requested services.

🖋 TEST YOURSELF 🖋

....

1. **Who are the potential users of a treatment plan?**
   (a) The clinician
   (b) The patient
   (c) The patient's insurer
   (d) a and b
   (e) a and c
   (f) All of the above

2. **Which of the following is *not* a common element of treatment planning?**
   (a) Problem identification
   (b) Treatment goals
   (c) Flexibility over the course of treatment
   (d) Approval by a consulting practitioner
   (e) Intervention strategies

3. **Only those problems identified by the patient should be included in the problem list.** True or False?

4. **Which of the following is an important characteristic of all goals and objectives?**

    (a) Easy to achieve within a short period of time

    (b) Progress toward them can be measured

    (c) Stated in negative language

    (d) Determined by the clinician

    (e) a and b

    (f) c and d

5. **Treatment should not be attempted when there are no empirically supported therapies for the patient's problem.** True or False?

6. **When considering how to treat the patient's problems, the clinician should**

    (a) use the same therapeutic approach consistently throughout the course of treatment.

    (b) consider each individual problem to determine whether different techniques are warranted.

    (c) always refer the patient to a psychiatrist to determine whether psychopharmacologic intervention is warranted.

    (d) always use a multimodal approach.

7. **As a general rule, treatment plans should be reviewed**

    (a) every 30 days.

    (b) no longer than 6 months after the initiation of treatment, and every 6 months thereafter if necessary.

    (c) only at those times required by the patient's insurance company.

    (d) whenever deemed appropriate by factors relevant to the individual patient.

8. **What could you do to get patients actively involved in setting their own treatment goals and objectives?** _____

9. **Thinking about the types of problems that are seen in general clinical practice, what are some examples of types of problems or diagnoses that would *generally* be amenable to short-term planned treatment? What types of interventions would you consider for each of those problems?** _____

(continued)

10. **Imagine that you are seeing two patients with the exact same problems. One is an out-of-pocket, self-pay patient with unlimited resources while the other is receiving prepaid services through an MBHO. All other things being equal, how might the treatment plans be developed differently, if at all?** _____

_____

Answers: 1. f; 2. d; 3. False; 4. b; 5. False; 6. b; 7. d; 8. have patients identify what problems they want to work on first, review the draft treatment plan with the patient for approval, explain the purpose of the plan, and obtain informed consent; 9. adjustment disorders, acute situational crises, specific phobias, mild anxiety and mild depression, with cognitive or behavioral therapy, or with effective means of providing relief from these problems in relatively short amounts of time; 10. more options with regard to treatment approach, duration of treatment, use of psychological testing, and more LOCs might be available to self-pay patients.

Six

MONITORING TREATMENT PROGRESS: IMPLICATIONS FOR TREATMENT PLANNING

Monitoring the progress of planned treatment is an essential component of behavioral health care quality assurance (Campbell, 1992). It is useful to all stakeholders in mental health and substance abuse care, but it is particularly valuable to clinicians and patients. This is especially the case with those patients who are seen over relatively long periods of time. In addition to enabling the tracking of improvement during treatment, information obtained from ongoing monitoring of patients can provide additional insights into them and their problems and, consequently, can facilitate needed revisions to the case formulation. Makover (1992) has noted that "continual reformulation of the case sharpens the focus of the therapy so that new revisions may achieve successive approximations to the truth" (p. 342). If the treatment has not resulted in the expected effects but a clearer picture of the patient is obtained, appropriate changes in the treatment plan can be formulated and deployed. Furthermore, Mumma (1998) has indicated that

> in order to capture the flexibility inherent in [case] formulation-based treatment planning . . . , the treatment plan and operationalization needs to be dynamic—to change and be responsive to information that becomes available as the treatment progresses. . . . Thus, the criteria for effective implementation of the plan may change as the therapy progresses and the formulation evolves. By implication, evaluation of adequacy of treatment implementation needs to be tied to the formulation and plan extant at a particular phase of treatment. (p. 269)

The adjustments to treatment plans may reflect the need for (a) more intensive or aggressive treatment (e.g., increased number of psychotherapeutic sessions each week, addition of a medication adjunct), (b) less intensive treatment (e.g., reduction or discontinuation of medication, transfer from inpatient to outpatient care), (c) a different therapeutic approach (e.g., changing from analytic therapy to cognitive-behavioral therapy), or (d) a combination of changes in the treatment plan. Regardless, any modifications require later reassessment of the patient to determine whether the treatment revisions have affected patient progress in the expected direction. This process may be repeated any number of times. These in-treatment reassessments also can provide information relevant to the decision of when to terminate treatment.

The development of a plan for monitoring treatment progress requires careful consideration of a number of issues if one is to obtain useful information. This chapter presents a discussion of the key issues that should be addressed in the course of developing, implementing, and effectively using a system for monitoring progress according to a plan of treatment.

GENERAL PROCESSES FOR TREATMENT MONITORING

Figure 6.1 presents a general process for treatment monitoring. In this particular paradigm, a screening process has been incorporated into the clinical assessment process. The results of the screening thus may serve as the source of the baseline data against which data obtained at other points in treatment can be compared. This assumes, of course, that the screening measure assesses variables that one wishes to use to monitor treatment progress, and that the same measure is used throughout the monitoring process.

Once baseline data are obtained, a reassessment of the patient on those variables selected for tracking occurs at regularly scheduled points in the therapeutic process. Those clinicians with the necessary resources also can generate an expected *recovery curve* for the patient (discussed later). This curve will enable the clinician to determine whether the patient is on the expected track for recovery throughout the episode of care, based on the amount and speed of recovery of other patients with similar characteristics. Absent the ability to generate recovery curves, the clinician can employ a variety of means to determine whether the patient is making appropriate progress toward recovery (also discussed later). Regardless of the approach, deviations noted on remeasurement are evaluated and modification of the treatment is considered. Modifications to the plan are implemented if necessary, and the planned monitoring continues.

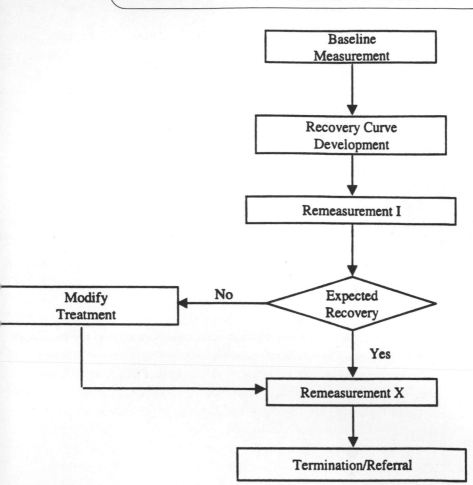

Figure 6.1. Flow chart for a general treatment monitoring process.

Note. From *Psychological Testing in the Age of Managed Behavioral Health Care* (p. 43), by M. E. Maruish, 2002, Mahwah, NJ: Lawrence Erlbaum Associates. Reprinted with permission.

Callaghan (2001) has recommended a series of steps for data-based treatment monitoring that provide useful supplements to the process just described. As summarized in Rapid Reference 6.1, these are as follows:

1. Select an appropriate intervention based on the findings of the clinical interview. However, as indicated in previous chapters of this

Rapid Reference 6.1

Steps to Monitoring Treatment Progress

1. Select an appropriate intervention.
2. Select useful instrumentation for monitoring.
3. Enlist the patient's cooperation in the treatment-monitoring process.
4. Gather baseline data.
5. Provide feedback to the patient after each assessment.
6. Determine whether treatment is effective, and modify treatment if necessary.
7. Monitor progress throughout the course of treatment.
8. If possible, monitor patient status after treatment termination.

Note. From Callaghan (2001).

book, data from other sources of information (e.g., psychological testing, collateral interviews, medical chart reviews) should be obtained and considered along with interview findings when determining the most appropriate intervention for any patient.

2. For the purpose of treatment monitoring, select instrumentation that would provide useful information to both the clinician and the patient during the course of treatment. Preference should be given to standardized instruments, but idiographic measures should be considered if standardized instrumentation appropriate to the patient's problems and goals is not available. Also consider using a combination of both types of instrumentation to allow both individualized assessment and comparison to the results of other patients, clinicians, and types of interventions.

3. Enlist the patient's cooperation in completing the instrumentation. Discuss the reason for wanting the patient to complete the monitoring instrument several times during treatment, including how it will help both parties to determine what does and does not work, to get past therapeutic impasses, and generally to stay on track and ensure treatment is progressing.

4. Begin gathering assessment data before treatment begins, or at least

as soon as possible afterwards. This will provide the baseline measure necessary for determining the meaning of data gathered at points later in treatment.

5. Provide the patient with feedback as soon as possible after each assessment. This will not only demonstrate to the patient how this information helps the clinician, but it will also help reinforce the patient's continued participation in the ongoing data-gathering process.

6. Use the data to determine what seems to be effective or is not resulting in the expected improvements. As necessary, modify the intervention.

7. Continue the treatment monitoring process (assessment, feedback to patient, treatment adjustment) throughout the course of therapy until treatment is terminated.

8. Whenever possible, schedule a posttreatment follow-up session to gather additional data about how the patient has been doing since the termination of treatment.

For those with necessary resources, Callaghan (2001) has two other recommendations. One is for the clinician to graphically or otherwise visually display individual patient data over time. The other is to create an electronic database for storing monitoring data and other patient information (e.g., problems, diagnoses, type or types of treatment). Both would facilitate the tracking of treatment progress over time. They also would enable the clinician to make comparisons across patients and on other selected variables, and thus to garner information about what works for whom.

Overall, the preceding discussion is intended to provide an overview of the important components needed to establish a means of monitoring a patient's progress through the course of treatment. The scheme presented in Figure 6.1 and that proposed by Callaghan are relatively broad and simplistic, but they serve as good starting points or frameworks from which to conceptualize a useful means of monitoring treatment. Developing and implementing a useful and effective treatment-tracking system requires careful consideration of a number of variables that can be easily overlooked or not be fully appreciated until its too late. The sections that follow address the more important of these factors.

WHAT TO MONITOR

Deciding to monitor treatment and then committing to that decision are the first hurdles in the development and implementation of any type of monitoring process or program. This can be a difficult process. Once these hurdles are met, the clinician must make another difficult decision—that is, which variables to monitor. Probably the most frequently monitored variable is symptomatology, or psychological or mental health status. This is because disruption in these dimensions is probably the most common reason people seek behavioral health care services in the first place. However, there are other reasons for seeking help. Common examples include difficulties in coping with various types of role expectations or life transitions (e.g., a new job, a recent marriage or divorce, other changes in the work or home environment), an inability to deal with the behavior of others (e.g., spouse, children), or general dissatisfaction with life. Thus, one may find that for some patients, improved functioning on the job, at school, or with family or friends is much more relevant and important than symptom reduction. For other patients, improvement in quality of life or sense of well-being may be more meaningful.

It is no simple matter to determine exactly what should be measured and monitored. In the end, the most important variables to monitor are those that are tied to the patient's goals and objectives. However, the issue is sometimes complicated by a desire to meet the needs of each individual patient and, for better or worse, those of the relevant third parties (e.g., insurers). At the same time, careful consideration of the following questions should greatly facilitate the decision.

What Are the Goals and Objectives of Treatment?

As suggested previously, the goals and objectives of the treatment plan should be the primary consideration in the selection of what to monitor. This is why it is important that one criterion for the selection of goals and objectives is that they be measurable (see chapter 5).

What Are the Clinician's Criteria for the Successful Completion of Treatment?

What the patient identifies as being important to accomplish during treatment might reflect a lack of insight into that person's problems, or it might be inconsistent with what an impartial, trained observer would consider indicative of meaningful improvement. Ideally, these issues would have been resolved during the goal-setting part of treatment planning. However, for any number of reasons, this resolution may not have occurred. In cases such as these, it may be appropriate for the clinician to determine what else constitutes therapeutic success and the variables associated with these criteria, and to measure progress toward these criteria along with the mutually agreed upon goals and objectives.

Will the Measurement of the Selected Variables Lead to Actionable Information?

There may be a number of variables that could provide information related to the degree to which the patient is benefiting from treatment. One will likely find, however, that only a relative few provide actionable information. For example, suppose a clinician frequently provides services to patients who experience work-related difficulties. Any number of behaviors could contribute to these problems. A detailed assessment of various aspects of these patients' work lives can uncover specific reasons they are experiencing impairment in on-the-job functioning. Thus, one would routinely want to assess variables such as relationships with peers, relationships with supervisors, productivity, tardiness, or absences with these types of patients. The results would provide clues as to what aspect of work functioning to focus the intervention efforts on and to monitor, thus increasing the probability of improved work functioning.

What Are Significant Third Parties' Criteria for the Successful Completion of the Treatment?

From a strict therapeutic perspective, this should be given the least amount of consideration. From a more realistic perspective, one cannot overlook the expectations and limitations that one or more third parties have for the treatment that is rendered. The expectations and limitations set by the patient's parents or guardian, significant other, health plan, employer, teacher, court system, third-party payer, practice guidelines, and possibly other external forces may significantly play into the decision about what is considered successful treatment or when to terminate treatment. Consequently, these expectations may dictate what is monitored.

Are There Any Organizational Initiatives for Treatment Monitoring?

In an organizational setting, one may not be able to ignore any ongoing, system-wide treatment-monitoring or quality-improvement programs in which data on specific domains of functioning are routinely gathered on *all* patients. This may not necessarily preclude monitoring additional, patient-specific variables, but doing so may have an impact on the burden to the patient and staff (discussed later).

Are the Selected Variables Meaningful or Useful Across the Levels of Care?

In cases of the more severely impaired or chronic patients, the clinician would be well advised to consider whether the measures chosen for tracking the selected variables are appropriate for use across the continuum of care. This would allow for a more accurate determination of improvement as the patient transitions from one LOC to another (e.g., from inpatient to partial hospitalization to outpatient). For example, the symptom domains assessed by symptom checklists such as the BSI might be better as monitoring measures than those domains assessed by the BPRS in settings where a relatively high percentage of patients begin an episode of care through inpatient treatment but later transition to outpatient treatment. Unlike those assessed by the BPRS, the symptom domains measured by the BSI are much more relevant across the continuum of care and thus lend themselves better to tracking a greater percentage of patients during an episode of care.

What is the Burden of Monitoring the Selected Variables?

The task of monitoring treatment progress should not become too burdensome in terms of the patient, clinician, or required financial resources. As a general rule, the more data one attempts to gather from a given patient or collateral, the more costly the endeavor will be and the less likely any data at all will be obtained. The key is to identify the point at which the amount of data that can be obtained (from a patient, collaterals, or both) and the ease and cost at which it can be gathered are optimized. The issue has to do not only with the number of variables, but also with the difficulty one might experience in obtaining data for a single variable or from a single source. For example, a clinician might choose to use data from a structured clinical interview. This type of data might provide excellent, useful information that meets the needs of several stakeholders. At the same time, the fact that obtaining this data would require a total of 2 hours of unreimbursed clinical staff time would prohibit the use of this method.

In addition to the cost and availability of clinical or administrative labor, burden might also present itself in other forms, such as training staff in how to obtain the desired data, getting patients to complete standardized measures on multiple occasions, or the need to develop customized instrumentation. Again, the issue here is one of practicality given patient, clinician, and organizational resources and capabilities.

> **DON'T FORGET**
>
> Variables that are monitored during the course of treatment should
>
> - provide information that tells the clinician and patient what aspects of treatment should be continued or changed.
> - provide an indication of progress toward successful treatment as defined by all stakeholders in the patient's treatment.
> - entail minimal burden.
> - be meaningful across all LOCs in which the patient is likely to receive care.

HOW TO MONITOR

One of the most important considerations related to how treatment monitoring data are obtained is from where or whom this data should come. Equally important is how that data will be elicited. The desire for certain types of data may necessitate the use of specific sources of information, whereas other types of data can be validly obtained from more than one source. The type of setting also may have a bearing on the selection of the best source of data (Berman, Hurt, & Heiss, 1996). Similarly, the available options for the means by which such data can be gathered can affect the choice of the method for monitoring the course of treatment.

Sources of Information

Just as during the clinical assessment phase, data obtained for the purpose of treatment monitoring may be obtained from any of several sources. The source determined to be most advantageous to use may be dependent on one or more variables related to the patient, the patient's particular circumstances, or the LOC in which the treatment is rendered.

Patient- versus Observer-Elicited Data

Issues related to the use of patient-completed versus observer-completed psychological instrumentation for clinical assessment purposes were discussed in chapter 3. The points made during that discussion are also pertinent to the use of these instruments for treatment monitoring and therefore will not be repeated here.

Self-Monitoring

Another source of treatment-monitoring data is the patient. According to Korotitsch and Nelson-Gray (1999), this form of patient self-report refers to "an assessment procedure that involves data collection made by the [patient] primarily within naturalistic settings" (*Introduction,* para. 1). On the continuum of directness of assessment, it falls between direct observation in a naturalistic setting (most direct) and interview and self-report measures (most indirect). Barton, Blanchard, and Veazey (1999) view it as the preferred choice of assessing symptoms and other internal, subjective states. Jackson (1999) states that at the minimum, a system of self-monitoring requires the specification of (a) behaviors, thoughts, or emotions targeted for monitoring; (b) the qualities of those dimensions to be monitored and recorded (e.g., frequency, duration); (c) the recording format (e.g., continuous, sample); and (d) the means of recording (e.g., notebook, hand-held digital assistant). The accurate recording of the target behaviors and evaluation of those recordings should also be included as important components of the system.

Self-monitoring as a treatment-monitoring tool has many advantages. As Korotitsch and Nelson-Gray (1999) point out, it is inexpensive, requires little in terms of resources, and allows for the assessment of both private or unobservable behaviors (e.g., sexual activity, paranoid ideation) and clinically relevant behaviors that occur in everyday life. It can inform the clinician about how well the patient is implementing the treatment interventions and can help identify difficulties in doing so. They also note Bornstein's observations that self-monitoring emphasizes the patient's control over his or her own behavior, provides the patient with continuous feedback about that behavior, and may allow for a more thorough description of the behavior than could otherwise be obtained.

Moreover, there is another potential benefit that can result from self-monitoring. In what Korotitsch and Nelson-Gray (1999) refer to as *reactivity*, the self-monitoring procedure becomes a therapeutic intervention because of the changes in the patient that occur as a result of the self-monitoring. As they point out, self-monitoring can lead to reactive effects on many types of symptoms and behaviors, including substance use, hallucinations, ruminative thinking, paranoid and suicidal ideation, and insomnia. This suggests that in addition to its use as an ongoing assessment procedure, self-monitoring can also be used as an adjunct to any other interventions that are included in the patient's treatment plan. Factors related to maximizing the potential for reactive effects through self-monitoring are presented in Rapid Reference 6.2.

Of course, just like any other procedure that might be used to monitor patient progress, the benefits that can accrue from self-monitoring depend a great deal on the accuracy of the data being provided by the patient. Based on their review of the literature, Korotitsch and Nelson-Gray (1999) have made recommendations for ways to maximize the accuracy of self-monitoring data. These are presented in Rapid Reference 6.3. Fortunately, they also note that ac-

Rapid Reference 6.2

Factors Related to Maximizing Reactivity Through Self-Monitoring

- Motivated patient
- Well-defined, motoric responses
- Explicit goals for change
- Reinforcement contingent on reactive effects
- Recordings made just prior to target behaviors
- Minimized concurrent response requirements

Note. From Korotitsch and Nelson-Gray (1999).

Rapid Reference 6.3

Means of Maximizing Accuracy of Self-Monitoring

- Well-defined, positive, and overt target responses
- Training provided to patient
- Patient's awareness that accuracy checks will be made
- Importance to treatment of accurate data stressed to patient
- Reinforcement of accurate data
- Minimized concurrent response requirements
- Recordings made just after target behaviors occur

Note. From Korotitsch and Nelson-Gray (1999).

curate reporting is not required in order for the patient to benefit from the reactive effects of self-monitoring.

Administrative Data

Another potential source of monitoring information is administrative data. In many of the larger clinical settings, this information can easily be retrieved through the organization's claims and authorization databases, data repositories and warehouses, and other databases that make up the organization's management information system (MIS). Data related to the patient's dose and regimen of medication, physical findings, medical and behavioral resource utilization, rehospitalization during a specific period of time, treatment costs, and other types of data typically stored in these systems can be useful in evaluating the progress of therapeutic interventions.

Multiple Sources

Many would agree that the ideal approach for gathering data would be the use of multiple sources (Berman et al., 1996; Berman, Rosen, Hurt, & Kolarz, 1998; Bieber et al., 1999; Lambert & Lambert, 1999; Strupp, 1996). Indeed, information based on data obtained from patients, collaterals, and administrative sources can provide enhanced insights into the effectiveness of the clinician's services. They also may facilitate the identification of root causes of problems within the treatment plan. Inherent in this approach, however, are increased costs and the potential for contradictory information and concomitant questions about how to proceed when contradictions occur. As Lambert and Lambert point out, "The data generated from these viewpoints are always subject to the limitations inherent in the methodology; none is 'objective' or most authoritative" (p. 116). Consequently, one must be prepared with approaches to resolving contradictory information.

CAUTION

- Administrative data are usually of limited utility. They should never be the sole means of monitoring treatment progress.

- Monitoring data obtained from multiple sources may yield contradictory information about the patient's treatment progress.

- The value of self-monitoring from patients who are poorly motivated or have not been adequately trained in the procedure will be of minimal value.

Selection of Psychological Tests for Treatment Monitoring

In addition to the general considerations for psychological measures discussed in chapter 3, the selection of test instruments for treatment-monitoring purposes requires considerations related to the fact that the instrument will be completed two or more times during the course of an episode of care. Based on this consideration alone, cost becomes a particularly important factor in the selection of a measure to be used for this purpose. However, other factors also come into play.

First, many instruments are designed to assess the patient's status at the time of testing. Items on these measures are generally worded in the present tense (e.g., "I feel tense and nervous," "I feel that my family loves and cares about me"). Changes from one day to the next on the constructs measured by these instruments should be reflected in the test results. Other instruments, however, ask the patient to indicate whether a variable of interest has been present, or how much or to what extent it has occurred *during a specific time period in the past*. The items usually are asked in the context of something like "During the past month, how often have you . . ." or "During the past week, to what extent has. . . ." Readministration of these interval-of-time–specific measures or subsets of items within them should be undertaken only after a period of time equivalent to or longer than the time interval to be considered in responding to the items has passed. For example, an instrument that asks the patient to consider the extent to which certain symptoms have been problematic during the past 7 days should not be readministered for at least 7 days. The responses from a readministration that occurs fewer than 7 days after the first administration would include the patient's consideration of his or her status during a portion of the previously considered time frame. This may make interpretation of the change of symptom status (if any) from the first to the second administration difficult, if not impossible.

Second, given that the purpose of repeated testing is to detect change in a patient's status on one or more domains of functioning, it is important that the selected instrument be sensitive to change that has

DON'T FORGET

General considerations for psychological instrument selection:

- Brevity
- Psychometric integrity
- Relevancy to the intended purpose of the assessment
- Availability of relevant normative data
- Cost
- Reading level
- Content
- Ease of use
- Comprehensibility of results

occurred over time. Here, good test-retest reliability is a key indicator of this sensitivity. Lambert and his colleagues (Burlingame, Lambert, Reisinger, Neff, & Mosier, 1995) indicate that the minimum acceptable reliability should be about .70. From this author's perspective, one would ideally want the reliability coefficients that are evaluated for acceptability for monitoring to be based on a demographically relevant *normal,* or community sample. It is difficult to tell what a stated reliability coefficient based on a patient sample really means. In these cases, is a low to moderate reliability on a given measure due to true change in the patient as a result of intervention, or is it a reflection of error variance that is built into the instrument? And what does high "patient-based reliability" mean? Does it indicate that the instrument is insensitive to change, or that the instrument was based on a sample that truly did not change as a result of intervention? For this reason, one should feel most confident with instruments with good community sample–based reliabilities.

WHEN TO MONITOR

The goal of monitoring is to determine whether treatment is on track with expected progress at a given point in time. When and how often one might assess the patient is dependent on a number of factors. The first is the expected length of treatment. Implementing a monitoring protocol with patients who are expected to be seen for only 4 or 5 sessions is not cost-effective and probably will not contribute much useful information. With patients who are likely to be seen for several sessions—for example, 10 or more—implementing a plan for regular, scheduled retesting during the episode of care can provide the clinician with information about whether the patient is adequately progressing toward recovery, given clinical expectations.

The second factor is the time frame that the patient must consider in responding to the items of an assessment instrument, or during which the presence or frequency of a monitored variable is counted. This issue was discussed earlier and thus will not be addressed again here.

The third consideration is the frequency at which the clinician finds monitoring activities useful. This can be dependent on any number of factors, such as expectations for speed of improvement based on clinical judgment, perceived impact of a critical life event (e.g., death of a spouse, loss of employment) on the patient's recovery, the clinician's past experience with monitoring similar patients, and the patient's reactions to repeated measurement of his or her psychological status. Because of the subjective nature of these variables, determination of the desired frequency of patient monitoring for any given patient is likely to vary from one clinician to another.

Finally, there are financial considerations. What will be the cost of reassessing patients? And how many reassessments are patients or their insurers willing to pay for (or is the clinician or provider organization willing to perform pro bono)? This may be more important to consider than the other three factors when determining how often to monitor patients, because multiple reassessments can be quite time consuming and expensive. They may also significantly impact the patient's available health care benefits.

HOW TO EVALUATE RESULTS

The types of analyses of treatment monitoring data can range from a simple charting of patient test scores or the frequency of target thoughts, emotions, or behaviors over time; to a comparison of a point-in-time performance, a normative standard or preselected treatment goal; to the calculation of inferential statistics that examine the significance of changes in the data from one measurement period to the next. It may also involve more sophisticated statistical procedures such as predictive modeling to identify at-risk patients. Knowing the types of analyses that need to be conducted will have a bearing on what, how, and when data are collected.

There are three general approaches to evaluating treatment-monitoring data. One is by determining whether the patient is making continuing progress toward a predetermined standard; another is by determining whether the patient has made progress based on a comparison of assessment results at one point in time to those from another assessment; and the third is through a combination of both types of comparisons.

Progress Toward a Standard

This means of analyzing treatment-monitoring data is the simplest, and it probably represents the most commonly employed means of tracking progress over time. It involves no more than monitoring patient progress through the trending of the data points during the course of treatment. The patient would be considered improving if the data trend toward some predetermined standard. A trend indicative of no improvement or deterioration of the patient's condition generally would call for the reevaluation and, most likely, revision of the treatment plan. There are a number of options for the standard that is selected for use with this method.

Individual Goals and Objectives

Whenever possible, the goals and objectives that are stated in the treatment plan should serve as the standard against which patient progress should be directly evaluated. Since this is not always possible, one may have to opt for a more indirect evaluation. For example, number of pounds lost each week during a 3-month period would serve as a direct measure for monitoring the treatment of obesity. On the other hand, elimination of depression is a common goal of treatment, but the construct of depression may not be easily monitored. In this case, tracking the number or frequency of occurrences of specific, measurable depressive symptoms (e.g., number of social activities engaged in, instances of sexual intercourse, or occurrences of suicidal ideation during a period of 1 week) can provide a valid indication of the progress that the patient is making toward the goal.

Normative Data

Population-specific normative data can serve as yet another standard against which to judge treatment progress. Standardized normative data that typically accompany published psychological tests is a good example. Most of these measures have nonpatient normative data that can be a useful (perhaps the most useful) source of comparison information. Many of these tests also include patient normative data that permit a fair comparison of similar behavioral health patients (e.g., inpatients vs. outpatients), thus eliminating some of the potential effects of confounding variables (e.g., symptom severity).

Organizational Performance Goals

Sometimes, the clinician will be practicing in an organization that sets its own standards for successful treatment. To some degree, these standards probably will be based on a combination of what the industry standard is and what the organization sees as being realistic, given the population it serves, the resources available, accreditation and regulatory requirements, the expectations of other stakeholders, and whatever other demands it must meet to remain successful and solvent.

Recovery Curves

Another approach to monitoring therapeutic change against a standard is *patient profiling* (Leon, Kopta, Howard, & Lutz, 1999). Patient profiling is yet another contribution stemming from the work of Howard and his colleagues. It is the product of two of their theories: the phase model of psychotherapy (described earlier) and the *dose-response model* of psychotherapeutic effectiveness (Howard et al., 1986; see also Lueger et al., 2001; Lutz, Lowry, Kopta, Einstein, & Howard, 2001). In this model, *dose* actually refers to what is more traditionally described as the duration or number of treatment sessions. The model theorizes "a lawful linear relationship between the log of the number of sessions and the normalized probability of patient improvement" (Howard et al., 1996, p. 1060). Howard and his colleagues thought that a log-normal model fit because the target of improvement changes during the course of treatment. In fact, this line of thinking led to their conceptualization of the phase model of psychotherapy.

Patient profiling essentially involves the generation of an expected curve of recovery over the course of psychotherapy along any measurable construct dimension that the clinician or investigator may choose (Howard et al., 1996; Leon et al., 1999). Individual profiles are generated from selected patient clinical characteristics (e.g., severity and chronicity of the problem, attitudes toward treatment, scores on treatment-relevant measures) present at the time of treatment onset. Simply put, the measure of the construct of interest is modeled as a log-linear function of the session number, based on data from a large sample of therapy patients with the same clinical characteristics. Howard et al. (1996) used scores from the Mental Health Index (MHI; Howard, Brill, Lueger, O'Mahoney, & Grissom, 1993; Sperry, Brill, Howard, & Grissom, 1996)—a composite of scores from three instruments measuring well-being, symptomatology, and life functioning—to demonstrate the generation and tracking of individual patient profiles. (The MHI was developed to reflect the important dimensions of the Howard's phase theory and thus provides an excellent measure for profiling purposes. However, one could choose to profile the patient on only a single domain, such as symptomatology, or other global constructs using other appropriate instrumentation.)

In patient profiling, hierarchical linear modeling is used to predict the course of improvement during treatment. Plotting of the results of multiple administrations of the monitoring measure during the course of treatment al lows a graphical comparison of the patient's actual score with the improvement trajectory that would be expected from similar individuals after the same number of treatment sessions. Howard and his colleagues (Lutz, Martinovich, & Howard, 1999) also developed a means for generating a *failure boundary* that is approximately two-thirds of a standard deviation below the expected recovery curve. The area between the recovery and failure curves provides a range in which patient recovery should proceed. Thus, the therapist knows when the treatment is working and when it is not so that necessary adjustments in the treatment strategy (and treatment plan) can be made. Lutz et al. found that patient performance falling below the failure boundary could be used as a predictor of treatment failure, with the occurrence of two of more failed assessment values during the treatment process warranting reconsideration of the treatment strategy. An example of a patient profile developed according to Howard's methodology is presented in Figure 6.2.

In summarizing the work of Howard and his colleagues, Lueger et al. (2001) report that studies conducted with various samples and outcomes measures generally support a treatment-duration effect for psychotherapy that results in approximately 50% of patients showing improvement by 8 treatment sessions, 75% by 26 sessions, and 85% by 60 sessions. As might be expected, however, variability in these findings is noted with regard to diagnoses, symptoms, and interpersonal problems. Using session-by-session data rather than mathematical extrapolations of pre- and posttreatment data, Kadera, Lambert, and Andrews (1996) derived treatment-duration effect curves that were more conservative than those generated by Howard and his colleagues. Those readers considering the use of dose-effect curves or patient profiling are encouraged to take note of the Kadera et al. findings.

Statistically Significant Change

Another approach to treatment monitoring is to determine whether changes in patient scores on monitoring measures are *statistically significant*. This represents an approach that is probably more in line with the training of behavioral scientists and thus is likely to be much more appealing than making comparisons to some standard. Probably one of the more popular means of determining whether a change on a measure from one point in time to another is statistically significant is through the use of the reliable change index (RCI).

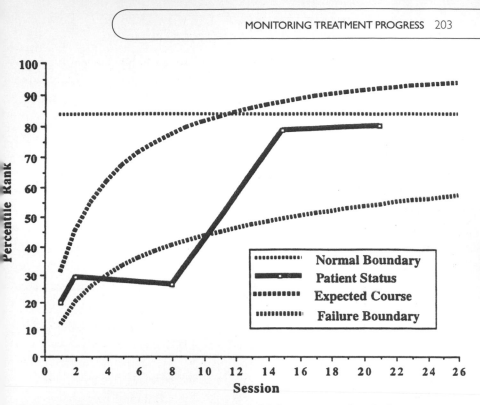

Figure 6.2. Treatment course for a case in which outcomes data led to a change in treatment strategy.

Note. From "Patient Profiling: An Application of Random Coefficient Regression Models to Depicting the Response of a Patient to Outpatient Psychotherapy," by W. Lutz, Z. Martinovich, and K. I. Howard, 1999, *Journal of Consulting and Clinical Psychology, 67,* p. 576. Copyright 1999 by the American Psychological Association. Reprinted with permission.

This index, initially espoused by Jacobson and his colleagues (Jacobson, Föllette, & Revenstorf, 1984) and later modified on the recommendation of Christensen and Mendoza (1986), is nothing more than the difference between two scores at two points in time, divided by the standard error of difference (S_{diff}). If a greater score, number, or frequency on a given measure is indicative of a greater level of psychopathology, then one can be 95% confident ($p < .05$) that real improvement has occurred if the resulting RCI value is less than -1.96. Conversely, if a lower score, number, or frequency on a given measure is indicative of a greater level of psychopathology, then one can be 95% confident that real improvement has occurred with an RCI value greater than $+1.96$.

Employing the RCI for determining statistically significant change during the course of treatment requires the use of measures with known psychometric properties, including reliability. This is one reason that standardized measures should be used by the clinician as the means of monitoring patient progress through the course of treatment.

Clinically Significant Change

The RCI allows clinicians to use standardized psychological measures to demonstrate whether treatment has resulted in statistically reliable change between scores from any two points in time. However, Jacobson and his colleagues (Jacobson et al., 1984) also acknowledged the importance of determining whether *clinically significant change* has occurred in evaluating the effectiveness of treatment. Jacobson and Truax (1991) broadly define the clinical significance of treatment as "its ability to meet standards of efficacy set by consumers, clinicians, and researchers" (p. 12). Furthermore, they noted that

> while there is little consensus in the field regarding what these standards should be, various criteria have been suggested: a high percentage of clients improving . . . ; a level of change that is recognizable by peers and significant others . . . ; an elimination of the presenting problem . . . ; normative levels of functioning at the end of therapy . . . ; high end-state functioning at the end of therapy . . . ; or changes that significantly reduce one's risk for various health problems. (p.12)

Viewed from a more practical standpoint, clinically significant change (i.e., improvement) may be described as change that both is statistically reliable and moves the patient from the range of dysfunction into or toward that of normal functioning. The issue of clinical significance has received a great deal of attention in psychotherapy research during the past several years. This is at least partially owing to the work of Jacobson and his colleagues (Jacobson & Truax, 1991; Jacobson et al., 1984, 1986) and others (e.g., Christensen & Mendoza, 1986; Speer, 1992; Wampold & Jenson, 1986). Their work came at a time when researchers began to recognize that traditional statistical comparisons do not reveal a great deal about the efficacy of therapy.

From their perspective, Jacobson and his colleagues (Jacobson et al., 1984; Jacobson, Roberts, Berns, & McGlinchey, 1999; Jacobson & Truax, 1991) felt that clinically significant change could be conceptualized in one of three ways. Thus, for clinically significant change to have occurred, the measured level of functioning following the therapeutic episode would have to be statistically reliable *and* either (a) fall outside the range of the dysfunctional population by at least 2 standard deviations from the mean of that population, in the direction of functionality; (b) fall within 2 standard deviations of the mean for the normal or functional population; or (c) be closer to the mean of the functional population than to that of the dysfunctional population. Jacobson et al. (1999) have offered suggestions for the use of each of these criteria, depending upon the availability of normative data. These suggestions are summarized in Rapid Reference 6.4. It is important to note that Jacobson et al. also indicated that their method allows only for the determination of clinically significant *improve-*

≣ Rapid Reference 6.4

Suggestions for Use of Jacobson's Criteria for Clinically Significant Change

Criterion for Clinical Significance[a]	Recommended Use
Measure falls outside the range of the dysfunctional population by at least 2 standard deviations from the mean of that population, in the direction of functionality	• Return to normal functioning is not feasible (e.g., schizophrenia, autism) • Current treatment technology is limited (e.g., some addictive behaviors) • Normative data are available for a dysfunctional population
Measure falls within 2 standard deviations of the mean for the normal or functional population	• Normative data are available for a functional population but unavailable for a dysfunctional population • No consensus about what is an appropriate measure
Measure is closer to the mean of the functional population than to that of the dysfunctional population	• Normative data are available for both functional and dysfunctional populations

Note. From Jacobson et al. (1999, p. 303).

[a]Change must also be reliable.

CAUTION

- According to Jacobson et al., clinical change that is not reliable should not be considered significant.

- Organizational goals that are less stringent than individual patient goals may result in premature termination of treatment.

- Patient profiling based on data from the patients who are dissimilar from the patient being treated will yield misleading or inaccurate information.

ment, because methods to establish cutoff points for identifying clinically significant deterioration have not been established.

Determining clinically significant change via the methods advocated by Jacobson and his colleagues is an example of the third approach to evaluating treatment monitoring data, that is, through a comparison of the patient's data to both a standard and patient data obtained from a previous measurement. There are other approaches to analyzing individual patient data for reliable change and clinically significant change. Excellent discussions of the RCI and other methods can be found in Hsu (1996, 1999), Jacobson et al. (1999), Kazdin (1999), Saunders, Howard, and Newman (1988), and Speer and Greenbaum (1995). Interested readers are encouraged to review these and other articles on the topic before deciding which approach to determining clinically significant change is best suited for their particular needs. In addition, the reader is also referred to an excellent discussion of analyzing individual patient change data in Newman and Dakof (1999).

REVISION VERSUS MAINTENANCE OF THE TREATMENT PLAN

With the data that are provided by regular monitoring of the patient's condition throughout the episode of care, the clinician is armed with information that can assist in the evaluation of the effectiveness of the current treatment plan at each instance of data gathering. What, however, should the clinician do with this information? How should it be used?

General Considerations

One advantage of using standardized measures and statistical procedures like those described earlier is that they can provide empirical support for the cli-

Rapid Reference 6.5

Questions for Evaluating the Findings from Remeasurement

- Were the measures used for monitoring valid and reliable?
- Was the planned intervention fully implemented?
- Has the patient completed the treatment activities that were required up to this point?
- Has enough time been allowed for change to occur?
- Are the goals and objectives realistic and achievable?
- Was there any component of the treatment plan that could have or should have been done differently?

nician's assessment of how the patient is progressing in treatment and, consequently, the need to modify the existing treatment plan. Thus, whenever possible, the use of psychometrically sound instrumentation and appropriate statistical procedures for analyzing monitoring data is always recommended. Regardless of whether standardized instruments and accepted analytic procedures are employed, however, deviations from the range of desired or expected performance require that the clinician decide whether there is a need to revise the case formulation, the plan of treatment, or both. In the end, it should always be a clinical decision based on available data and other aspects of the patient and the care that he or she has received.

Rapid Reference 6.5 presents several questions that clinicians should ask themselves when reviewing reassessment findings that suggest that no improvement or deterioration in a patient's condition has occurred. Answers to these questions may indicate that despite the findings, the patient should continue on the same course of treatment.

The Effects of Providing Feedback to the Therapist

Intuitively, one would expect that having the type of information that Howard and his colleagues demonstrated would result in positive outcomes for the patient—but is this really the case? Lambert, Whipple, et al. (2001) sought to answer this question by conducting a study that they hoped would show that patients whose therapists receive feedback about their patients' progress would have better outcomes and better treatment attendance (an indicator of cost-effective psychotherapy) than those patients whose therapists did not receive this same type of feedback.

Approximately half of the 609 patient participants in the Lambert, Whipple, et al. (2001) study were assigned to a feedback (experimental) group while the other half comprised a no feedback (control) group. The feedback provided to the experimental group's therapists came in the form of a weekly updated report of the baseline and current Total scale scores of the OQ-45 and the number of sessions that the patient had completed. The feedback report also contained one of four possible color-coded interpretations of the patient's progress: (a) functioning in the normal range, consider termination; (b) adequate change being made, no treatment plan changes recommended; (c) rate of change inadequate, consider altering treatment plan, patient may achieve no significant benefit from treatment; or (d) not making expected level of progress, may have negative outcome or drop out of treatment, consider revised or new treatment plan, reassess readiness for change. Predictions of patients' leaving treatment early or being at risk for a negative treatment outcome were based on algorithms developed by Lambert (1998).

The findings from this study were mixed. Although the outcome (i.e., post-treatment OQ-45 scores) for those cases that were predicted not to benefit from or to drop out of therapy *(signal cases)* was better for those whose therapists received feedback, the difference was not significant. However, two other findings are noteworthy. First, the percentage of signal cases with feedback that demonstrated statistically or clinically significant change (Jacobson & Truax, 1991) was twice that of signal cases for whom no feedback was provided (26% vs. 13%, respectively). Surprisingly, the deterioration rates for the two signal groups were approximately the same. Moreover, signal cases with feedback received significantly more sessions than their non-feedback signal counterparts, whereas non-signal patients with feedback received significantly fewer sessions than the non-signal, no-feedback subsample. Lambert, Whipple, et al. (2001) felt that the results did not support the routine use of their predictive algorithms. Possibly this was due to the fact that therapists did not systematically seek consultation for signal cases when the feedback report recommended it. Also, there apparently was no way of determining whether the report led to changes in type or intensity of the treatment provided by the therapist. They did see the session-attendance findings as being appropriate.

When feedback on patient progress was positive, patients were seen for fewer sessions; when it was negative, patients were seen for more sessions.

In a follow-up study, Lambert et al. (in press) sought to replicate these findings using the OQ-45 with a larger university sample. The findings were generally supportive of those of the original study. Those patients identified to their therapists as not on track in terms of their expected treatment progress were found to make greater subsequent gains than similar patients whose therapists did not receive such feedback. Also, among the two nonprogressing groups, fewer of the feedback group deteriorated by the end of treatment whereas more of this same group showed reliable or clinically significant improvement in their conditions. Other data suggested that at least to some degree, the feedback led to changes in treatment by those therapists receiving it. Together, these two investigations (Lambert, Whipple, et al., 2001; Lambert et al., in press) lend support for benefits accruing from the use of assessment-based feedback provided to clinicians during treatment. At the same time, Lambert, Hansen, and Finch (2001) point out that in order to be effective, the feedback needs to be timely and to provide information that is action oriented.

Notwithstanding whether it is used as fodder for generating complex statistical predictions or for simple point-in-time comparisons, the work of Howard, Lambert, and their colleagues demonstrates that psychological test data obtained for treatment monitoring can provide an empirically based means of determining the effectiveness of mental health and substance abuse treatment during an episode of care. The value of these data lies in their ability to support ongoing treatment decisions that must be made using objective means. Consequently, they allow for improved patient care while supporting efforts to demonstrate accountability to the patient and interested third parties.

SUMMARY

Campbell (1992) has identified the treatment-monitoring process as an application of single-subject design evaluation procedures. Its implementation in a clinical setting reflects the need for clinicians to continually review the validity of their patients' case formulations and to be flexible in their approach to treatment. Overall, the treatment-monitoring process is relatively straightfor-

Putting It Into Practice

Case Study of Mary Smith (*continued*)

TREATMENT SUMMARY

Mary Smith

The treatment plan was implemented the week after it was finalized and approved both by Ms. Smith and by the treatment team at the weekly case conference meeting. As per the plan, she was seen for weekly sessions over a 6-month period, with monitoring data being gathered at the beginning of every other treatment session. These data included the OQ-45 Total and subscale raw scores obtained during that day's administration of the instrument; Ms. Smith's report of the average daily occurrences of both obsessive thinking and compulsive behavior during the previous week; and her rating of her ability to concentrate during the previous week. During the first treatment session, Ms. Smith was instructed in self-monitoring techniques for identifying and tracking both obsessions and compulsions. For the purpose of monitoring, an *obsession* was operationally defined as an undesirable intrusive thought that lasted for a minimum of 15 sec. A *compulsion* was defined as a physical behavior that Ms. Smith felt compelled to perform in order to alleviate an intrusive thought. Ms. Smith was also provided with instructions for using a 7-point rating scale for rating concentration impairment (1 = *Concentration problems do not interfere with my schoolwork;* 4 = *Can study for at least an 30 minutes without concentration problems;* 7 = *Can't study for more than 5 minutes without concentration problems*).

The monitoring data obtained over the 6 months of treatment are presented in Table 6.1. Measurement data obtained at the time of the second session revealed that little or no change in the raw scores that were obtained for the four OQ-45 scales at the time of their initial administration. Baseline measurement of the average daily occurrence of obsessions and compulsions (75 and 56, respectively) reflected the degree to which each of these types of symptoms were problematic for Ms. Smith. As well, the average self-rating of her ability to concentrate (6 = *Can't study for more than 10 minutes without concentration problems*) was consistent with the stated complaint that led her to seek treatment.

Remeasurement of Ms. Smith on the variables used for tracking treatment progress reflected the improvement that was apparent to the clinician during the sessions that occurred during the first 2 months. Statistically significant symptomatic improvement was indicated by the scores obtained on the OQ-45 Total and Symptom Distress scales for the 8th session. Part of this improvement could be attributed to the decision of the consulting psychiatrist to initiate a course of antidepressant medication as an adjunct to psychotherapy. However, Ms. Smith suffered a setback in her progress when her father died.

This occurred a few days after the 9th session. Its effects were reflected in the measurements taken for all tracking variables taken during the 10th session. The scheduled 3-month evaluation of the treatment plan took place just prior to the 12th session during the clinic's weekly case conference meeting. All staff agreed that the setback in Ms. Smith's condition was not unexpected given her history, and that she was likely to recover relatively quickly. Consequently, the consensus of the staff was to continue with the original treatment plan without modification.

As expected, Ms. Smith was able to recover her lost therapeutic gains during the next six sessions and from there, to continue with steady increases in symptomatic relief. By the 22nd session, all four OQ-45 scale scores were within the nonpatient population range. In fact, her scores indicated that she had attained clinically significant improvement on the Total, Symptom Distress, and Social Role scales, according to Jacobson and Truax's (1991) criteria. Moreover, her obsessional thinking and compulsive behaviors diminished in frequency to less than half of the baseline occurrences. Perhaps most important to Ms. Smith was the fact that her rating of concentration difficulties dropped from 6 to 2, a level that she said was probably an improvement over her premorbid ability to concentrate.

The gains exhibited during the 22nd session were maintained through the 24th session. During that session, termination of treatment (as per the treatment plan) was discussed. Ms. Smith indicated that she had received the help she was seeking, was functioning much better than before, and was optimistic about the future and her ability to deal more effectively with the demands and pressures imposed on her by others. The clinician concurred with her, and both agreed to terminate treatment. However, the clinician encouraged her to contact him again should other problems arise, or even if she simply needed a booster shot (so to speak) of treatment to ensure that she maintained the gains she had made during the previous 6 months.

ward. A baseline of patient functioning is taken at the beginning of treatment. The patient is reassessed at a later date and the results are examined for evidence of progress. Based on this evaluation, the treatment plan remains the same or is modified. The patient is reassessed at regular intervals throughout treatment, with modifications to the treatment plan being made as necessary.

However simple the process itself may seem, establishing an effective system for treatment monitoring that yields useful information requires much forethought. A number of issues must be taken into consideration when one is developing a plan for monitoring the treatment of an individual patient. The first is *what* will be monitored. Although the goals and objectives of treatment should have the greatest influence in this decision, other factors cannot be ig-

Table 6.1 Summary of Ms. Smith's OQ-45, Self-Monitoring, and Self-Rating Scores During Treatment

Measure	Treatment Session											
	2	4	6	8	10	12	14	16	18	20	22	2
OQ-45												
T	86	79	74	67	83	77	70	65	60	57	54	5
SD	51	45	42	38	49	46	40	38	33	32	29	2
IR	14	14	13	12	15	13	13	12	12	11	12	1
SR	21	20	19	17	19	18	17	15	15	14	12	1
Obs	75	69	61	55	70	68	60	53	47	42	37	3
Cm	56	51	45	40	49	48	42	38	33	30	28	2
Cn	6	5	4	4	7	6	5	4	3	3	2	

Note: "Measure" is the variable measured and tracked. T = Total scale raw score (clinical cut-off = 63, RCI = 14); SD = Symptom Distress scale raw score (clinical cutoff = 30, RCI = 10); IR = Interpersonal Relations scale raw score (clinical cutoff = 15, RCI = 8); SR = Social Role scale raw score (clinical cutoff = 15, RCI = 7); Obs = average number of daily self-monitored obsessional thoughts; Cm = average number of daily self-monitored compulsive behavior; Cn = average self-rating of concentration ability (1 = *Concentration problems do not interfere with my schoolwork*, 4 = *Can study for at least 30 minutes without concentration problems*, 7 = *Can't study for more than 5 minutes without concentration problems*).

nored. One must also take into account what the clinician or significant third parties consider to be important for treatment success; whether the variables that will be monitored are meaningful across different LOCs and will provide actionable information; and the burden of measuring those variables.

Next is the issue of *how* treatment progress will be monitored. There may be several options for the source from which the monitoring data can be obtained. These may include patient's self-report measures (e.g., symptom checklists), patient self-monitoring outside of the treatment setting, observer-completed measures, and administrative data (e.g., number of emergency room visits or prescription refills). Use of standardized, self-report psychological test instrumentation is a common means of eliciting desired monitoring data for many patients. In selecting this type of measure, one should consider the recommendations provided in chapter 3 as well as other factors that are important for measures that are administered to the same patient multiple times (i.e., test-retest reliability, interval of consideration for the presence or severity of a symptom or behavior, and cost).

Cost should also play an important part in the decision about *when* the patient will be reassessed. Monitoring involves more than one reassessment beyond the baseline measurement. Depending on the procedure or instrumentation chosen for the task, monitoring can become quite expensive. However, cost should not be the only factor considered when deciding on the frequency of monitoring. One also needs to take into account the expected length of treatment, the frequency at which the clinician feels monitoring information will be useful, and again, the interval of consideration that is built into the instrumentation chosen for the task.

Finally, the clinician must decide on the *method of evaluating the obtained results*. One option is to compare the patient's progress against a preselected standard. The standard may be directly related to the patient's specific goals or objectives, normative data such those accompanying published psychological tests, standards set by the provider organization, or those established through individual patient profiling and recovery curves. Alternately, the clinician may wish to determine whether the changes that occur are statistically significant (reliable) or clinically significant. The results of the selected method of evaluation will serve as the basis for deciding whether to continue along the same course of treatment. Modifications in the treatment plan, however, should be based not only on the results of these data, but also on other factors that can play into a lack of progress or even deterioration in the patient's condition during treatment (e.g., lack of patient involvement, poor execution of the treatment plan, occurrence of a significant crisis or life event).

Formal treatment monitoring is an often-overlooked component of the treatment-planning process. Certainly, clinicians monitor their patients' progress informally, either by asking them or collaterals if they are feeling better, doing something more (or less) than before, or thinking or doing something differently from session to session; or by noting changes in their presentation during the treatment session. Although providing important information, these informal procedures can be rather hit-or-miss in terms of what is attended to and what is really going on with the patient. Use of a well thought out process that utilizes standardized measures to gather relevant patient data at predetermined points in time, along with objective means of analyzing that data, can provide much more useful information. As a result, it can help clinicians feel much more confident in their decisions about the care they are providing to their patients.

⚔ TEST YOURSELF ⚔

1. **What type of adjustment to treatment might monitoring data *not* indicate needs to occur?**
   (a) No change in treatment plan
   (b) Treatment at a higher or lower LOC
   (c) Change in the type of psychotherapy the patient is receiving
   (d) Need for evaluation for medication
   (e) Treatment termination
   (f) None of the above

2. **What is the *most* important consideration in selecting the variable to be monitored during treatment?**
   (a) The interests of third-party stakeholders in the patient's care
   (b) The goals and objectives of the treatment
   (c) The meaningfulness of the variables across LOCs
   (d) What the clinician thinks should be monitored
   (e) What the patient thinks should be monitored

3. **Self-monitoring data are one type of which of the following?**
   (a) Clinically significant data
   (b) Statistically significant data
   (c) Patient-reported data
   (d) Administrative data
   (e) Data obtained by a trained observer

4. **Which of the following is an example of the burden associated with treatment monitoring?**

   (a) Cost of training staff in data gathering methods

   (b) Clinician time

   (c) Patient time

   (d) Administrative support staff time

   (e) Cost of the monitoring instrumentation

   (f) All of the above

5. **Which of the following is not a potential limitation of a psychological measure being considered for treatment monitoring?**

   (a) Test-retest reliability based on a patient normative sample

   (b) Test-retest reliability based on a nonpatient or community sample

   (c) An interval of consideration for monitored symptoms that is longer than the frequency at which the clinician plans to monitor the symptoms

   (d) An interval of consideration for monitored symptoms that is shorter than the frequency at which the clinician plans to monitor the symptoms

   (e) a and c

   (f) b and d

   (g) All of the above

6. **Which of the following is not a standard nor involves a standard against which patient progress can be monitored?**

   (a) Patient goals

   (b) Normative data

   (c) Recovery curves

   (d) Organization standards

   (e) Statistically significant change

   (f) Clinically significant change

7. **What types of patient variables would be most appropriate to monitor for patients who probably will receive services across the LOC continuum?** _____

   _____

8. **Besides the cost, interval of consideration, and test-retest reliability, what other specific factors would be important to consider in selecting instrumentation for treatment monitoring?** _____

   _____

(continued)

9. **With what types of patients should one be satisfied with reliable change, even though clinically significant change has not been achieved?** _____

10. **In general, what variables might be important to monitor for patients with major depressive disorder? What sources of data would one use to obtain information about these variables?** _____

Answers: 1. f; 2. b; 3. c; 4. f; 5. f; 6. e; 7. symptom severity, general level of distress, role functioning, and well-being; 8. brevity, psychometric integrity, relevancy to the intended purpose of the assessment, availability of relevant normative data, reading level, content, ease of use, and comprehensibility of results; 9. patients with conditions that are chronic, severe, or generally refractory to treatment; 10. mood (self-report and observer data), weight change (self-monitoring data), sleep (self-monitoring data), psychomotor agitation (observer data), energy level (self-monitoring data), feelings of guilt and worthlessness (self-report and self-monitoring data), role functioning (self-report and observer data), engagement in pleasurable activities (self-monitoring and observer data), and health care resource utilization (administrative data).

References

Abrahamson, D. J. (1999). Outcomes, guidelines, and manuals: On leading horses to water. *Clinical Psychology: Science and Practice, 6,* 467–471.

Addis, M. E., & Krasnow, A. D. (2000). A national survey of practicing psychologists' attitudes toward psychotherapy treatment manuals. *Journal of Consulting and Clinical Psychology, 68,* 331–339.

Addis, M. E., Wade, W. A., & Hatgis, C. (1999). Barriers to dissemination of evidence-based practices: Addressing practitioners' concerns about manual-based psychotherapies. *Clinical Psychology: Science and Practice, 6,* 430–441.

Ambrose, P. A. (1997). Challenges for mental health service providers: The perspective of managed care organizations. In J. N. Butcher (Ed.), *Personality assessment in managed health care* (pp. 61–72). New York: Oxford University Press.

Amchin, J. (1991). *Psychiatric diagnosis: A biopsychosocial approach using DSM-III-R.* Washington, DC: American Psychiatric Press.

American Educational Research Association, American Psychological Association, & National Council on Measurement in Education. (1999). *Standards for educational and psychological testing.* Washington, DC: American Educational Research Association.

American Psychiatric Association. (1994). *Diagnostic and statistical manual of mental disorders* (4th ed.). Washington, DC: Author.

American Psychiatric Association. (2000). *Diagnostic and statistical manual of mental disorders* (4th ed.; text rev.). Washington, DC: Author.

American Psychological Association. (1992). Ethical principles of psychologists and code of conduct. *American Psychologist, 47,* 1597–1611.

American Psychological Association, Task Force on Psychological Intervention Guidelines. (1995). *Template for developing guidelines: Interventions for mental disorders and psychosocial aspects of physical disorders.* Washington, DC: Author.

American Psychological Association, Template Implementation Work Group. (2000). *Criteria for evaluating treatment guidelines.* Washington, DC: Author.

Appelbaum, S. A. (1990). The relationship between assessment and psychotherapy. *Journal of Personality Assessment, 54,* 791–801.

Barton, K. A., Blanchard, E. B., & Veazey, C. (1999). Self-monitoring as an assessment strategy in behavioral medicine. *Psychological Assessment, 11,* 490–497.

Beck, A. T., Steer, R. A., & Brown, G. K. (1996). *Manual for the Beck Depression Inventory–II.* San Antonio, TX: Psychological Corporation.

Ben-Porath, Y. S. (1997). Use of personality assessment instruments in empirically guided treatment planning. *Psychological Assessment, 9,* 361–367.

Berg, A. O., Atkins, D., & Tierney, W. (1997). Clinical practice guidelines in practice and education. *JGIM, 12*(Suppl. 2), S25–S33.

Bergner, R. M. (1998). Characteristics of optimal clinical case formulations: The linchpin concept. *American Journal of Psychotherapy, 52,* 287–300.

Berman, W. H., Hurt, S. W., & Heiss, G. E (1996). Outcomes assessment in behavioral healthcare. In C. E. Stout, G. A. Theis, & J. Oher (Eds.), *The complete guide to managed behavioral care* (pp. II-D.1–II-D.10). New York: Wiley.

Berman, W. H., Rosen, C. S., Hurt, S. W., & Kolarz, C. M. (1998). Toto, we're not in Kansas anymore: Measuring and using outcomes in behavioral health care. *Clinical Psychology: Science and Practice, 5,* 115–133.

Beutler, L. E. (1989). Differential treatment selection: The role of diagnosis in psychotherapy. *Psychotherapy, 26,* 271–281.

Beutler, L. E. (1991). Selective treatment matching: Systematic eclectic psychotherapy. *Psychotherapy, 28,* 457–462.

Beutler, L. E. (1995). The clinical interview. In L. E. Beutler & M. R. Berren (Eds.), *Integrative assessment of adult personality* (pp. 94–120). New York: Guilford Press.

Beutler, L. E. (1998). Identifying empirically supported treatments: What if we didn't? *Journal of Consulting and Clinical Psychology, 66,* 113–120.

Beutler, L. E. (2001). Comparisons among quality assurance systems from outcome assessment to clinical utility. *Journal of Consulting and Clinical Psychology, 69,* 197–204. Retrieved July 10, 2001 from PsycARTICLES database.

Beutler, L. E., & Clarkin, J. F. (1990). *Systematic treatment selection: Toward targeted therapeutic interventions.* New York: Brunner/Mazel.

Beutler, L. E., Goodrich, G., Fisher, D., & Williams, O. B. (1999). Use of psychological tests/instruments for treatment planning. In M. E. Maruish (Ed.), *The use of psychological testing for treatment planning and outcomes assessment* (2nd ed., pp. 81–113). Mahwah, NJ: Erlbaum.

Beutler, L. E., Wakefield, P., & Williams, R. E. (1994). Use of psychological tests/instruments for treatment planning. In M. E. Maruish (Ed.), *The use of psychological testing for treatment planning and outcome assessment* (pp. 55–74). Hillsdale, NJ: Erlbaum.

Beutler, L. E., & Williams, O. B. (1995). Computer applications for the selection of optimal psychosocial therapeutic interventions. *Behavioral Healthcare Tomorrow, 4,* 66–68.

Bieber, J., Wroblewski, J. M., & Barber, C. A. (1999). Design and implementation of an outcomes management system within inpatient and outpatient behavioral health settings. In M. E. Maruish (Ed.), *The use of psychological testing for treatment planning and outcomes assessment* (2nd ed., pp. 171–210). Mahwah, NJ: Erlbaum.

Bloom, B. L. (1992). Planned short-term psychotherapy: Current status and future challenges. *Applied and Preventive Psychology, 1,* 157–164.

Brogan, M. M., Prochaska, J. O., & Prochaska, J. M. (1999). Predicting termination and continuation status in psychotherapy using the transtheoretical model. *Psychotherapy, 36,* 105–113.

Brown, R. L. (1992). Identification and office management of alcohol and drug disorders. In M. F. Fleming & K. L. Barry (Eds.), *Addictive disorders* (pp. 25–43). St. Louis, MO: Mosby Year Book.

Brown, R. L., & Rounds, L. A. (1995). Conjoint screening questionnaires for alcohol and other drug abuse: Criterion validity in a primary care practice. *Wisconsin Medical Journal, 94,* 135–140.

Budman, S. H., & Gurman, A. S. (1988). *Theory and practice of brief psychotherapy.* New York: Guilford Press.

Burlingame, G. M., Lambert, M. J., Reisinger, C. W., Neff, W. M., & Mosier, J. (1995).

Pragmatics of tracking mental health outcomes in a managed care setting. *Journal of Mental Health Administration, 22,* 226–236.

Butcher, J. N. (1990). *The MMPI-2 in psychological treatment.* New York: Oxford University Press.

Butcher, J. N. (1997). Introduction to the special section on psychological assessment: A necessary step for effective intervention. *Psychological Assessment, 9,* 331–333.

Butcher, J. N., Dahlstrom, W. G., Graham, J. R., Tellegen, A. M., & Kaemmer, B. (1989). *MMPI-2: Manual for administration and scoring.* Minneapolis, MN: Univeristy of Minnesota Press.

Butcher, J. N., Graham, J. R., Williams, C. L., & Ben-Porath, Y. S. (1989). *Development and use of the MMPI-2 content scales.* Minneapolis, MN: University of Minnesota Press.

Butcher, J. N., & Williams, C. L. (1992). *Esssentials of MMPI-2 and MMPI-A interpretation.* Minneapolis, MN: University of Minnesota Press.

Callaghan, G. M. (2001). Demonstrating clinical effectiveness for individual practitioners and clinics. *Professional Psychology: Research and Practice, 32,* 289–297.

Campbell, J. A. (1992). Single-subject designs for treatment planning and evaluation. *Administration and Policy in Mental Health, 19,* 335–343.

Chambless, D. L. (1996). In defense of dissemination of empirically supported psychological interventions. *Clinical Psychology: Science and Practice, 3,* 230–235.

Chambless, D. L., Baker, M. J., Baucom, D. H., Beutler, L. E., Calhoun, K. S., Crits-Christoph, P., Daiuto, A., DeRubeis, R., Detweiler, J., Haaga, D. A., Johnson, S. B., McCurry, S., Mueser, K. T., Pope, K. S., Sanderson, W. C., Shoham, V., Stickle, T., Williams, D. A., & Woody, S. R. (1997). *Update on empirically validated therapies, II.* Manuscript submitted for publication. [Online] Available from http://www.apa.org/divisions/div12/est/97REPORT.SS.htm

Chambless, D. L., & Hollon, S. D. (1998). Defining empirically supported therapies. *Journal of Consulting and Clinical Psychology, 66,* 7–18. Retrieved June 26, 2001 from PsycARTICLES database.

Chambless, D. L., Sanderson, W. C., Shoham, V., Johnson, S. B., Pope, K. S., Crits-Christoph, P., Baker, M., Johnson, B., Woody, S. R., Sue, S., Beutler, L., Williams, D. A., & McCurry, S. (1996). An update on empirically validated therapies. *The Clinical Psychologist, 49,* 5–18.

Christensen, L., & Mendoza, J. L. (1986). A method of assessing change in a single subject: An alteration of the RC index [Letter to the editor]. *Behavior Therapy, 17,* 305–308.

Cicchetti, D. V. (1994). Guidelines, criteria, and rules of thumb for evaluating normed and standardized assessment instruments in psychology. *Psychological Assessment, 6,* 284–290.

CIGNA Behavioral Health. (1999). *Level of care guidelines for mental health and substance abuse treatment.* Eden Prairie, MN: Author.

Citrome, L. (1998). Practice protocols, parameters, pathways, and guidelines: A review. *Administration and Policy in Mental Health, 25,* 257–269.

Clarkin, J. F., & Kendall, P. C. (1992). Comorbidity and treatment planning: Summary and future directions. *Journal of Consulting and Clinical Psychology, 60,* 904–908.

Clinton, J. J., McCormick, K., & Besteman, J. (1994). Enhancing clinical practice: The role of practice guidelines. *American Psychologist, 49,* 30–33.

Davies, A. R., & Ware, J. E. (1991). *GHAA's Consumer Satsifaction Survey and user's manual.* Washington, DC: Group Health Association of America.

Derogatis, L. R. (1983). *SCL-90-R: Administration, scoring and procedures manual–II.* Baltimore: Clinical Psychometric Research.

Derogatis, L. R. (1992). *BSI: Administration, scoring and procedures manual–II.* Baltimore: Clinical Psychometric Research.

Derogatis, L. R. (1994). *SCL-90-R: Symptom Checklist-90-R administration, scoring, and procedures manual.* Minneapolis, MN: National Computer Systems.

Derogatis, L. R., Lipman, R. S., & Covi, L. (1973). SCL-90: An outpatient psychiatric rating scale—preliminary report. *Psychopharmacology Bulletin, 9,* 13–27.

Derogatis, L. R., & Savitz, K. L. (1999). The SCL-90-R, Brief Symptom Inventory, and matching clinical rating scales. In M. E. Maruish (Ed.), *The use of psychological testing for treatment planning and outcomes assessment* (2nd ed., pp. 679–724). Mahwah, NJ: Erlbaum.

DiClemente, C. C., & Hughes, S. O. (1990). Stages of change profiles in outpatient alcoholism treatment. *Journal of Substance Abuse, 2,* 217–235.

DiClemente, C. C., & Prochaska, J. O. (1998). Toward a comprehensive, transtheoretical model of change. In W. R. Miller & N. Healther (Eds.), *Treating addictive behaviors* (pp. 3–24). New York: Plenum Press.

Dowd, E. T., Milne, C. R., & Wise, S. L. (1991). The Therapeutic Reactance Scale: A measure of psychological reactance. *Journal of Counseling and Development, 69,* 541–545.

Eifert, G. H., Evans, I. M., & McKendrick, V. G. (1990). Matching treatments to client problems not diagnostic labels: A case for paradigmatic behavior therapy. *Journal of Behavior Therapy and Experimental Psychiatry, 21,* 163–172.

Eisen, S. V. (1996). Behavior and Symptom Identification Scale (BASIS-32). In L. I. Sederer & B. Dickey (Eds.), *Outcomes assessment in clinical practice* (pp. 65–69). Baltimore: Williams & Wilkins.

Eisen, S. V., & Culhane, M. A. (1999). Behavior and Symptom Identification Scale. In M. E. Maruish (Ed.), *The use of psychological testing for treatment planning and outcomes assessment* (2nd ed., pp. 759–790). Mahwah, NJ: Erlbaum.

Eisen, S. V., Dill, D. L., & Grob, M. C. (1994). Reliability and validity of a brief patient-report instrument for psychiatric outcome evaluation. *Hospital and Community Psychiatry, 45,* 242–247.

Eisen, S. V., Wilcox, M., Leff, H. S., Schaefer, E., & Culhane, M. A. (1999). Assessing behavioral health outcomes in outpatient programs: Reliability and validity of the BASIS-32. *Journal of Behavioral Health Services and Research, 26,* 5–17.

Eisen, S. V., Wilcox, M., Schaefer, E., Culhane, M. A., & Leff, H. S. (1997). *Use of BASIS-32 for outcome assessment of recipients of outpatient mental health services.* Report to Human Services Research Institute, Cambridge, MA.

Eisman, E. J., Dies, R. R., Finn, S. E., Eyde, L. D., Kay, G. G., Kubiszyn, T. W., Meyer, G. J., & Moreland, K. L. (1998). *Problems and limitations in the use of psychological assessment in contemporary healthcare delivery: Report to the Board of Professional Affairs, Psychological Assessment Work Group, Part II.* Washington, DC: American Psychological Association.

Eisman, E. J., Dies, R. R., Finn, S. E., Eyde, L. D., Kay, G. G., Kubiszyn, T. W., Meyer, G. J., & Moreland, K. L. (2000). Problems and limitations in the use of psychological assessment in contemporary healthcare delivery. *Professional Psychology: Research and Practice, 31,* 131–140.

Field, M. J., & Lohr, K. N. (Eds.). (1990). *Clinical practice guidelines*. Washington, DC: National Academy Press.

Finn, S. E. (1996). *Manual for using the MMPI-2 as a therapeutic intervention*. Minneapolis, MN: University of Minnesota Press.

Fisher, D., Beutler, L. E., & Williams, O. B. (1999). Making assessment relevant to treatment planning: The STS Clinician Rating Form. *Journal of Clinical Psychology, 55,* 825–842.

Frank, A., Eisenthal, S., & Lazare, A. (1978). Are there social class differences in patients' treatment conceptions? Myths and facts. *Archives of General Psychiatry, 35,* 61–69.

Friedman, A. F., Lewak, R., Nichols, D. S., & Webb, J. T. (2001). *Psychological assessment with the MMPI-2*. Mahwah, NJ: Erlbaum.

Garfield, S. L. (1996). Some problems with "validated" forms of psychotherapy. *Clinical Psychology: Science and Practice, 3,* 218–229.

Gaw, K. F., & Beutler, L. E. (1995). Integrating treatment recommendations: The clinical interview. In L. E. Beutler & M. R. Berren (Eds.), *Integrative assessment of adult personality* (pp. 94–120). New York: Guilford Press.

Ginsberg, G. L. (1985). Psychiatric history and mental status examination. In H. I. Kaplan & B. J. Sadock (Eds.), *Comprehensive textbook of psychiatry/IV* (4th ed., pp. 487–495). Baltimore: Williams & Wilkins.

Gough, H. G., McClosky, H., & Meehl, P. E. (1951). A personality scale for dominance. *Journal of Abnormal and Social Psychology, 46,* 360–366.

Gough, H. G., McClosky, H., & Meehl, P. E. (1952). A personality scale for social responsibility. *Journal of Abnormal and Social Psychology, 47,* 73–80.

Graham, J. R. (2000). *MMPI-2: Assessing personality and psychopathology* (3rd ed.). New York: Oxford University Press.

Greene, R. L. (1991). *The MMPI-2/MMPI: An interpretive manual*. Boston: Allyn & Bacon.

Greene, R. L. (2000). *The MMPI-2: An interpretive manual* (2nd ed.). Boston: Allyn & Bacon.

Greene, R. L., & Clopton, J. R. (1999). Minnesota Multiphasic Personality Inventory–2 (MMPI-2). In M. E. Maruish (Ed.), *The use of psychological testing for treatment planning and outcomes assessment* (2nd ed., pp. 1023–1049). Mahwah, NJ: Erlbaum.

Hamilton, M. (1967). Development of a rating scale for primary depressive illness. *British Journal of Social and Clinical Psychology, 6,* 278–296.

Harkness, A. R., & Lilienfeld, S. O. (1997). Individual differences science for treatment planning: Personality traits. *Psychological Assessment, 9,* 349–360.

Hathaway, S. R., & McKinley, J. C. (1943). *The Minnesota Multiphasic Personality Inventory manual*. Minneapolis, MN: University of Minnesota Press.

Havik, O. E., & VandenBos, G. R. (1996). Limitations of manualized psychotherapy for everyday clinical practice. *Clinical Psychology: Science and Practice, 3,* 264–267.

Hayes, O. W. (1994). Clinical practice guidelines: A review. *Journal of the American Osteopathic Association, 94,* 732–738.

Hays, R. D., Davies, A. R., & Ware, J. E. (1987). *Scoring the Medical Outcomes Study Patient Satisfaction Questionnaire–III* (Unpublished MOS memorandum). Santa Monica, CA: RAND Corporation.

Heimberg, R. C. (1998). Manual-based treatment: An essential ingredient of clinical practice in the 21st century. *Clinical Psychology: Science and Practice, 5,* 387–390.

Hoffman, F. L., Capelli, K., & Mastrianni, X. (1997). Measuring treatment outcome for adults and adolescents: Reliability and validity of BASIS-32. *Journal of Mental Health Administration, 24,* 316–331.

Howard, K. I., Brill, P. L., Lueger, R. J., O'Mahoney, M. T., & Grissom, G. R. (1993). *Integra outpatient tracking assessment.* Philadelphia: Compass Information Services.

Howard, K. I., Kopta, S. M., Krause, M. S., & Orlinsky, D. E. (1986). The dose-effect relationship in psychotherapy. *American Psychologist, 41,* 154–159.

Howard, K. I., Lueger, R. J., Maling, M. S., & Martinovich, Z. (1993). A phase model of psychotherapy outcome: Causal mediation of change. *Journal of Consulting and Clinical Psychology, 61,* 678–685.

Howard, K. I., Moras, K., Brill, P. B., Martinovich, Z., & Lutz, W. (1996). Evaluation of psychotherapy: Efficacy, effectiveness, and patient progress. *American Psychologist, 51,* 1059–1064.

Hsu, L. M. (1996). On the identification of clinically significant client changes: Reinterpretation of Jacobson's cut scores. *Journal of Psychopathology and Behavioral Assessment, 18,* 371–385.

Hsu, L. M. (1999). Caveats concerning comparisons of change rates obtained with five models of identifying significant client changes: Comment on Speer and Greenbaum (1995). *Journal of Consulting and Clinical Psychology, 67,* 594–598.

Institute of Medicine, Committee on Clinical Practice Guidelines, Field, M. J., & Lohr, K. N. (Eds.). (1990). *Guidelines for clinical practice: From development to use.* Washington, DC: National Academy Press.

Jackson, J. L. (1999). Psychometric considerations in self-monitoring assessment. *Psychological Assessment, 11,* 439–447.

Jacobson, N. S., Follette, W. C., & Revenstorf, D. (1984). Psychotherapy outcome research: Methods for reporting variability and evaluating clinical significance. *Behavior Therapy, 15,* 336–352.

Jacobson, N. S., Follette, W. C., & Revenstorf, D. (1986). Toward a standard definition of clinically significant change [Letter to the editor]. *Behavior Therapy, 17,* 309–311.

Jacobson, N. S., Roberts, L. J., Berns, S. B., & McGlinchey, J. B. (1999). Methods for defining and determining the clinical significance of treatment effects: Description, application, and alternatives. *Journal of Consulting and Clinical Psychology, 67,* 300–307.

Jacobson, N. S., & Truax, P. (1991). Clinical significance: A statistical approach defining meaningful change in psychotherapy research. *Journal of Consulting and Clinical Psychology, 59,* 12–19.

Jongsma, A. E., & Peterson, L. M. (1999). *The complete adult psychotherapy treatment planner* (2nd ed.). New York: Wiley.

Kadera, S. W., Lambert, M. J., & Andrews, A. A. (1996). How much therapy is really enough? A session-by-session analysis of the psychotherapy dose-effect relationship. *Journal of Psychotherapy Practice and Research, 5,* 132–151.

Kazdin, A. E. (1999). The meanings and measurement of clinical significance. *Journal of Consulting and Clinical Psychology, 67,* 332–339.

Kazdin, A. E., & Kendall, P. C. (1998). Current progress and future plans for developing effective treatments: Comments and perspectives. *Journal of Clinical Child Psychology, 27,* 217–226.

Keller, S. D., & Ware, J. E. (1996). Questions and answers about SF-36 and SF-12. *Medical Outcomes Trust Bulletin, 4,* 3.

Kessler, L. G., McGonagle, K. M., Zhao, S., Nelson., C. B., Hughes, M., Eshelman, S., Wittchen, H. U., & Kendler, K. S. (1994). Lifetime and 12-month prevalence of DSM-III-R disorders in the U.S.: Results from the National Comorbidity Study. *Archives of General Psychiatry, 51,* 8–20.

Kiesler, C. A. (2000). The next wave of change for psychology and mental health services in the health care revolution. *American Psychologist, 55,* 481–487.

Korotitsch, W. J., & Nelson-Gray, R. O. (1999). An overview of self-monitoring research in assessment and treatment. *Psychological Assessment, 11,* 415–425. Retrieved July 6, 2001 from PsycARTICLES database.

Kubiszyn, T. W., Meyer, G. J., Finn, S. E., Eyde, L. D., Kay, G. G., Moreland, K. L., Dies, R. R., & Eisman, E. J. (2000). Empirical support for psychological assessment in clinical health care settings. *Professional Psychology: Research and Practice, 31,* 119–130.

Lachar, D., Bailley, S. E., Rhoades, H. M., Espadas, A., Aponte, M., Cowan, K. A., Gummattira, P., Kopecky, C. R., & Wassef, A. (2001). New subscales for an anchored version of the Brief Psychiatric Rating Scale: Construction, reliability, and validity in acute psychitric admissions. *Psychological Assessment, 13,* 384–395.

Lachar, D., Bailley, S. E., Rhoades, H. M., & Varner, R. V. (1999). Use of BPRS-A percent change scores to identify significant clinical improvement: Accuracy of treatment response classification in acute psychiatric inpatients. *Psychiatry Research, 89,* 259–268.

Lambert, M. J. (1998). Manual-based treatment and clinical practice: Hangman of life or promising development? *Clinical Psychology: Science and Practice, 5,* 391–395.

Lambert, M. J., & Finch, A. E. (1999). The Outcome Questionnaire. In M. E. Maruish (Ed.), *The use of psychological testing for treatment planning and outcomes assessment* (2nd ed., pp. 831–869). Mahwah, NJ: Erlbaum.

Lambert, M. J., Hansen, N. B., & Finch, A. E. (2001). Patient-focused research: Using patient outcome data to enhance treatment effects. *Journal of Consulting and Clinical Psychology, 69,* 159–172.

Lambert, M. J., Hansen, N. B., Umphress, V., Lunnen, K., Okiishi, J., Burlingame, G., Huefner, J. C., & Reisinger , C. W. (1996). *Administration and scoring manual for the Outcome Questionnaire (OQ 45.2).* Wilmington, DE: American Professional Credentialing Services.

Lambert, M. J., & Lambert, J. M. (1999). Use of psychological tests for assessing treatment outcome. In M. E. Maruish (Ed.), *The use of psychological testing for treatment planning and outcomes assessment* (2nd ed., pp. 115–151). Mahwah, NJ: Erlbaum.

Lambert, M. J., Whipple, J. L., Smart, D. W., Vermeesch, D. A., Nielsen, S. L., & Hawkins, E. J. (2001). The effects of providing therapists with feedback on patient progress during psychotherapy: Are outcomes enhanced? *Psychotherapy Research, 11,* 49–68.

Lambert, M. J., Whipple, J. L., Vermeesch, D. A., Smart, D. W., Hawkins, E. J., Nielsen, S. L., & Goates, M. (in press). Enhancing psychotherapy outcomes via providing feedback on client progress: A replication. *Clinical Psychology and Psychotherapy.*

Lehnhoff, J. (1991). Assessment and utilization of patient strengths in acute care treatment planning. *The Psychiatric Hospital, 22,* 11–15.

Leon, S. C., Kopta, S. M., Howard, K. I., & Lutz, W. (1999). Predicting patients' responses to psychotherapy: Are some more predictable than others? *Journal of Consulting and Clinical Psychology, 67,* 698–704.

Luborsky, L., & Crits-Christoph, P. (Eds.). (1990). *The core conflictual relationship theme.* New York: Basic Books.

Lueger, R. J., Howard, K. I., Martinovich, Z., Lutz, W., Anderson, E. E., & Grissom, G. (2001). Assessing treatment progress of individual patients using expected treatment response models. *Journal of Consulting and Clinical Psychology, 69,* 150–158.

Lutz, W., Lowry, J., Kopta, S. M., Einstein, D. A., & Howard, K. I. (2001). Prediction of dose-response relations based on patient characteristics. *Journal of Clinical Psychology, 57,* 889–900.

Lutz, W., Martinovich, Z., & Howard, K. I. (1999). Patient profiling: An application of random coefficient regression models to depicting the response of a patient to outpatient psychotherapy. *Journal of Consulting and Clinical Psychology, 67,* 571–577.

Makover, R. B. (1992). Training psychotherapists in hierarchical treatment planning. *Journal of Psychotherapy Practice and Research, 1,* 337–350.

Marques, C. (1998). Manual-based treatment and clinical practice. *Clinical Psychology: Science and Practice, 5,* 400–402.

Maruish, M. E. (1999). Introduction. In M. E. Maruish (Ed.), *The use of psychological testing for treatment planning and outcomes assessment* (2nd ed., pp. 1–39). Mahwah, NJ: Erlbaum.

Maruish, M. E. (2000). Introduction. In M. E. Maruish (Ed.), *Handbook of psychological assessment in primary care settings* (pp. 3–41). Mahwah, NJ: Erlbaum.

Maruish, M. E. (2002). *Psychological testing in the age of managed behavioral health care.* Mahwah, NJ: Erlbaum.

McConnaughy, E. A., DiClemente, C. C., Prochaska, J. O., & Velicer, W. F. (1989). Stages of change in psychotherapy. *Psychotherapy, 26,* 494–503.

McConnaughy, E. A., Prochaska, J. O., & Velicer, W. F. (1983). Stages of change in psychotherapy: Measurement and sample profiles. *Psychotherapy: Theory, Research and Practice, 20,* 368–375.

McHorney, C. A., & Tarlov, A. R. (1995). Individual-patient monitoring in clinical practice: Are available health status surveys adequate? *Quality of Life Research, 4,* 293–307.

McIntyre, J. S. (1996). The role of psychotherapy in the treatment of depression [Commentary]. *Archives of General Psychiatry, 53,* 291–293.

Meyer, G. J., Finn, S. E., Eyde, L. D., Kay, G. G., Moreland, K. L., Dies, R. R., Eisman, E. J., Kubiszyn, T. W., & Reed, G. M. (2001). Psychological testing and psychological assessment: A review of evidence and issues. *American Psychologist, 56,* 128–165.

Miller, I. J. (1996). Managed care is harmful to outpatient mental health services: A call for accountability. *Professional Psychology: Research and Practice, 27,* 349–363.

Moreland, K. L. (1996). How psychological testing can reinstate its value in an era of cost containment. *Behavioral Healthcare Tomorrow, 5,* 59–61.

Morey, L. C. (1991). *The Personality Assessment Inventory professional manual.* Odessa, FL: Psychological Assessment Resources.

Morey, L. C. (1999). Personality Assessment Inventory. In M. E. Maruish (Ed.), *The use of psychological testing for treatment planning and outcomes assessment* (2nd ed., pp. 1083–1121). Mahwah, NJ: Erlbaum.

Morey, L. C., & Henry, W. (1994). Personality Assessment Inventory. In M. E. Maruish

(Ed.), *The use of psychological testing for treatment planning and outcome assessment* (pp. 185–216). Hillsdale, NJ: Erlbaum.

Mueller, R. M., Lambert, M. J., & Burlingame, G. M. (1998). Construct validity of the Outcome Questionnaire: A confirmatory factor analysis. *Journal of Personality Assessment, 70,* 248–262.

Mumma, G. H. (1998). Improving cognitive case formulations and treatment planning in clinical practice and research. *Journal of Cognitive Psychotherapy: An International Quarterly, 12,* 251–274.

Munich, R. L., Hurley, B., & Delaney, J. (1990). Quality assurance and quality of care: I. Monitoring treatment. *The Psychiatric Hospital, 21,* 71–75.

Murphy, M. J., DeBernardo, C. R., & Shoemaker, W. E. (1998). Impact of managed care on independent practice and professional ethics: A survey of independent practitioners. *Professional Psychology: Research and Practice, 29,* 43–51.

Naglieri, J. A., & Pfeiffer, S. I. (1999). Use of the Devereux Scales of Mental Disorders for diagnosis, treatment planning, and outcome assessment. In M. E. Maruish (Ed.), *The use of psychological testing for treatment planning and outcomes assessment* (2nd ed., pp. 535–561). Mahwah, NJ: Erlbaum.

Najavits, L. M., Weiss, R. D., Shaw, S. R., & Dierberger, A. E. (2000). Psychotherapists' views of treatment manuals. *Professional Psychology: Research and Practice, 31,* 404–408.

Nathan, P. E. (1998). Practice guidelines: Not yet ideal. *American Psychologist, 53,* 290–299.

Newman, F. L., & Dakof, G. A. (1999). Progress and outcomes assessment of individual patient data: Selecting single-subject design and statistical procedures. In M. E. Maruish (Ed.), *The use of psychological testing for treatment planning and outcomes assessment* (2nd ed., pp. 211–223). Mahwah, NJ: Erlbaum.

Newman, F. L., & Tejeda, M. J. (1999). Selecting statistical procedures for progress and outcome assessment: The analysis of group data. In M. E. Maruish (Ed.), *The use of psychological testing for treatment planning and outcomes assessment* (2nd ed., pp. 225–266). Mahwah, NJ: Erlbaum.

Nichols, D. S. (2001). *Essentials of MMPI-2 assessment.* New York: Wiley.

Overall, J. E., & Gorham, D. R. (1962). The Brief Psychiatric Rating Scale. *Psychological Reports, 10,* 799–812.

Overall, J. E., & Gorham, D. R. (1988). The Brief Psychiatric Rating Scale: Recent developments in ascertainment and scaling. *Psychopharmacology Bulletin, 24,* 97–99.

Overall, J. E., & Klett, C. J. (1972). *Applied multivariate analysis.* New York: McGraw-Hill.

Parloff, M. B. (1998). Is psychotherapy more than manual labor? *Clinical Psychology: Science and Practice, 5,* 376–381.

Persons, J. B. (1989). *Cognitive therapy in practice: A case formulation approach.* New York: Norton.

Phelps, R., Eisman, E. J., & Kohout, J. (1998). Psychological practice and managed care: Results of the CAPP practitioner survey. *Professional Psychology: Research and Practice, 29,* 31–36.

Prochaska, J. O. (1995). Common problems: Common solutions. *Clinical Psychology: Science and Practice, 2,* 101–105.

Prochaska, J. O., & DiClemente, C. C. (1982). Transtheoretical therapy: Toward a more integrative model of change. *Psychotherapy: Theory, Research and Practice, 19,* 276–288.

Prochaska, J. O., & DiClemente, C. C. (1992). The transtheoretical approach. In J. C.

Norcross & M. R. Goldfried (Eds.), *Handbook of psychotherapy integration* (pp. 300–334). New York: Basic Books.

Prochaska, J. O., DiClemente, C. C., & Norcross, J. C. (1992). In search of how people change: Applications to addictive behaviors. *American Psychologist, 47,* 1102–1114.

Prochaska, J. O., Velicer, W. F., DiClemente, C. C., & Fava, J. (1988). Measuring processes of change: Applications to the cessation of smoking. *Journal of Consulting and Clinical Psychology, 56,* 520–528.

QualityMetric, Inc., 2000, QMetric SFV2™ (SF-36®/SF-12® Version 2 (n.d.). Retrieved December 11, 2000, from http://www.qualitymetric.com/innohome/sfv2.shtml

Radosevich, D. M., Werni, T. L., & Cords, J. (1994). *Assessment of visit-specific satisfaction.* Bloomington, MN: Health Outcomes Institute.

Rains, N. E., Kukor, T., Myers, D., Bobbitt, B., & Davis, K. (1996). *Suicide and its aftermath.* Minneapolis, MN: United Behavioral Systems.

Robins, L. N., Helzer, J. E., Croughan, J., & Ratcliff, K. S. (1981). National Institute of Mental Health Diagnostic Interview Schedule: Its history, characteristics, and validity. *Archives of General Psychiatry, 38,* 381–389.

Rothbaum, P. A., Bernstein, D. M., Haller, O., Phelps, R., & Kohout, J. (1998). New Jersey psychologists' report on managed mental health care. *Professional Psychology: Research and Practice, 29,* 37–42.

Rubin, H. R., Gandek, B., Rogers, W. H., Kosinski, M., McHorney, C. A., & Ware, J. E. (1993). Patients' ratings of outpatient visits in different practice settings. *Journal of the American Medical Association, 270,* 835–840.

Sanchez, H. G. (2001). Risk factor model for suicide assessment and intervention. *Professional Psychology: Research and Practice, 32,* 351–358.

Saunders, S. M., Howard, H. I., & Newman, F. L. (1988). Evaluating the clinical significance of treatment effects: Norms and normality. *Behavioral Assessment, 10,* 207–218.

Schaefer, M., Murphy, R., Westerveld, M., & Gewirtz, A. (2000, August). *Psychological assessment and managed care: Guidelines for practice with children and adolescents.* Continuing education workshop presented at the annual meeting of the American Psychological Association, Washington, DC.

Schreter, R. K. (1997). Essential skills for managed behavioral health care. *Psychiatric Services, 48,* 653–658.

Sechrest, L. B. (2001). Managed, be managed, or find something else to do. *The National Psychologist, 10*(5), 1, 17.

Seligman, L. (1993). Teaching treatment planning. *Counselor Education and Supervision, 32,* 287–297.

Shoham-Salomon, V., & Hannah, M. T. (1991). Client-treatment interaction in the study of differential change processes. *Journal of Consulting and Clinical Psychology, 59,* 217–225.

Sifneos, P. E. (1987). *Short-term dynamic psychotherapy: Evaluation and technique* (2nd ed.). New York: Plenum Press.

Smith, B., & Sechrest, L. (1991). Treatment of aptitude × treatment interactions. *Journal of Consulting and Clinical Psychology, 59,* 233–244.

Sommers-Flanagan, J., & Sommers-Flanagan, R. (1995). Intake interviewing with suicidal patients: A systematic approach. *Professional Psychology: Research and Practice, 26,* 41–47.

Speer, D. C. (1992). Clinically significant change: Jacobson and Truax (1991) revisited. *Journal of Consulting and Clinical Psychology, 60,* 402–408.

Speer, D. C., & Greenbaum, P. E. (1995). Five methods for computing signficant individual client change and improvement rates: Support for an individual growth curve approach. *Journal of Consulting and Clinical Psychology, 63,* 1044–1048.

Sperry, L., Brill, P. L., Howard, K. I., & Grissom, G. R. (1996). *Treatment outcomes in psychotherapy and psychiatric interventions.* New York: Brunner/Mazel.

Spitzer, R. L., Williams, J. B., & Gibbon, M. (1986). *The Structured Clinical Interview for DSM-III-R—Patient version.* New York: Biometrics Research Department, New York State Psychiatric Institute.

Stricker, G., Abrahamson, D. J., Bologna, N. C., Hollon, S. D., Robinson, E. A., & Reed, G. M. (1999). Treatment guidelines: The good, the bad, and the ugly. *Psychotherapy, 36,* 69–79.

Strosahl, K. (1998). The dissemination of manual-based psychotherapies in managed care: Promises, problems, and prospects. *Clinical Psychology: Science and Practice, 5,* 382–386.

Strupp, H. H. (1996). The tripartite model and the *Consumer Reports* study. *American Psychologist, 51,* 1017–1024.

Task Force on Promotion and Dissemination of Psychological Procedures. (1995). Training in and dissemination of empirically-validated psychological treatments. *The Clinical Psychologist, 48,* 3–23.

Tickle-Degnen, L. (1998). Communicating with clients about treatment outcomes: The use of meta-analytic evidence in collaborative treatment planning. *American Journal of Occupational Therapy, 52,* 526–530.

Tillett, R. (1996). Psychotherapy assessment and treatment selection. *British Journal of Psychiatry, 168,* 10–15.

Tompkins, M. A. (1999). Using a case formulation to manage treatment nonresponse. *Journal of Cognitive Psychotherapy: An International Quarterly, 13,* 317–330.

Trzepacz, P. T., & Baker, R. W. (1993). *The psychiatric mental status examination.* New York: Oxford University Press.

Umphress, V. J., Lambert, M. J., Smart, D. W., Barlow, S. H., & Clouse, G. (1997). Concurrent and construct validity of the Outcome Questionnaire. *Journal of Psychoeducational Assessment, 15,* 40–55.

United Behavioral Systems. (1994). *Writing effective treatment plans.* Unpublished training manual.

United Behavioral Health. (2000). *General treatment planning.* [Online]. Available from http://ubhweb.uhc.com/ubh/clinical-guidelines/gen_tx_planning.html

United Behavioral Health. (2001). *United Behavioral Health level of care guidelines.* [Online]. Available from http://www.provweb.com/html/LevelOfCareGuidelines/index.html

Velicer, W. F., Hughes, S. L., Fava, J. L., Prochaska, J. O., & DiClemente, C. C. (1995). An empirical typology of subjects within stage of change. *Addictive Behaviors, 20,* 299–320.

Velicer, W. F., Norman, G. J., Fava, J. L., & Prochaska, J. O. (1999). Testing 40 predictions from the transtheoretical model. *Addictive Behaviors, 24,* 455–469.

Velicer, W. F., Prochaska, J. O., Fava, J. L., Rossi, J. S., Redding, C. A., Laforge, R. G., & Robbins, M. L. (2000). Using the transtheoretical model for population-based approaches to health promotion and disease prevention. *Homeostasis in Health and Disease, 40,* 174–193.

Wampold, B. E., & Jenson, W. R. (1986). Clinical significance revisited [Letter to the editor]. *Behavior Therapy, 17,* 302–305.

Ware, J. E. (1999a). Future directions in health status assessment. *Journal of Clinical Outcomes Management, 6,* 34–37.

Ware, J. E. (1999b). SF-36 Health Survey. In M. E. Maruish (Ed.), *The use of psychological testing for treatment planning and outcomes assessment* (2nd ed., pp. 1227–1246). Mahwah, NJ: Erlbaum.

Ware, J. E., & Hays, R. D. (1988). Methods for measuring patient satisfaction with specific medical encounters. *Medical Care, 26,* 393–402.

Ware, J. E., Kosinski, M., & Keller, S. D. (1994). *SF-36 Physical and Mental summary scales: A user's manual.* Boston: The Health Institute.

Ware, J. E., Kosinski, M., & Keller, S. D. (1995). *SF-12: How to score the SF-12 Physical and Mental summary scales* (2nd ed.). Boston: New England Medical Center, The Health Institute.

Ware, J. E., Snow, K. K., Kosinski, M., & Gandek, B. (1993). *SF-36 Health Survey manual and interpretation guide.* Boston: New England Medical Center, The Health Institute.

Weiner, I. B. (1999). Rorschach inkblot technique. In M. E. Maruish (Ed.), *The use of psychological testing for treatment planning and outcomes assessment* (2nd ed., pp. 1123–1156). Mahwah, NJ: Erlbaum.

Weiner, I. B., & Exner, J. E., Jr. (1991). Rorschach changes in long-term and short-term psychotherapy. *Journal of Personality Assessment, 56,* 453–465.

Wenning, K. (1993). Long-term psychotherapy and informed consent. *Hospital and Community Psychiatry, 44,* 364–367.

Wetzler, H. P., Lum, D. L., & Bush, D. M. (2000). Using the SF-36 Health Survey in primary care. In M. E. Maruish (Ed.), *Handbook of psychological testing in primary care settings* (pp. 583–621). Mahwah, NJ: Erlbaum.

Wilson, G. T. (1998). Manual-based treatment and clinical practice. *Clinical Psychology: Science and Practice, 5,* 363–375.

Woerner, M. G., Mannuzza, S., & Kane, J. M. (1988). Anchoring the BPRS: An aid to improved reliability. *Psychopharmacology Bulletin, 24,* 112–117.

Wolfe, J. (1999). Overcoming barriers to evidence-based practice: Lessons from medical practitioners. *Clinical Psychology: Science and Practice, 6,* 445–448.

World Health Organization (1992). *International Classification of Diseases, Tenth Revision.* Geneva, Switzerland: Author.

Yesavage, J. A., Brink, T. L., Rose, T. L., Lum, O., Huang, V., Adey, M., & Leirer, V. O. (1983). Development and validation of a geriatric depression screening scale: A preliminary report. *Journal of Psychiatric Research, 17,* 37–49.

Annotated Bibliography

Beutler, L. E. (1995). The clinical interview. In L. E. Beutler & M. R. Berren (Eds.), *Integrative assessment of adult personality* (pp. 94–120). New York: Guilford Press.

This chapter provides a general guide for conducting a clinical interview. Specific content areas to be covered in the interview are detailed. Included are specific questions for eliciting the information as well as examples of patient-therapist dialogue related to specific interview content areas.

DiClemente, C. C., & Prochaska, J. O. (1998). Toward a comprehensive, transtheoretical model of change. In W. R. Miller & N. Healthier (Eds.), *Treating addictive behaviors* (pp. 3–24). New York: Plenum Press.

This chapter provides a summary of Prochaska's transtheoretical model of change. It includes informative discussions of the levels, stages, and processes of change; their implications for planning interventions; current status of research on the transtheoretical model; and implications for the future.

Gaw, K. F., & Beutler, L. E. (1995). Integrating treatment recommendations: The clinical interview. In L. E. Beutler & M. R. Berren (Eds.), *Integrative assessment of adult personality* (pp. 280–319). New York: Guilford Press.

This chapter presents a discussion of the assessment of the five dimensions of the systematic treatment selection model developed by Beutler and Clarkin (1990), using both clinical indicators and the results of psychological testing. A general approach for integrating these findings into an integrated treatment plan is also presented.

Hsu, L. M. (1999). Caveats concerning comparisons of change rates obtained with five models of identifying significant client changes: Comment on Speer and Greenbaum (1995). *Journal of Consulting and Clinical Psychology, 67,* 594–598.

This article presents a comment on the findings of Speer and Greenbaum (1995; discussed in this bibliography) with regard to their comparison of rates of pre- and posttreatment change for five methods of determining significant patient change. The author identifies problems related to the meaning of the findings and the implications of recommendations that were made as a result of those findings.

Jacobson, N. S., Roberts, L. J., Berns, S. B., & McGlinchey, J. B. (1999). Methods for defining and determining the clinical significance of treatment effects: Description, application, and alternatives. *Journal of Consulting and Clinical Psychology, 67,* 300–307.

This article provides further discussion on the important topic of how to determine clinically significant change. A discussion of future directions in this area is also included.

Lueger, R. J., Howard, K. I., Martinovich, Z., Lutz, W., Anderson, E. E., & Grissom, G. (2001). Assessing treatment progress of individual patients using expected treatment response models. *Journal of Consulting and Clinical Psychology, 69,* 150–158.

This article discusses the use of Howard's dosage-response and phase models and expected treatment response curves as the basis of a treatment quality assessment system. A case example is provided.

Makover, R. B. (1992). Training psychotherapists in hierarchical treatment planning. *Journal of Psychotherapy Practice and Research, 1,* 337–350.

In this article, the author describes a four-level hierarchical treatment-planning model that includes aims, goals, strategies, and tactics. A discussion of the type of assessment that should precede treatment planning and a case study are also included.

Maruish, M. E. (Ed.). (1999). *The use of psychological testing for treatment planning and outcomes assessment* (2nd ed.). Mahwah, NJ: Erlbaum.

This four-part edited book presents a comprehensive overview of the use of psychological testing for treatment planning, treatment monitoring, and outcomes assessment purposes in behavioral health care settings. Part I contains chapters on general considerations related to the book's topic. Parts II and III contain chapters that deal with the use of specific psychological test instruments for treatment planning and outcomes assessment. Part II addresses the use of specific child and adolescent instruments, whereas Part III is concerned with adult instrumentation. Part IV presents a discussion of the use of psychological assessment in the future.

Maruish, M. E. (Ed.). (2000). *Handbook of psychological assessment in primary care settings.* Mahwah, NJ: Erlbaum.

This four-part edited book presents an overview of the use of psychological assessment in primary and other medical care settings. Part I contains chapters on general considerations related to the book's topic. Part II contains chapters that deal with the use of specific psychological test instruments for screening, treatment planning, and treatment monitoring in primary care settings. Part III presents an overview of three primary and behavioral health care integration projects. Part IV presents a discussion of future directions in the use of psychological assessment in primary care settings.

Maruish, M. E. (2002). *Psychological testing in the age of managed behavioral health care.* Mahwah, NJ: Erlbaum.

This book presents a comprehensive overview of how psychological testing can be used and demonstrate its value in managed behavioral health care settings. Attention is given to its use for screening, treatment planning, treatment monitoring, and outcomes assessment. Tests that have demonstrated value for these purposes are discussed in some detail.

Meyer, G. J., Finn, S. E., Eyde, L. D., Kay, G. G., Moreland, K. L., Dies, R. R., Eisman, E. J., Kubiszyn, T. W., & Reed, G. M. (2001). Psychological testing and psychological assessment: A review of evidence and issues. *American Psychologist, 56,* 128–165.

This article presents a comprehensive look at the utility of psychological testing and psychological assessment. The results of relevant empirical data are reviewed and presented to support the use of testing and assessment and to identify limitations thereof. Recommendations for future research in the area are indicated.

Nathan, P. E. (1998). Practice guidelines: Not yet ideal. *American Psychologist, 53,* 290–299.

This article addresses issues related to the development and use of clinical practice guidelines. Included is a brief history of attempts to identify treatments that are empirically supported. Guidelines developed by AHCPR, the American Psychiatric Association, and Division 12 of the American Psychological Association are discussed and compared.

Persons, J. B. (1989). *Cognitive therapy in practice: A case formulation approach.* New York: Norton.

> *Although developed specifically for cognitive-behavioral therapists, this book has several chapters that have general applicability to the development of clinical problem lists and case formulations, regardless of the clinician's theoretical orientation to the conceptualization and treatment of behavioral problems.*

Sanchez, H. G. (2001). Risk factor model for suicide assessment and intervention. *Professional Psychology: Research and Practice, 32,* 351–358.

> *This article presents a model for assessing, intervening with, and managing suicidal patients based on risk factors and protective factors. A checklist to assist in the assessment of suicide risk is included as an appendix.*

Speer, D. C., & Greenbaum, P. E. (1995). Five methods for computing significant individual client change and improvement rates: Support for an individual growth curve approach. *Journal of Consulting and Clinical Psychology, 63,* 1044–1048.

> *This article presents five methods for determining clinically significant change in patients using pre- and posttreatment difference scores. The results of a sample of 73 outpatients on a measure of well-being were analyzed by each of the five methods. Comparison of the findings from the five methods indicated that a growth curve approach yielded the highest rate of improvement.*

Trzepacz, P. T., & Baker, R. W. (1993). *The psychiatric mental status examination.* New York: Oxford University Press.

> *This book is a detailed guide to conducting a comprehensive mental status examination. A glossary is presented at the end of each content area chapter. In addition, a chapter with eight case vignettes and accompanying mental status examination findings is included.*

Index

Accreditation:
   quality of care and, 57
   third-party payers and, 1–2
   treatment plans and, 176
Action, as a stage of change, 152, 155
Activities of daily living (ADLs), 66
Affective disorders, 58
Agoraphobia, 147
Alcoholics Anonymous:
   clinical interviews and, 17
   as a type of intervention, 162
Algorithms. *See* Clinical practice
   guidelines
American Psychological Association
   (APA):
   clinical practice guidelines, 143
   diagnosis, 40
   empirically supported treatments,
     149, 150
   informed consent, 129
   psychological testing, 61
Anorexia nervosa, 170
Anxiety disorders, 58
Aptitude X Treatment Interactions
   (ATIs), 156–157
Assessment, 51–53
   case study, 46–51
   clinical interviews and, 16–21
   content areas for, 21–23
     diagnosis, 40–42
     education, 26

     employment, 26
     family/social history, 24–26
     history of problem, 24
     medical history, 27–28
     mental health/substance abuse,
       27
     mental status examination
       (MSE), 37–38
     motivation to change, 31–32,
       33, 45
     patient characteristics, 28–35, 36
     patient strengths, 35–37, 54
     presenting problem, 23–24, 31
     suicidal/homicidal ideation,
       39–40
     treatment goals, 42–45
   importance of, 14–15
   means of, 15–16 (*see also under*
     Psychological testing; *and specific*
     tests)
   psychological testing vs.
     psychological assessment, 55
Asthma, comorbid disorders and, 156
Attention-deficit/hyperactivity disorder (ADHD):
   medication trials and, 64
   psychological testing and, 60
   resource limitations and, 170

Beck Depression Inventory-II
   (BDI-II), 73

Behavior and Symptom Identifica-
    tion Scale (BASIS-32), 92–93
Behavior modification program, 169
Brief Psychiatric Rating Scale
    (BPRS):
    general information, 94–95
    monitoring treatment progress
        and, 192
Brief Symptom Inventory (BSI):
    general information, 86, 88–89
    monitoring treatment progress
        and, 192
Bulimia:
    resource limitations and, 170
    selecting appropriate staff, 175

CAGE-AID, 100–101
Care manager, 175
Carve-out plan, 55
Case formulation:
    case study, 119
    defined, 108–109
    development, 112–113
        steps to, 113–117
    limitations, 118
    overview, 107–108, 118, 120–121
    role of, 109–111
    sharing with patients, 111–112
Catholic Charities, 171
Central nervous system disorders,
    16–17
Change:
    motivation to, 31–32, 33, 45
    stages of, 152–155
CIGNA, 158
Clinical efficacy, 146

Clinical interviews:
    different structures for, 18–20
    goals of, 17–18
    helpful hints, 20–21
    as part of assessment, 16–17
Clinical management, 161
Clinical pathways. See Clinical prac-
    tice guidelines
Clinical practice guidelines:
    definition of, 143–144
    differences in, 145–146
    overview, 142–143
    purpose of, 144–145
Clinical Psychology: Science and Practice,
    149
Clinical utility, 146
Clinically significant change, 204–
    206. See also Statistically signifi-
    cant change
Clinicians:
    long-term therapy and, 167
    problem list length and, 137
    professional training and assess-
        ment, 15, 23
    short-term therapy and availability
        of, 166–167
    theoretical orientation and assess-
        ment, 15
Collaterals, 77
    assessment and, 15, 24
    contracts, 16
    interviews, 16
    monitoring treatment progress
        and, 196
    treatment expectations and, 4
Congestive heart failure, 156

Contemplation, as a stage of change, 152, 155
Continuous quality improvement (CQI) process, 117
Coping styles, 34–35, 36
    in case study, 49
Cost:
    monitoring treatment progress and, 192–193
    reassessment and, 199
        determining when to, 213
Cost-benefit analysis, 165

Delusions, problem list and, 135
Desensitization, 162
Development, treatment plan:
    flexibility, 132
    goals, 130–131
    intended users, 125–127
    overview, 132–133, 178, 181–184
    patient involvement, 127–130
    presenting problem, 134
    problem identification, 130
    purposes of, 122–124
    referrals, 133
    strategies, 131
Diabetes:
    comorbid disorders and, 156
    medical intervention and, 161
Diagnostic Interview Schedule (DIS), 18
Diagnostic and Statistical Manual of Mental Disorders–Fourth Edition, Text Revision (DSM-IV-TR):
    appropriate LOC and, 158
    in case study, 50, 179

clinical interviews and, 18
diagnostic classification, 41, 137, 138
functional impairment and, 29
patient strengths and, 35
Division 12:
    of APA, 149, 150
Dose-response model, 201
Dream interpretation, 163
Dysthymic disorder, 51, 179

Education:
    intervention, 161–162
    psychological testing and, 74–75
    referrals and, 172
    treatment and, 26
Electroconvulsive therapy (ECT), 161
Electroencephalogram (EEG), 15, 23
Electronic database, 189
Emphysema, 156
Empirically supported treatments (ESTs):
    criteria for, 151
    diagnosis and, 40
    overview, 149–151
Employment assistance program (EAP):
    OQ-45 and, 90
    referrals, 133
Employment:
    history, treatment and, 26
    OQ-45 and, 90
    referrals and, 172
    treatment goals and, 139
Ethical Principles of Psychologists and Code of Conduct, 129

Externalization:
    explanation of, 35–36
    psychological testing and, 68
    See also Internalization
Eye movement desensitization and
    reprocessing (EMDR), 163

Failure boundary, 202
Family Services, 171
Formal treatment plan, 132
Free association, 163
Functional impairment, 29

Geriatric Depression Scale (GDS),
    74
Global Assessment of Functioning
    (GAF), 29. See also *Diagnostic
    and Statistical Manual of Mental
    Disorders–Fourth Edition, Text
    Revision (DSM-IV-TR)*
Goals:
    patient-identified, 42–43, 44
    third-party, 44–45
    treatment, 4, 69, 130, 138–142
    assessment and, 14–15
Group Health Association of Amer-
    ica (GHAA), 99

Hallucinations:
    problem list and, 135
    referrals, 171
    self-monitoring, 195
Hamilton Rating Scale for Depres-
    sion (HRSD), 19
Health Insurance Experiment
    (HIE), 95, 96

Hierarchical treatment-planning
    structure, 130–131
Homicidal ideation:
    assessment and, 39–40
    problem severity and, 65
Horizontal exploration, 19–20

Implosion, 162
Informed consent:
    explanation of, 128–130
    strategies for treatment planning
    and, 163
Insomnia, 195
Institute of Medicine (IOM), 143,
    144
Intensive outpatient (IOP) care, 158
Interactive voice response (IVR)
    system, 75
Internalization:
    in case study, 49
    explanation of, 35–36
    psychological testing and, 68
    See also Externalization
*International Classification of Diseases
    and Related Health Problems, Tenth
    Edition (ICD-10)*, 41
    diagnosis classification, 137
Intervention strategy, 110

Joint Commission for the Accredita-
    tion of Healthcare Organiza-
    tions (JCAHO):
    general information about, 1–2, 5,
    7
    MBHO interest in psychological
    testing and, 57

resource limitations and, 169
writing treatment plans for MB-
    HOs and, 176
Juvenile detention, 10

Level of care (LOC):
    monitoring treatment progress
        and, 192
    overview, 6, 158–159, 178
    resource limitations and, 170
    selecting appropriate staff, 174
    stepping down, 174, 181
    treatment transfer/termination,
        172, 174
Linchpin approach, 112–113
Litigation:
    clinical practice guidelines and, 145
    informed consent and, 129–130
    protection against, 8

Maintenance, as a stage of change,
    152, 155
Major depressive disorder, 42
Managed behavioral health care or-
    ganizations (MBHOs):
    assessment and, 16
    case formulation and, limitations,
        118
    clinical interviews and, 17
    communication with external re-
        viewers, 3, 7
    diagnosis and, 42
    LOC, appropriate, 158, 159
    OQ-45 and, 89, 90
    psychological testing
        attitude toward, 61–63

brevity of, 72
cost, 60–61, 63, 74
diagnosis, assisting in, 58–60
medication trials and diagnosis,
    63–64
overview, 55–57, 101
performance measures, de-
    mands for, 57
population-based performance,
    57
program development, 57–58
streamlining interventions and,
    60–61
treatment planning, assisting in,
    60
value of assessment, 63
resource limitations and, 170
quality of care, 6–7
short-term therapy and, 165, 166,
    167
strategies for treatment planning
    and, 163
treatment authorization and, 6
treatment goals and, 43, 44
treatment planning, emphasis on,
    3–5
VSQ and, 100
writing treatment plans for, 176–
    178, 182
See also Third-party payers
Management information system
    (MIS), 196
Marital therapy:
    in case study, 180
    treatment goals and, 139
    treatment modality and, 110, 160

Medical intervention, 161
Medical Outcomes Study (MOS):
  SF-36 and, 95–96
  VSQ and, 99, 100
Memory lapses, 16–17, 171
Mental Health Index (MHI), 201
Mental Status Examination(MSE),
  19, 37–38
Methylphenidate. *See* Ritalin
Minnesota Multiphasic Personality
  Inventory-2 (MMPI-2), 23
  benefits of, 54
  in case study, 102, 103
  general information, 79, 80–85
  patient characteristics and, 65
  problem identification and, 65
Monitoring, treatment plan, 185–
  189, 209, 211–216
  appropriate time for, 198–199
  case study, 210–211
  clinically significant change, 204–
  206
  elements, 190–193
  evaluating results, 199–200
    individual goals, 200
    normative data, 200
    organizational performance
    data, 200
    recovery curves, 201–202
  psychological tests, selecting,
  196–198
  revision vs. maintenance, 206–207
  feedback and, 207–209
  sources of information, 193–194
    administrative data, 196
    multiple, 196

patient/observer data, 194
  self-monitoring, 194–196
  statistically significant change,
  202–204
Multiple providers, 5

National Committee for Quality Assurance (NCQA):
  general information about, 2, 5, 7
  MBHO interest in psychological
  testing and, 57
  resource limitations and, 169
  writing treatment plans for
  MBHOs and, 176
Neurologists, 171

Objective social support, 33–34
Obsessive-compulsive personality
  disorder, 49, 51, 179, 210
Omnibus diagnostic interview, 18
Outcome Questionnaire–45 (OQ-
  45):
  BASIS-32, compared to, 92
  in case study, 102, 103, 180, 181,
  210, 211, 212
  general information, 89–92
  monitoring treatment progress
  and, 208, 209

Panic disorder, 147
Paranoia, 195
Patient profiling, 201
Patient Satisfaction Questionnaire-
  III, 99
Personality Assessment Inventory
  (PAI)

patient characteristics and, 67
problem identification and, 65
Phase model of psychotherapy:
overview, 153–154, 155
recovery curves and, 201
Planned brief therapy. *See* Planned
short-term therapy
Planned Parenthood, 171
Planned short-term therapy, 164–
167
Posttraumatic stress disorder
(PTSD), 163
Practice parameters. *See* Clinical
practice guidelines
Practice policy. *See* Clinical practice
guidelines
Precontemplation, as a stage of
change, 152, 155
Preparation, as a stage of change,
152, 155
Primary care physician (PCP):
clinical interview and, 17
communication with, 7
quality care and, 6
selecting appropriate staff, 174–
175
treatment barriers and, 171
Principle of parsimony, 61
Problem complexity, 30–31, 32
Problem-focused treatment, 58
Psychiatrists:
approach to assessment, 15, 23
treatment barriers and, 171
See also Clinicians
Psychological Assessment Work
Group (PAWG), 61–63

Psychological testing:
assessment data
advantages over, 68–69
combining with other, 69–70
case study, 102–103
clarification of problems, 65–66
criteria for selection of, 70–72
brevity, 72–73
comprehensiveness, 75
content, 75
cost, 74
ease of use, 75
normative data and, 74
patient/observer-completed,
76–78
reading level, 74–75
relevancy, 73
validity/reliability, 73
identification of problems, 64–65
instruments, 78–101 (*see also under
specific tests*)
MBHO impact on, 55–64
monitoring treatment progress
and, 196–198
overview, 54–55, 101, 104–106
patient characteristics, identifying,
66–68
progress, monitoring, 68
Psychologists:
approach to assessment, 15, 23
MBHOs and, 55, 58
neurologist referrals and, 171
See also Clinicians
Psychopharmacologic intervention,
160–161
Psychotherapeutic intervention, 160

Rational emotive therapy, 162
Reactivity, 195
Reactance, 32–33
Recovery curve, 186, 201–202
Referrals:
   barriers to treatment and, 170–172
   treatment plans and, 133, 134
Rehabilitation, as a phase of psychotherapy, 154, 155
Relaxation training:
   in case study, 180
   treatment modality and, 110
Reliable change index (RCI), 202–204
Remediation, as a phase of psychotherapy, 154, 155
Remoralization, as a phase of psychotherapy, 153–154, 155
Resistance, 32–33
Ritalin, 64
Rorschach Inkblot Method:
   adjustment difficulty indices, 87–88
   overview, 79, 85–86
Routine testing, 58
Ruminative thinking, self-monitoring, 195

Schizophrenia:
   BPRS and, 94
   diagnosis, 42
   frequency/duration of treatment and, 164
   length of treatment and, 177
   treatment goals and, 139

Seizures, concomitant, 16–17
Self-monitoring:
   in case study, 180, 210, 212
   treatment progress and, 194–196
Self-report instruments:
   in case study, 102
   overview, 76–78
   See also specific tests
Semistructured interview, 19–20, 22
SF-12 Health Survey (SF-12), 98–99
SF-36 Health Survey (SF-36):
   general information, 95–98
   problem severity and, 66
   psychological testing costs and, 74
   SF-12 vs., 98–99
Signal cases, 208
Smoking, treatment goals and, 139
Social workers, approach to assessment, 15
Socioeconomics, referrals and, 171
Standards for Educational and Psychological Testing, 73
Statistically significant change, 202–204. See also Clinically significant change
Strength-focused assessment, 35–37
Stroke, 156
Structured Clinical Interview for DSM-III-R (SCID), 18
Structured interview, 18–19
Subjective distress, 30
Subjective social support, 33–34
Substance abuse disorders, cooccurrence with mental health disorders, 27

Suicidality, 39–40
  in case study, 102
  monitoring treatment progress and, 200
  problem severity and, 65
  self-monitoring, 195
Support groups, as a type of intervention, 17, 162
Symptom Checklist–90-R (SCL-90-R), general information, 86, 88–89
Systematic treatment selection model, 29

Talk therapy, 160
Task Force on Promotion and Dissemination of Psychological Procedures, 149
Task Force on Psychological Interventions, 149
Template Implementation Work Group, 143–144
Test-retest reliability, 104, 198
Therapeutic Reactance Scale, 67
Third-party payers:
  appropriate LOC and, 159
  case formulation and, 107
  diagnosis and, 41
  monitoring treatment progress and, 190
    criteria for completion of treatment, 191
  psychological testing and, 62, 63
  resource limitations and, 170
  selecting appropriate staff, 175

strategies for treatment planning and, 163
  treatment goals and, 44–45
  See also Managed behavioral health care organizations (MBHOs)
Thought-stopping, in case study, 180
Transference:
  analysis of, 163
  patient barriers and, 168
Transtheoretical model of change, 152–153, 155, 157
Treatment manuals, 146–149
  advantages/disadvantages, 148
Treatment modality, 110
Treatment plan:
  assumptions about, 9–10
  overview of, 1–9
  See also Assessment; Case formulation; Development, treatment plan; Monitoring, treatment plan; Psychological testing
Treatment, involuntary, 10, 142, 169

United Behavioral Systems (UBS), 43–44
  appropriate LOC and, 158
  psychopharmacologic intervention and, 161
  stepping down LOC and, 174
  treatment goals and, 140
Unplanned short-term therapy, 164
Unstructured interview, 18–19

Vertical exploration, semistructured
    interviews and, 19–20
Visit-Specific Satisfaction Question-
    naire (VSQ), 99–100

Women, CAGE-AID and, 101
World Health Organization (WHO),
    41

About the Author

Mark Maruish, PhD, earned his doctoral degree in clinical psychology from United States International University (now Alliant International University) in San Diego, California. He also completed a postdoctoral fellowship in clinical neuropsychology at the University of Nebraska Medical Center. He practiced as a clinical neuropsychologist in both private and rehabilitation settings before spending almost a decade in the psychological test publishing field. He subsequently worked for several health care outcomes management companies in the Minneapolis area. He currently holds the position of Director of Quality Improvement for the Health Plan Division of United Behavioral Health, a large, nationwide managed behavioral health care organization. A frequent presenter at professional meetings, Maruish has published several books on the topic of psychological testing and assessment in behavioral health and primary care settings. He is currently in the process of preparing the third edition of his edited book, *The Use of Psychological Testing for Treatment Planning and Outcomes Assessment.*